RESEARCH
STRATEGIES
FOR A
DIGITAL AGE

Second Edition

BONNIE L. TENSEN
Seminole Community College

THOMSON

WADSWORTH

Australia   Brazil   Canada   Mexico   Singapore   Spain   United Kingdom   United States

Research Strategies for a Digital Age
Second Edition
Bonnie L. Tensen

Publisher: *Michael Rosenberg*
Development Editor: *Cheryl Forman*
Managing Marketing Manager: *Mandee Eckersley*
Associate Marketing Communications Manager: *Patrick Rooney*
Associate Content Project Manager: *Jennifer Kostka*
Production Service/Compositor: *Pre-Press Company, Inc.*

Print Buyer: *Mary Beth Hennebury*
Photo Manager: *Sheri Blaney*
Photo Researcher: *Cheri Throop*
Text/Cover Designer: *Yvo Riezebos*
Cover Photo: © *Daniel Gilbey/ istockphoto.com*
Text/Cover Printer: *Transcontinental Printing/Louiseville*

ISBN-13: 978-1-4130-1923-0
ISBN-10: 1-4130-1923-4

Every effort has been made to verify the authenticity and sources of URLs listed in this book. All URLs were correctly linked to their websites at the time of publication. Due to the quickly evolving nature of the Internet, it is possible that a link may break or a URL may change or become obsolete. Should you discover any inconsistencies, please contact http://www.thomsonedu.com/support and a correction will be made for the next printing.

Credits appear on pages 247–248, which constitute a continuation of the copyright page.

Thomson Higher Education
25 Thomson Place
Boston, MA 02210-1202
USA

For more information about our products, contact us at:

Thomson Learning
Academic Resource Center
1-800-423-0563

For permission to use material from this text or product, submit a request online at
http://www.thomsonrights.com

Any additional questions about permissions can be submitted by e-mail to
thomsonrights@thomson.com

Printed in Canada
3 4 5 6 7 10 09 08 07

Library of Congress Control Number: 2006924766

Contents

PART THREE
RESEARCH DOCUMENTATION

Preface

When I wrote the first edition of this book, I thought there soon would come a time when the information and instruction it provided no longer would be necessary. The world is rapidly becoming Internet proficient—even Internet dependent—and our students are on the leading edge of the digital learning curve. They are more computer-savvy than ever, but even in the midst of this "information explosion," I've been astonished to discover they need even *more* "coaching" than ever in research strategies.

Many, if not most, of our students are masterful "digital researchers" when it comes to purchasing a ringtone of the current number one hit, obtaining the lowest airfare for a weekend getaway to New York City, discovering whether or not that cutie they "met" on *MySpace* is unattached, reserving a ticket to the latest blockbuster a week before it premieres, or finding out where their favorite local band is playing that weekend. It's not surprising, then, that they approach research with great confidence (sometimes even disdaining the advice of teachers whom they perceive as "technochallenged"). Their ever-twitching fingertips continuously affixed to keyboards, students feel that no information is beyond reach of their broadband connections.

Nevertheless, despite the tremendous quantity of information easily accessible via the World Wide Web and students' proficiency at obtaining answers to their personal questions and needs, this generation is no better at conducting academic research than those of us who as undergraduates had to rummage through unwieldy card catalogs. (In fact, they face new and daunting challenges.) I would never have anticipated that the information in this book would be more relevant, important, and necessary *today* than ever before.

The "information superhighway" has invaded our lives, radically changing the way information is stored and disseminated. Internet technology has transformed the library of the twenty-first century, making *more* information *more* accessible to *more* students. Although no one can dispute that the Internet has greatly increased our access to information, it also creates a special set of problems for students who do not (or cannot) distinguish between the credible sources available via the electronic library and the morass of unregulated information on the World Wide Web. The aim of this book is to teach students the following:

- Basic research strategies and library skills that will enable them to proficiently use online catalogs and databases to locate credible sources in the new, "digital" library
- Researching and evaluative skills that will enable them to identify reliable and academically appropriate information on the World Wide Web
- Proper methods of incorporating and documenting these resources in their research papers

v

The idea for this text arose from my experiences teaching research and composition in the networked classroom. At first I focused on the use of the electronic tools and neglected the teaching of basic research competencies. When my students handed in their research projects, I began to realize that the two are inextricably intertwined. Given their increased access to information, I expected that they would locate sources that were fair, accurate, *and* scholarly. Instead, their resources tended to be personal web pages containing biased or unsupported opinion, short newspaper or popular magazine articles that were written by journalists rather than experts, and abstracts of articles (instead of the articles themselves). Many of my students had advanced Internet "surfing" skills, but they lacked research acumen. In the end they were reduced to the scholarly equivalent of "roadkill" on the information superhighway because the sources they located contained inaccurate, incomplete, or misleading information. These experiences convinced me that the traditional must be taught simultaneously with the high tech. Technological ability is now inseparable from information literacy—at least when it comes to writing college papers that require research. The second edition of *Research Strategies for a Digital Age* emphasizes traditional research strategies and skills in the context of new and emerging technologies.

As a quick glance at the table of contents will show, *Research Strategies for a Digital Age* is divided into three major sections. The first section explains a process for beginning and sustaining a research project. Students are instructed how to use the online library catalog as a starting point to learn:

- the basics of creating *matching terms* and *search phrases* (e.g., keyword and Boolean phrases)
- the art of research *sleuthing* (the way one scholarly source leads to other valuable resources)
- the basics of *source evaluation* (whether a resource is relevant, reliable, and unbiased).

The search phrases students develop with the help of the online catalog are then used to explore electronic databases (indices and collections of articles from popular and academic periodicals). This edition features an expanded explanation of the distinctions between bibliographic and full-text databases (and the growing breed of databases that offer both types of results). It also includes instruction on how to use advanced search features to refine a search by more precisely delineating the types of sources required.

The second section of this text teaches students to use these same, time-tested research strategies to cautiously explore the World Wide Web—first, by casting their research nets in "well-stocked ponds" (i.e., search engines, directories, and subject guides), and then by evaluating this information to confirm that it meets the stringent requirements of academic research. The section concludes with a chapter on field research (interviews and surveys) with suggestions about how to maximize use of the Internet to efficiently conduct these studies. In this new edition, there are more exercises for both "smart" and traditional classroom activities.

The final section of *Research Strategies for a Digital Age,* Second Edition, begins with a comprehensive warning against plagiarizing. The Internet poses a dilemma for teachers as well as students. Most professors list academic dishonesty in the "top 5" of the challenges they face in the classroom. The brief one- to two-paragraph-long admonition against plagiarism that appears in most handbooks is not sufficient to warn today's students. Most students find it very difficult to resist "borrowing" from the vast amount of text available to them on the WWW, and they remain confused about what constitutes plagiarism. For this reason, this second edition includes an expanded caution against academic dishonesty. The text describes the "many faces" of plagiarism now made possible by the "cut-and-paste" nature of the World Wide Web and offers examples of improper paraphrasing and summarizing. This section also includes greatly expanded chapters on documentation. Many instructors and students indicated that the documentation chapters are extremely helpful, since they offer examples of the types of sources that students *really use* in their research projects (i.e., articles from databases and web pages). Therefore, these chapters have been expanded and now feature the most current information on how to document conventional "hard" print sources as well as the new types of electronic resources available in school libraries. Documentation has become confusing because digital resources are constantly morphing into new forms. For instance, databases once exclusively packaged in CD-ROMs are now delivered over the Internet. This text offers the most up-to-date documentation models for the Modern Language Association (MLA), American Psychological Association (APA), Council of Science Editors (CSE), and *The Chicago Manual of Style* (CMS) formats. It includes sample student essays in each of these formats that offer marginal notations to explain the intricacies of in-text and works-cited documentation choices. New to this edition is an annotated sample literary-analysis research paper.

Research Strategies for a Digital Age, Second Edition, is a unique text. There are many guides to the Internet available. This is *not* one of them. The ideal starting place for scholarly research has always been, and still is, the academic library; this text teaches students to maximize their use of the new technologies available in our "wired" libraries as well as on the web. The research paper is a staple of many academic classes, yet most handbooks provide only a cursory explanation of the research process; this text offers a step-by-step progression that enables students to build researching and evaluative skills while introducing them to a variety of research tools. Proper documentation is fundamental to the research project, yet few handbooks or guides provide sufficient examples of the newer forms (e.g., websites, database articles) by which information is made available. This text provides an abundance of sample entries of the types of documents students are now using in *four* different styles. Most importantly, *Research Strategies for a Digital Age,* Second Edition, is written to appeal to students and actively engage them in the research process.

New to the Second Edition

- Additional cautions against plagiarism that convey the importance of performing sound, ethical online research
- Extended examples of Works Cited entries of the types of resources that students are using
- New exercises for both networked and nonnetworked classrooms, in recognition of the evolving nature of today's classroom
- Expanded explanations of advanced search features to enable students to refine their searches using current search tools
- Revised "e-tip" boxes that reflect the most current Internet search tools
- Updated "Writing Tips" that cover how to skillfully incorporate direct quotations
- New website screenshots and examples that provide students with the most current technological information
- Extensive coverage of current MLA, APA, CSE, and CMS documentation styles, including new individual chapters on CSE and CMS
- New sample research papers in CSE, CMS, and literary styles that demonstrate correct in-text and reference list documentation methods
- Citation directories in each documentation chapter that allow students to quickly locate instruction and examples for the type of source they're citing

If a course includes a research component, *Research Strategies for a Digital Age*, Second Edition, is the perfect ancillary text that will help students develop research methods and habits (skills that will serve them well throughout their college careers) that are conducive to the "libraries" of today—whether virtual or real.

Acknowledgments

I would like to thank my colleagues at SCC for the support and suggestions they have made so that this second edition could better address the needs of students. I also want to thank all those instructors whose feedback has aided me in making improvements. My thanks go to my students, as well, whose moments of confusion and enlightenment have helped me to find better ways to explain the strategies in this text. I'd also like to thank the folks at Thomson Wadsworth and Pre-Press Company, Inc. (especially Cheryl Forman, Jennifer Kostka, and Crystal Spath) for their support and help with this new edition. And I really can't find the words to thank Karen Kaivola for all the help she has given me in writing and in life (but when I do, I'm sure she'll help me edit them for greater clarity and impact).

PART

1

RESEARCH BASICS

Get Off to a Good Start

"The beginning

is the most

important part

of the work."

PLATO, *The Republic*

Perhaps you will find no college assignment more difficult than the research paper. After all, for most course projects, your instructor provides the "raw materials" (class readings, lectures, demonstrations, instructions) you need to successfully complete the assignment. But the research paper requires you to strike out on your own: You must determine the topic (sometimes with little or no guidance), develop an approach that works for you, and base your claims and analysis on reliable information. Finally, after having expended much effort on these invisible but essential "behind-the-scenes" tasks, you must present your findings—accurately, cleverly, persuasively, and intelligently—in an essay, report, or argument. No wonder so many students find the research project daunting!

Choosing a topic that will enable you to produce a strong essay and locating credible, relevant sources to support your points convincingly are challenging and time-consuming steps in the process, but both are absolutely essential. Because the final written or oral presentation is often the only graded part of the process, some students (foolishly) minimize the amount of effort they expend at the beginning of the process. However, if you have ever tried to write a detailed, informative, and well-supported essay without first focusing and thoroughly researching your topic— without really *knowing* what's important about that topic—you are already well aware of this. You know from your own experience how difficult it is to sustain anything resembling an intelligent discussion beyond the first paragraph or two. Fortunately, there are tried-and-true methods that can help you get started. This chapter offers strategies for developing a topic that is

3

interesting and researchable. Later chapters will talk about how to develop an argument or analysis of that topic that is convincing and persuasive.

Step 1: Choose a Topic

Choose a Topic You Care About

I frequently tell my students that the key to good writing is to write about something you care about. However, in a general requirement class—a class that is mandated rather than freely chosen—coming up with a topic that will sustain your interest (let alone your passion) for the duration of the project requires careful thought.

Some research projects have built-in parameters regarding both topic and method. Projects for a class in a specific discipline (e.g., environmental science, astronomy, sociology, psychology, humanities) will be about some aspect of the subject of the course itself. Even if the professor doesn't assign a particular topic, the readings and materials of the class will help you determine what you might want to learn more about. The situation in a first-year English composition class is different, and often more challenging, at least in terms of developing a good topic. In such courses, often the only requirement for topics is that the subject must be researchable, controversial, or "arguable." The work of figuring out what exactly to write about is frequently left entirely up to you.

A common mistake that many students make when faced with such an "open" assignment is choosing a topic too quickly, without a careful or honest exploration of their real interests. Either they choose something currently in the news, something they think a college paper "should" address, or something they know other students are writing about. Such papers rarely demonstrate a writer's best thinking or writing.

In my English I composition class, I purposely make many of the most controversial topics (e.g., abortion, euthanasia, capital punishment, cloning, gun control, stem cell research) off limits. Whether or not your instructor does the same, I encourage caution about choosing these topics. For one thing, given the restrictions of most undergraduate research assignments (which generally require papers between 8 and 12 pages), a student would be hard-pressed to mount a convincing case (and by this I mean an argument capable of persuading a reader to seriously reconsider his or her views on the subject) about such potentially emotional topics. These are subjects that have been argued intensely in our society, often in polarizing ways, and are still far from being resolved. Even a cursory review of the basic arguments would require more than 10 pages to be persuasive to a broad audience. (You should always assume that your readers are educated people, many of whom will not automatically agree with your views or assumptions and who will therefore need to be persuaded by careful, reasoned argument rather than by emotional appeal or unsupported claims.) It is foolish to take on a project that is doomed from the start—and that is exactly what an argument that can never persuade is: doomed. Furthermore, it is all too easy to fall into "groupthink" when dealing with such questions. Rather than encouraging you to acquire information to formulate your own unique perspective on the issue, such papers tend to re-hearse established opinions. They simply put forth the "party line" whether from the conservative or liberal point of view, avoiding the hard work of original analysis.

Finally, most students who quickly choose one of these topics do not really feel a compelling need to learn more about it. They already know what they think—or at least they *think* they do. Thus, in the end, their papers are simply reiterations of what others have written before (or, worse, what they've heard on talk radio or seen on network TV) rather than any sustained engagement that leads to fresh insights. They don't really *care* about the project (other than completing it for a grade), and their writing suffers as a result.

Discover a Topic You Want to Know More About

Research is all about finding answers to an intriguing question or set of questions. A few years ago, one of my students wrote one of the worst research papers I have ever received. It argued that 18-year-olds should be granted the legal right to drink alcohol. The subject itself is a worthy one (over the years I have received numerous convincing essays that have argued this same point), but this particular essay of-fered no factual evidence or justification, and it was composed entirely of unsup-ported (and illogical) conjecture. As I discussed these problems with the student, it became apparent that he had absolutely no interest in the topic (he had chosen it because he thought *I* would find it fascinating). But it's virtually impossible to make a reader care about a topic if you don't care about it yourself. Even if readers are interested before they start reading your essay, if your writing does not express a personal enthusiasm, they will soon lose interest. I don't usually allow students to abandon their research projects in the middle of the semester, but I made an ex-ception in this case. In the end, the student produced a meticulously researched essay on methods for conserving the lobster population. His family is in the lob-stering business, and the diminishing crustacean population is a real threat to their livelihood. Once he discovered a topic he truly cared about, this student's research skills blossomed.

Therefore, your first challenge is to discover a topic that captivates your attention—something that you are curious about—perhaps something that you have some personal connection to (as was the case with my student who wrote about lobsters). Determining what this might be is not easy, but here is one strat-egy: Start by making a list of things in your own ordinary experience that "tick you off." Frustration is a strong emotion that can be redirected into more productive channels; you can use it to energize your desire to know more about something. Of course, not everything on your list will prove to be an appropriate or effective topic for an academic paper. That's okay. The point of the exercise is to free your-self up to generate ideas. However, with a little more creative/analytical thought, it is surprising how many times at least one of these "annoyances" can be trans-formed into an interesting, engaging, and researchable project.

One time when I used this exercise in a class, a student listed as one of her "pet peeves" the fact that movie theaters charge $3.00 for a 12-ounce bottle of water. In revisiting her list, she initially dismissed movie theater snack prices as an un-promising topic for a research paper. But then she started thinking about the topic from a slightly different angle. *Why* was she willing to pay for something that is free at the theater drinking fountain? The student was a confirmed bottled water drinker, convinced that bottled water is somehow healthier for her, but suddenly she found herself questioning things that she had never considered before. Where does bottled water come from? What is in bottled water? Is it healthier than tap water? Are there any significant differences between brands of bottled water? In this way, an idea that seemed like a "dead end" at first triggered an idea that led her to examine the nature of bottled water—a study that shattered many of her initial assumptions.

Because coming up with a good topic is often a real challenge, some students are most comfortable when instructors assign a specific subject to be researched. They are terrified if they must choose their own. Others chafe at any restrictions and want to determine their own direction. Whichever group you fall into— whether you prefer more structure or greater freedom—the success of your project depends on your active involvement and interest. A research project is hard work, and it is even more difficult if you don't care about your topic from the start. Re-gardless of whether the topic is assigned or you have the freedom to choose your own, make your research project relevant to *you*.

QUICK CHECK

Make Your Project Relevant

Make your project relevant by answering these questions:

- How does this topic relate to past/present concerns in my life?
- How does this subject relate to issues I have recently been studying or thinking about?
- How might this subject be important to me in the future?
- How can I use this subject to explore something that I want to know more about?

Needless to say, if you are not invested in the topic, you will find it difficult to sustain an attitude that will energize and encourage you throughout the process. That lack of passionate involvement also will be obvious to your readers who will, in turn, feel less interest than they otherwise would. Even if a research assignment seems mind-numbingly boring, you can find a way to transform it into a subject you care about.

Adapt Topics to Your Own Interests

Even assigned subjects often allow flexibility so you can adapt them to reflect your own particular interests. And although you might feel more comfortable when your instructor specifies the topic, you should never forfeit the opportunity to ex-plore an issue that you are genuinely interested in knowing more about. The trick is to find an angle or perspective that makes the topic come alive for *you*.

If the subject is assigned, try to shape your approach so that it reflects something that appeals to you, intrigues you, or even annoys you. You should at least experience a spark of curiosity. You should *want* to know more. Ideally, you'll feel much more than a spark of interest, and you'll discover that the assignment provides an opportunity for you to learn more about the world, yourself, other people, and/or other cultures. Coming up with your own angle on a topic is simply a matter of learning how to ask good questions—and, of course, of knowing yourself.

Turn a "Boring" Topic into an Interesting One. Suppose your American history instructor assigns a research project on "The Effects of the Vietnam War." Your first reaction might be to dismiss this topic as essentially boring—as something that might have appealed to the baby-boomer generation but not to you. However, unless the professor is very specific about what *types* of effects he/she expects you to study (e.g., the effects of the war on subsequent U.S. presidential elections), you can find a way to connect the subject with something you really *do* find interesting. If you are majoring in the biological sciences or pursuing a career in a medical field, for instance, you might research the long-term effects of Agent Orange on soldiers who fought in the Vietnam conflict. Someone interested in film or the arts might compare the different ways this war has been represented in film in the decades following the conclusion of American involvement. A sociology major could investigate some of the reasons why popular opinion concerning this war has changed since the 1960s. A student of architecture might consider the factors that influenced the design and construction of the *Vietnam Veterans Memorial* in Washington, D.C. It all comes back to knowing yourself and making connections that initially might not seem obvious.

Stumped? Ask Others. Sometimes answers to questions such as the ones listed earlier might come with virtually no conscious effort on your part. When that happens, the experience can seem almost magical. More often, especially for novice writers, your thinking will seem blocked. You might sit at the computer for hours without accomplishing anything that feels like real progress. That is a perfectly normal (if not particularly pleasant) experience. After all, a research project involves multiple tasks, each of which is complex, and only some of which are tangible features of the final product. In the inevitable moments of frustration—moments common to experienced writers as well as novices—it helps to remember that good thinking rarely occurs in a vacuum. If you can't come up with a good topic on your own, seek aid elsewhere.

Help can come in various forms. One option is to discuss the project with others.

- Make an appointment with your instructor. Explore your interests in conversation and ask for suggestions.
- Discuss the project with an instructor who teaches in your major or minor.
- Talk to other students in the class. After all, they are familiar with the assignment and will probably be eager to bounce ideas off you as well.
- Explain the assignment to friends and family members. Perhaps they can suggest a particular angle on the topic that combines your interests with the assignment.

Talking to someone or writing down your thoughts is a great way to move beyond a mental block. Forcing yourself to articulate your thoughts (even if you still feel confused) can lead to unexpected connections and even surprising breakthroughs.

-TIPS

Using E-Mail to Generate Ideas

E-mail is a wonderful way to solicit opinions from others. Some people find it easier to write down their questions than to communicate them face-to-face. Also, you might forget a suggestion you hear, but an e-mail response can be printed out. Many instructors include their e-mail addresses on course syllabi. If so, you should feel free to contact them. Exchange e-mail addresses with other students in your class. Sometimes class and work schedules make it difficult to meet to talk, but everybody reads his or her e-mail. E-mail is also an easy way to connect with people (e.g., family members, friends from home, former teachers) who might be able to offer suggestions as well.

Still Stumped? Browse. If you've tried all the preceding strategies and still haven't settled on a topic that seems interesting enough, try browsing an encyclopedia. The information given will probably prove too general to include in your final project, but the entries can help you discover an angle on a topic in order to personalize a research assignment. You will do more extensive research once you determine what your topic will be, but sometimes an encyclopedia article on a general topic can spark an idea or help you make connections that would not have occurred to you otherwise.

-TIPS

Online Encyclopedias

Britannica.com and *MSN Encarta*, once the most commonly used free online encyclopedias, now require subscriptions. However, *Britannica.com* <http://www.britannica.com/> still offers a "Best of the Web" search engine. *Encyclopedia.com* <http://www.encyclopedia.com/> and *Columbia Online Encyclopedia* <http://www.bartleby.com/65/> are free. *Wikipedia* <http://www.wikipedia.com> has become very popular with Internet users. However, because additions and edits can be made by *anyone* it cannot be considered an authoritative source and it should *not* be used in an academic research paper.

For instance, the results of a search using the terms "Vietnam War" and "film" in *Britannica.com* furnishes a link on this online encyclopedia's "Best of the Web" that includes a bibliography of over a hundred books and articles (in addition to an annotated "videography" of Vietnam War–themed movies) about how depictions of the war in popular films have changed over the years **(see Figure 1.1)**.

Using an online encyclopedia combines the assigned topic with a more personal concern to generate a possible research topic (and potential resources for further study). At this stage, you're not really looking for sources (although you might take a few minutes to bookmark or print them out for later use), but most importantly, you're looking for ideas. Time used to develop your ideas is always time well spent.

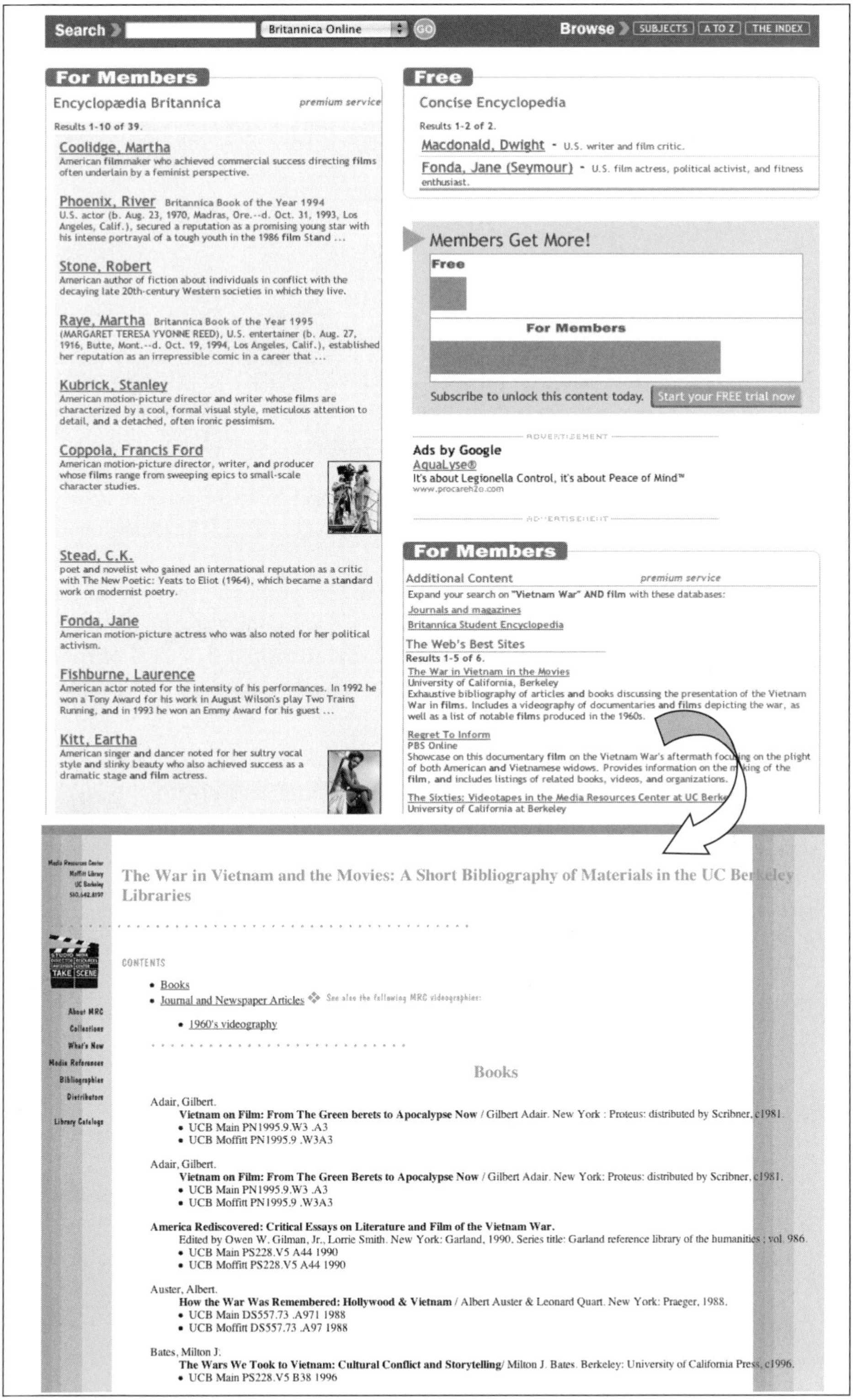

FIGURE 1.1 This website, found using an online encyclopedia as the search tool, provides over 100 potential sources for further research.

Another source for new ideas is a large daily newspaper, such as the *New York Times,* the *Washington Post,* the *Wall Street Journal,* or the *Chicago Tribune.* Newspapers, because they are published daily and reflect issues of contemporary concern, provide an almost endless supply of "hot" topics (i.e., subjects that are currently of interest and/or under debate).

e-TIPS

Online Newspapers

Many school libraries now have the *New York Times* and/or the *Wall Street Journal* available on-line or on a CD-ROM. You might be able to access full-text articles through your online reference system, or your library might have a computer station dedicated to a *Times* or *Journal* database.

A search using the terms "Vietnam War" and "architecture" on the *NewsBank NewsFile* database turned up an interview with Maya Lin, the designer of the Vietnam War Memorial **(see Figure 1.2).**

The article reveals that when the memorial was first proposed, many Vietnam veterans were outraged by the design. An analysis of their concerns, the compromises that were made, and the present popularity of the memorial (it is one of the most visited sites in the nation's capital) would be one way of relating the two subjects.

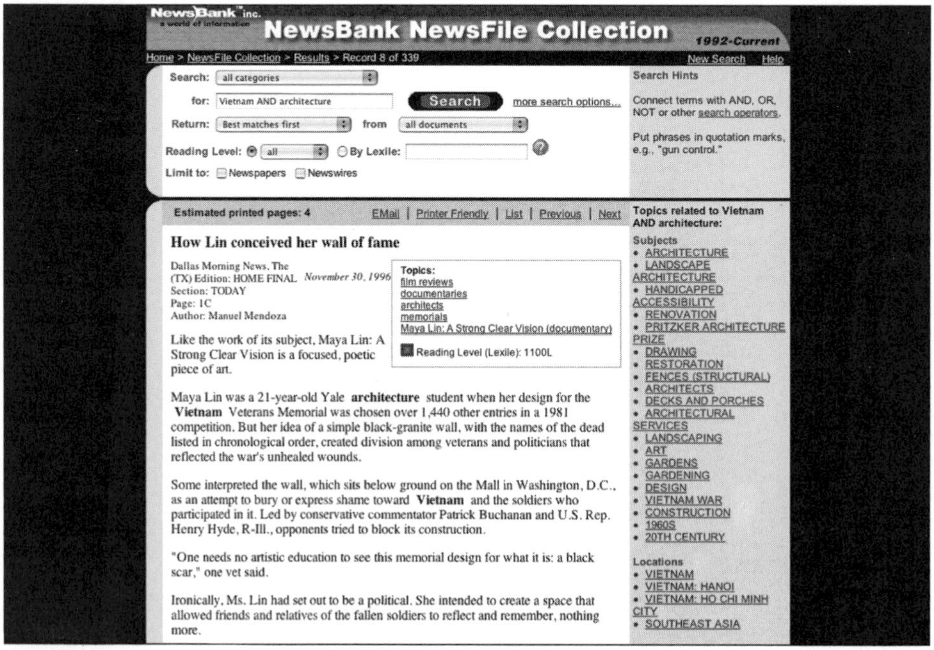

FIGURE 1.2 This database provides the full-text of the article. Some libraries have on-site computer stations dedicated to a *New York Times* database.

Although an article like this might generate an idea for a topic, you should be aware that, like an encyclopedia entry, a newspaper article might not be the best source of information for the final research project. Journalists are not usually experts on a topic (although they rely on experts). You would eventually need to learn what experts (i.e., scholars or scientists) are saying through further research. However, this article does supply the seed ideas for a research project that merges an assigned subject (the Vietnam War) with an individual interest (architecture).

The Internet is not usually the best starting point for extensive research on a topic because it is frequently difficult to determine whether information on a website is reliable. But if you have tried everything else and are still casting about for an idea, the web (like an encyclopedia or popular periodical) can help you determine a direction for your project. A simple keyword search will sometimes reveal interesting viewpoints and ideas.

For example, a quick search using the key terms "Vietnam War" and "medicine" turned up this informative website on the effects of Agent Orange **(see Figure 1.3)**. Compiled by four veterans who are interested in getting information to others who might have been affected by Agent Orange, this site documents that although America's involvement in the war ended in 1975, the U.S. government did not take definitive action to aid ailing veterans until the release of a study in 1993. This study linked Agent Orange to a host of serious health problems. One research question that arises immediately would be "Why the delay?" An investigation of the reasons for this time lapse might intrigue a premed or a prelaw student.

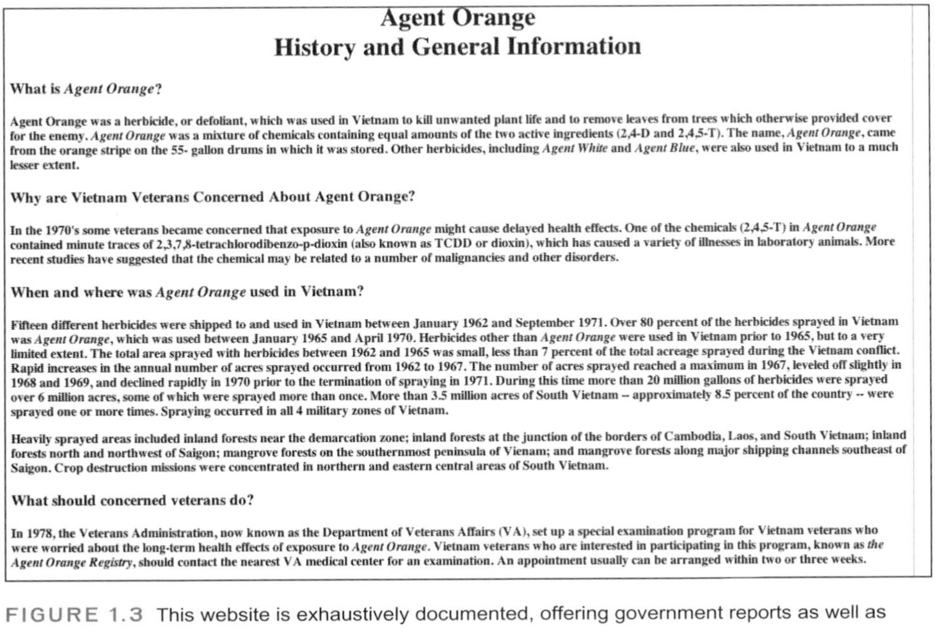

Agent Orange
History and General Information

What is *Agent Orange*?

Agent Orange was a herbicide, or defoliant, which was used in Vietnam to kill unwanted plant life and to remove leaves from trees which otherwise provided cover for the enemy. *Agent Orange* was a mixture of chemicals containing equal amounts of the two active ingredients (2,4-D and 2,4,5-T). The name, *Agent Orange*, came from the orange stripe on the 55-gallon drums in which it was stored. Other herbicides, including *Agent White* and *Agent Blue*, were also used in Vietnam to a much lesser extent.

Why are Vietnam Veterans Concerned About Agent Orange?

In the 1970's some veterans became concerned that exposure to *Agent Orange* might cause delayed health effects. One of the chemicals (2,4,5-T) in *Agent Orange* contained minute traces of 2,3,7,8-tetrachlorodibenzo-p-dioxin (also known as TCDD or dioxin), which has caused a variety of illnesses in laboratory animals. More recent studies have suggested that the chemical may be related to a number of malignancies and other disorders.

When and where was *Agent Orange* used in Vietnam?

Fifteen different herbicides were shipped to and used in Vietnam between January 1962 and September 1971. Over 80 percent of the herbicides sprayed in Vietnam was *Agent Orange*, which was used between January 1965 and April 1970. Herbicides other than *Agent Orange* were used in Vietnam prior to 1965, but to a very limited extent. The total area sprayed with herbicides between 1962 and 1965 was small, less than 7 percent of the total acreage sprayed during the Vietnam conflict. Rapid increases in the annual number of acres sprayed occurred from 1962 to 1967. The number of acres sprayed reached a maximum in 1967, leveled off slightly in 1968 and 1969, and declined rapidly in 1970 prior to the termination of spraying in 1971. During this time more than 20 million gallons of herbicides were sprayed over 6 million acres, some of which were sprayed more than once. More than 3.5 million acres of South Vietnam -- approximately 8.5 percent of the country -- were sprayed one or more times. Spraying occurred in all 4 military zones of Vietnam.

Heavily sprayed areas included inland forests near the demarcation zone; inland forests at the junction of the borders of Cambodia, Laos, and South Vietnam; inland forests north and northwest of Saigon; mangrove forests on the southernmost peninsula of Vienam; and mangrove forests along major shipping channels southeast of Saigon. Crop destruction missions were concentrated in northern and eastern central areas of South Vietnam.

What should concerned veterans do?

In 1978, the Veterans Administration, now known as the Department of Veterans Affairs (VA), set up a special examination program for Vietnam veterans who were worried about the long-term health effects of exposure to *Agent Orange*. Vietnam veterans who are interested in participating in this program, known as *the Agent Orange Registry*, should contact the nearest VA medical center for an examination. An appointment usually can be arranged within two or three weeks.

FIGURE 1.3 This website is exhaustively documented, offering government reports as well as analysis and opinion.

If you choose to use the Internet at this stage, remember that you are just *browsing* to find a topic. You will need to focus your topic more fully before you can begin to research in earnest.

e-TIPS

Search Engines

All search engines are not created equal. Some search word for word through the entire text, some organize websites into categories, and some are directories that do not search the entire web. When **browsing**, your best choice would be a subject directory such as **Librarians' Index** <http://www.lii.org>, **Infomine** <http://infomine.ucr.edu/>, **The Internet Public Library** <http://www.ipl.org>, or **The Virtual Library** <http://vlib.org>.

QUICK CHECK

Discover a Topic

Discover a topic you want to know more about.

- Discuss the project with your instructor, other students, family, and/or friends.
- Browse encyclopedias, newspapers, the Internet.
- Consider topics or issues you've encountered in other classes.

Choose a Worthwhile Topic

In addition to being relevant to you personally, an academic research project must fulfill the expectations of your instructor and conform to established practices in a particular discipline. The best topics invite discussion or debate and don't just recycle popular opinion (which may or may not be knowledgeable or informed) or regurgitate facts. You should choose a topic that will involve you in an interesting quest for knowledge and understanding rather than a simple fact-finding mission. Your research project should be stimulating for the reader as well as the writer, and the best ones almost always ask questions about the *how* or *why* of something—not just *what* or *where*.

Too Simple:

What TV shows contain violence?

What e-commerce businesses have proven successful?

Where are the best hospitals located?

Worthwhile:

Should television networks restrict violent programming in response to objections by religious and parental advocacy groups?

Why have certain e-commerce businesses been successful?

How have the best hospitals in the country achieved their superior status?

So think of the research project as an opportunity to find out something new about an issue that intrigues you. Think of it as an opportunity to help you to think more complexly about important issues, events, and ideas. It might be tempting to choose a topic quickly so you can get to the "real" work of finding books and articles and writing your report. However, if you rush this initial stage of the project, you might soon become discouraged and bored. Even more importantly, the resulting project will not reflect your best work.

Step 2: Narrow Your Focus

Even if you choose a focus for your paper that is personally interesting, if you do not adequately narrow the subject of your research in order to make it manageable, you can sabotage your project. Students often make the mistake of keeping their topics very broad and general, reasoning that they will run out of things to say if they choose a more focused or narrow subject. The problem with this strategy is that it leads students to choose topics that would best be subjects of an entire book rather than a short paper. The best research papers begin with a carefully delineated and focused assertion that is then methodically substantiated by specific examples, evidence, and analysis. If you begin with a broad assertion, you will be hard-pressed to provide adequate (or interesting) support for all that you claim. When it comes to research papers, it is generally better to say *a lot about a little* rather than *a little about a lot*.

> *Too Broad:*
> Children should have rights in our society.
>
> *Focused:*
> School locker searches are unconstitutional.
>
> *or* Drug testing should be banned from high school sports.
>
> *or* Teen curfews are undemocratic.
>
> *or* High school newspapers should not be censored by the administration.

Remember three important factors when determining the scope of your project.

1. *The assigned length of the project:* From the beginning, choose a topic that suits the limits of your assignment. If your instructor expects a 10-page essay, then your topic needs to be both focused and sufficiently complex. On the other hand, choose a less-involved subject—or just part of one—if the assignment is only 3 to 5 pages long; otherwise, you will merely scratch the surface of your topic. Superficial treatments are never effective in academic writing. For example, in 10 to 15 pages you could create a credible argument supporting the need for laws that require children to wear helmets when bicycling. If the assigned length is 3 pages, you might choose to narrow your subject to a discussion of how helmets have proven to protect children involved in bicycling accidents.

2. *The time you have to complete the project:* Any research project is time consuming. Certain topics will require even greater amounts of time. If your topic requires interviewing experts or conducting surveys and compiling

results, you need to allow time for this. Regardless of the type of research you are doing, make sure you limit your topic so you will have enough time to gather the necessary information. For instance, you might be interested in investigating the effectiveness of stalking laws. One way to make this subject more manageable would be to limit your discussion to the success rate of such laws in your own state or municipality.

3. *The resources you have at your disposal:* The Internet has made it possible to obtain a great deal of information that was formerly inaccessible or available only through interlibrary loan. Nevertheless, if you choose a topic that is so current or unstudied that little information about it exists, you will not be able to find enough information to support a research paper.

QUICK CHECK
Determine Project Scope
The BEST topics are specific and focused.
- Restrict your project to a topic or task you can complete successfully.
- Determine the scope of your topic to meet
  - □ the assigned length of the project
  - □ the time you have to complete the project
  - □ the resources you have at your disposal

A few years ago, MP3s (digital recordings available via the Internet) were just beginning to surface, and little information (beyond explanations of what they are and how they operate) existed about them. A researcher would have been frustrated by the quantity and quality of the information available. However, because of the threat MP3s pose to the multimillion-dollar recording industry, recently there has been a great deal of discussion about the commercial impact and ethical concerns surrounding this phenomenon. Today, a student who chose this topic would find numerous sources with far-ranging opinions (**see Figure 1.4**).

To research a topic conscientiously, you must become acquainted with a variety of perspectives on your subject. Therefore, if after extensive investigation you discover there is insufficient discussion of your subject, you must reject this topic or refocus it in a more promising direction. If you discover there is, on the other hand, an overwhelming amount of information, you must also proceed carefully: You must decide what is most important without misrepresenting or oversimplifying the subject.

Once you have chosen a topic and narrowed your focus, you are ready to begin to explore the different types of sources available (e.g., books, periodicals, websites, interviews, surveys). As your familiarity with these various resources develops, you may find that you develop an individualized approach to this process—methods and tactics that work especially well for you. However, certain time-tested strategies will remain constant. These research strategies are discussed in later chapters.

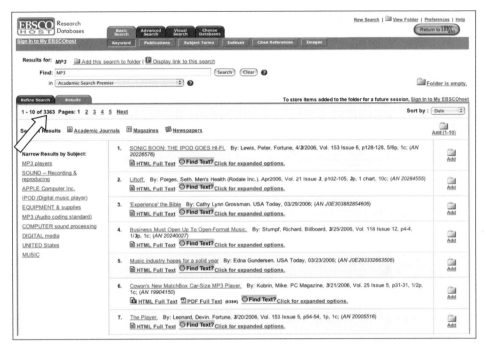

FIGURE 1.4 A search in this database revealed 3,363 periodical articles on MP3s. Prior to 1999 (when MP3s were first marketed), there was very little written about these recordings.

EXERCISES

1. People write best when they write about topics *they* consider interesting, but to choose a relevant topic, you must know yourself. To help you understand your interests, complete the following phrases as honestly and completely as you can.
   - The subject I most enjoy reading about is . . .
   - My favorite hobby or pastime is . . .
   - If I won the lottery, I would use the money to . . .
   - The type of volunteer activity I prefer is . . .
   - My favorite school subject has always been . . .
   - If I ran the world, the first thing I would change would be . . .

2. Make a list of four or five things that "tick you off." (Choose significant things that others might experience, as well. For instance, your little brother or your mother-in-law might tick you off, but there is little chance that this annoyance will yield a possible paper topic.) Meet in a small group (four or five) of other classmates and share your lists. Brainstorm together about how to transform these frustrations into viable research topics.

3. Your biology professor has assigned a research paper on "biological warfare." To get an overview of this topic and to begin to determine the specific focus

for your project, access an online encyclopedia (<www.britannica.com>; <www.encyclopedia.com>) and enter the search phrase "biological warfare." Make full use of the features provided by these tools (see the "e-tip" on page 8; consult the "Best of the Web" in ***Britannica.com***; check the *HighBeam* in ***Encyclopedia.com***) to locate as much current information as possible. As you browse these resources, keep in mind the interests you identified in Exercise 1 and list two potential topics or research questions that combine your personal interests with the issue of biological warfare.

4. The InfoTrac® College Edition database can also help you determine a particular focus for a project. If you are using the InfoTrac College Edition database in your course, use the passcode provided with this text to access the database and conduct a search using the same phrase ("biological warfare") as in the previous exercise. (Use the "Easy Search" function and conduct a "Subject Guide" search.) Browse down the results page and click on the listing entitled "Subdivisions." Review this inventory of categories and select three that interest you for further study. List these, and briefly (in a sentence or two) explain why they attracted your attention.

5. Return to the same "results" list from your InfoTrac College Edition database search on "biological warfare" in Exercise 4 and click on "Related Subjects" (this appears just below the "Subdivisions" link). Choose ONE of these related subjects (the one that seems most intriguing to you) and then click on the "Subdivisions" link for this topic. Write a paragraph that explains why you chose this particular "Related Subject" (stipulate what made it more interesting to you than the others). Also indicate which ONE of the subdivisions under this subject seems most interesting to you and why.

If you are not using the Info-Trac database, exercises 4 and 5 could be adapted for your school's full-text databases.

Find the Perfect Match

"What is

research, but a

blind date with

knowledge?"

WILLIAM HENRY

Don't let the chapter title fool you—we're still talking about research projects, not dating. But once you choose a topic for your project, you must still locate the information you need to answer your research questions and present a convincing analysis or argument. This means you will need to determine which key terms and phrases will lead you to that information. Sometimes that can be almost as difficult as finding Mr. or Ms. Right.

Where Do You Find the Perfect Match?

The Internet: Great Source or Source of Great Confusion?

In many ways, the Internet has made it easier to conduct research. The "Information Superhighway" can, with the click of a mouse, help you connect and communicate with countless potential sources for your investigation. Before the development of this system, students were usually limited to the resources available in their school and public libraries or through interlibrary loan. (Back then, even if the information was available, it usually took longer to find.) Today you have even more options: You can access library resources at other colleges and universities **(see Figure 2.1)**. You can e-mail (or conduct an online discussion with) a noted expert on your topic; you can join a listserv comprised of others—including experts—who share an interest in your subject; and you can browse a billion web pages. However, while the Internet has greatly expanded your choices for conducting research and accessing information, it has also created new problems for the novice researcher.

Three Common Problems with Internet Searches

So Many Websites, So Little Time! The most common complaint students have about doing research on the web is the sheer number of "hits" they get when conducting a keyword search. A search for a specific subject or item can turn up hundreds, or even thousands, of websites, and sifting through all of these options to evaluate their relevance for your particular project is a time-consuming—if not a daunting and overwhelming—task. Although search engines are great for obtaining certain types of information (e.g., which camera is best suited to your photography needs), much of the research you will be required to do during your academic career might be too complex and nuanced for a simple search using *Google, Yahoo!,* or any of the other commercial search engines commonly used to surf the web.

Unsuitable Websites. Another related problem is that your search will probably return numerous sites that are totally unrelated to your topic. This is because search engines are operated by "robots" (sometimes called "spiders" or "worms")—computer programs that roam the web, locating and cataloging sites with little or no human intervention. These robots rely on word choice and frequency of word use to determine what constitutes a match, but they have little sense of context. In addition, because many web editors want to increase the number of visitors to their sites for advertising purposes, they often embed invisible word lists that deceive these robots into making false matches. As a result, if your primary way of accessing information for your project is a web search, you will waste a great deal of time looking at irrelevant sites **(see Figure 2.2)**.

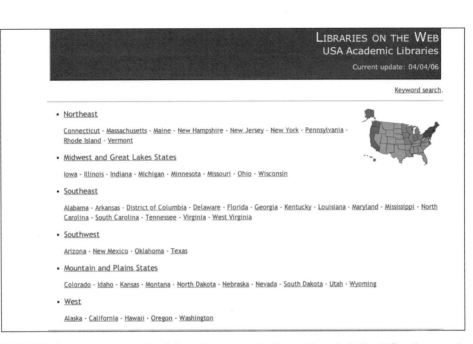

FIGURE 2.1 This website offers links to thousands of online catalogs, including U.S. colleges and universities, public libraries, and international libraries.

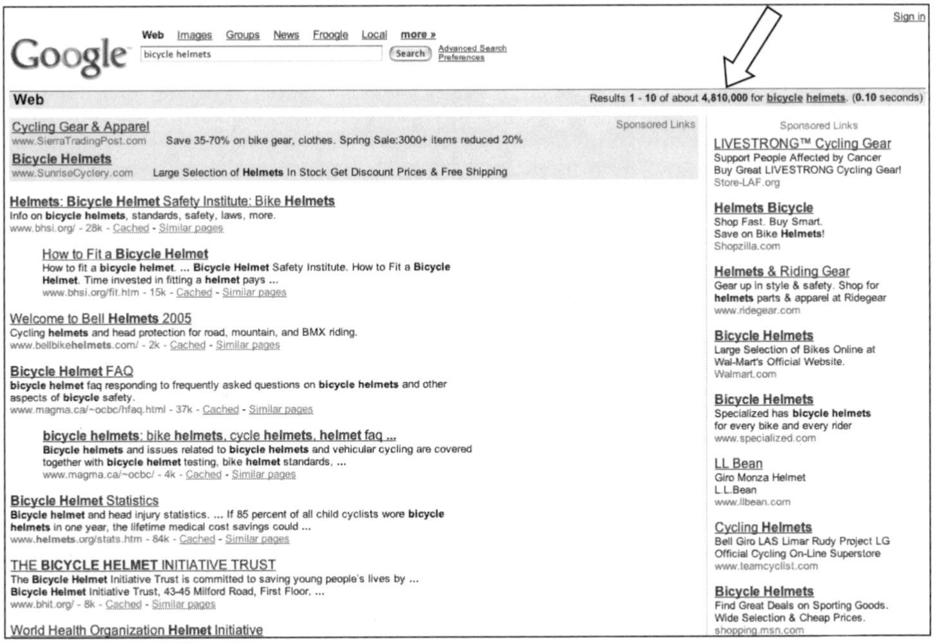

FIGURE 2.2 A simple Internet search using the keywords "bicycle helmets" resulted in 4,810,000 matches.

Unreliable Websites. While the previous problems may make your Internet searches frustrating and time consuming, perhaps nothing undermines the legitimacy of an academic research project more absolutely than unreliable websites. The Internet has made it possible for anyone with rudimentary computer skills and a URL to publish information accessible to a vast audience. In the past, students collected the bulk of their information from school or public libraries. They could be assured that these resources were reliable because editors of publishing companies, experts in the field, and librarians had already evaluated them and found them legitimate. However, no such methods of control determine what's published on many, if not most, websites. A student must evaluate each web page herself or himself to determine if the information published there is accurate and reliable. This is not always easy to discern, and it makes any research done on the web particularly challenging. A strong case must, after all, be based on reliable information.

The Solution: Begin Your Research in the Library

For the reasons just given, and despite the fact that you may eventually discover helpful resources on the Internet, *the library remains the best starting point* for conducting academic research. Now, I realize that not using the web to find answers to your research questions probably seems counterintuitive. The Internet has infiltrated our lives so completely that it has become a "first stop" whenever we need something (i.e., directions to a store, a phone number, a recipe for dinner). And what could be easier than typing in a few search terms and clicking the "enter" key? The impulse to head straight to the WWW when you want to begin your research project, although understandable, is a mistake.

Let me explain by offering an analogy. When I began to drive, I was taught that if I needed to stop a car quickly in slippery or wet conditions, I should "pump" the brakes (rather than simply stomping down on them) because this would give me more control and prevent the car from going into an uncontrolled slide. (Obviously, this was before the invention of "antilock" brakes.) A few years ago I was driving my elderly parents' ancient Toyota (no antilock brakes, no air bags) in the rain, when a Volvo station wagon made a sharp left turn right in front of me. I mashed down on the brake pedal and steered to the left, trying to go around the tanklike Volvo that now filled my entire lane and field of vision. I was sliding toward what seemed like an inevitable collision when a little voice in my brain told me that I *must* take my foot off the brake if I wanted the car to respond to the steering wheel. It took all my willpower and self-control to lift my foot off the brake (every ounce of energy in my body seemed directed at ramming that pedal to the floor), but when I did, the car jerked to the left, narrowly missing the back half of the Volvo. I had done what years of training had told me I should do even though it was completely opposite to what my instincts were crying out to do.

In the same way, if you want to do your best work on an academic research project, you *must* resist the allure and deceptive ease of the web. It's worth repeating: **For virtually every research project you will undertake in college, the best place to *begin* your search is your school library's online reference catalog.**

Internet technologies have transformed our libraries, making it possible to conduct searches more quickly and to access materials more easily. However, unlike the World Wide Web, your library's online reference system and bank of databases will most likely be current, credible, and relevant because they are largely devoted to scholarly and/or reputable sources. And here's the good news: As with the Internet, you can access most of this information via your home computer.

e-TIPS

Using an Online Library Catalog

Some online reference catalogs can be accessed only from computer terminals located in the school's library, but most colleges and universities have connected their catalogs to the web, making it possible for students to conduct research from non-networked computers. You still have to visit the library to check out books and access many of the holdings, but for numerous activities you are no longer restricted to the hours your library is open.

Also, college and university libraries often charge fees for printing research materials from school computers. Printing bibliographies of potential resources or full-text articles can be expensive. However, many online systems allow you to e-mail your search findings (which you can then print at your home computer). You may want to do the bulk of your searching from a computer with free or relatively inexpensive printing.

Types of Library Resources. Computers have changed the way we use our libraries. They have made it easier to access library resources whenever, and from wherever, we choose. Nonetheless, to a great extent library holdings have remained the same. There are still three main types of resources: general and special reference materials, books, and periodicals. What can be confusing is differentiating between your school's physical library (the actual building where books and periodicals are housed) and the virtual library (that usually includes the online catalog and databases as well as many additional study aids). Internet technology has made it possible for even the smallest college libraries to offer impressive collections, and it has made it easier, once you know how they work, to access them.

You will probably still need to visit your library in person to check out books, periodicals, and other printed materials, but with today's technology, library resources (and your access to them) have been dramatically expanded. You might already have a preference for the types of materials you like to use (probably because you have experienced success with one type when doing a research project in the past), but don't limit yourself. *Explore.* Expand your knowledge of what's available to you. One way to gain a less-biased perspective in your research is to gather information from a variety of sources. To do that, you should learn to use all of the resources available to you.

- *General and Special Reference Works.* Every library has a reference section. It is usually located in an especially accessible area, often near the front of the library, and it is staffed by reference librarians who can assist you. Books in this section (which include encyclopedias, dictionaries, atlases, almanacs, and biographical references) cannot be checked out. You may not realize it, but reference sections also include special reference works. These include not only general encyclopedias and dictionaries, but materials devoted to specific disciplines. At some point early in your college career, browse the reference section to get a sense of the resources available, especially those specific to your major and related areas of interest. Some of these reference works (like general encyclopedias and dictionaries) are now available online (see the "e-tips" on pages 8 and 10 about online encyclopedias and newspapers), but many special reference works are available only at the library. Here are some of the special reference works that might be housed in the general reference section.

- □ *Business and the Environment: A Resource Guide*
- □ *The Bulfinch Guide to Art History: A Comprehensive Survey and Dictionary of Western Art and Architecture*
- □ *From Suffrage to the Senate: An Encyclopedia of American Women in Politics*
- □ *Dictionary of Mathematics*

Because its resources will provide general overviews of your topic, the reference section can be an excellent starting point for your research. However, because the information contained in these works is so general, you will want to extend your search beyond them.

- *Books.* You are probably most familiar with these holdings. In fact, when you hear the word "library," books are what probably leap to mind. Library books are housed in the "stacks" (the main bookcases of the library), are arranged according to subject categories determined by the Library of Congress, and can be checked out and removed from the library. Sometimes they are written by one author; sometimes they contain collections of essays or chapters written by many experts, not all of whom necessarily share the same point of view or perspective.

e-TIPS

Interlibrary Loan

The Internet has made interlibrary loans easier and quicker. Some schools even allow you to order interlibrary loans online. Also, check to see if your school has agreements with other colleges or universities to share library resources. In my state, the colleges have linked their online catalogs so students can search just their own or all of the libraries for materials. It also has an arrangement with a neighboring four-year state university so that students can check out books from its much larger collection. Interlibrary loans from these schools often take less than a week to complete.

- *Periodicals.* Periodicals are publications like newspapers, magazines, and scholarly journals that are issued at regular intervals (e.g., daily, weekly, monthly). You might be familiar with periodicals like the *New York Times, Newsweek,* and *U.S. News and World Report,* but you may be less familiar with the many scholarly periodicals available in your library. The articles in these journals are written by experts in their fields, rather than reporters, and often provide the most up-to-date information on a subject because they are published more quickly than books. Periodicals, because they are frequently published on more perishable materials, are also the most "polymorphous" holdings in the library—you may find them available in their original "hard" (or printed on paper) state, on microfiche, on microfilm, or, increasingly, in computer databases.

e-TIPS

Full-Text Databases

Many smaller libraries have limited periodical resources. However, a new breed of databases (e.g., WilsonSelect, SIRSResearcher, Academic Search Elite [EBSCOhost], InfoTrac College Edition [Gale]) offers full-text periodical articles. How to use these databases will be discussed more fully in future chapters.

How Do You Find the Perfect Match?

Become Familiar with Your Library's Online Reference Catalog

Library research used to require hours spent shuffling through stacks of index cards in drawer after drawer of the card catalog—and taking note of potentially promising call numbers. However, computers have made the card catalog a thing of the past, and almost all library reference systems are now electronic. Learning to use your school's online catalog has a number of benefits that go beyond the obvious one of locating books, journal articles, or other resources available through your library system. It offers the perfect starting point for learning to effectively use electronic search tools.

Understand Electronic Search Tools

Although computer search tools may differ slightly in appearance and the features they offer, they all operate similarly. Whether you are using an Internet search engine, a database, or an online reference catalog, you simply type in a keyword or phrase that identifies your subject, click on a "begin search" button, and then wait for the computer to list all of the documents that match your request.

When you are using an online reference catalog search tool, you can search according to a keyword, an author's name, the title of a work, or a subject category. Some search tools offer other options as well, but these are the main categories for which you will usually search. At the beginning of a research project, you will primarily use the **keyword** or **subject** option **(see Figure 2.3).**

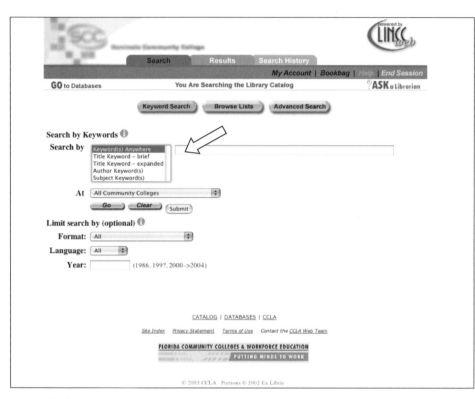

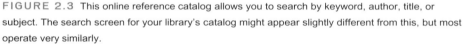

FIGURE 2.3 This online reference catalog allows you to search by keyword, author, title, or subject. The search screen for your library's catalog might appear slightly different from this, but most operate very similarly.

It is important to understand the difference between keyword and subject searches. A **keyword** search retrieves all documents that include the specified word(s), whether the words appear in the subject headings, title, or description of the article or book. In an online database or Internet search engine, a keyword search might search the entire text of the document. A **subject** search, on the other hand, retrieves documents that have been cataloged under that particular subject heading. In an online catalog and some databases, such headings are determined by the Library of Congress. There are advantages and drawbacks to both types of searches (see the "e-tip" on page 25).

While the operation seems very simple, if you have used such a search tool, you know that success or failure depends on your ability to match your search terms with the documents you are trying to retrieve. Even simple spelling errors can block your efforts. A student in one of my classes once spent a very frustrating 40 minutes in the online reference catalog and then brusquely informed me that our library contained absolutely nothing about Albert Einstein. I was a bit mystified until I looked at his computer screen and saw that he had been using the search terms "Albert Einstine." When he corrected his error, he, of course, had a wide range of documents to choose from. Even if you spell correctly, the most effective search terms may not be the ones that immediately come to mind.

e-TIPS

Keyword and Subject Searches

Keyword searches are different from subject searches. Understanding the differences will enable you to conduct the most effective searches.

Keyword Search

- Any words that *could* be used to describe your topic *can* be used (extremely flexible and broad)
- May retrieve many results that aren't relevant to your topic
- Most useful at the beginning of a project when you don't know the exact language used by experts on your topic

Subject Search

- The *exact* terms that describe a topic as determined by the Library of Congress or subject index must be used
- Search will fail completely if you don't locate or guess the correct subject headings
- Definitely the most effective type of search if you know the exact terms because it retrieves only the most relevant documents

e-TIPS

Common Search Mistakes

Electronic search tools seek precise matches to your search terms or phrases. Besides spelling mistakes, another common error students sometimes make is capitalizing words that are not proper nouns. Remember that some search engines are *case sensitive;* only capitalize when appropriate.

Formulate Effective Search Terms

The problem with electronic search tools is that although they are much quicker, and usually more thorough, than humans, they can't think. That is your job. However, this is not to say that you are confined to your own (perhaps, at least initially, limited) understanding of your topic. There are numerous support systems available to help you assemble a list of possible search words and phrases. Here's a useful tip: **Remember to keep a running list of possible search terms and phrases as you try, by trial and error, to find keywords that match your topic.** A keyword that was unsuccessful in the online catalog might work in a database or Internet search engine. It takes very little time to jot down a word or phrase, and it could save you much time and effort later. There are a number of ways you can expand your list of keywords.

Identify Synonyms or Related Words or Ideas. You might have chosen a topic for which you can readily identify keywords. For example, if you chose to research reasons why marijuana should be legalized for medical purposes, the key terms "marijuana," "legalization," and "medicine" almost leap out at you. Even in this fairly straightforward example, however, there are certain pitfalls you need to be familiar with. For instance, marijuana can also be spelled *marihuana.*

However, not all topics translate so quickly into search terms that will result in finding the information you need. If, for instance, you chose to investigate how communities regulate dog and cat populations, you might try the term "animal control." While this might seem like the obvious term (after all, agencies responsible for catching stray dogs and cats are often called "animal control" by local governments), a search using this phrase turned up documents that dealt with livestock, laboratory animals, and wild animals, but nothing about controlling stray or homeless pets.

You have two choices at this point. On the one hand, you could (like my student who informed me that he couldn't locate anything about Albert Einstein) foolishly decide that your library has no information on your topic. The better solution is to discover alternative words or phrases that relate to your subject. For instance, stray cats and dogs are frequently held in "animal shelters," and in some areas of the country these shelters are run by "humane societies."

Sometimes a dictionary or thesaurus can help you locate a successful keyword. One of my students wanted to examine how U.S. colleges and universities are responding to the special problems of foreign students who choose to study here. Searches using the phrase "foreign students" resulted in no matches. After consulting a thesaurus for synonyms, she experienced success with the phrase "international students."

e-TIPS

Use a Thesaurus

Most word-processing programs include a thesaurus. These computer versions often have shorter lists of optional words than their hard-copy counterparts, but they are much easier to use. Also, scanning alternative words for the synonyms in the original list can lead you to additional lists of possible keywords. You can also use the *Merriam-Webster Online Thesaurus* at <http://www.m-w.com/>.

Refer to the Library of Congress Classification System. Since all materials in the library are organized according to standardized categories (unlike the Internet, which is a wild and unregulated virtual space in which documents might be organized under any number of terms or phrases), the Library of Congress classification system can help you discover the key terms and phrases used by academics to describe your topic and match you up with the best resources available. You will find the *Library of Congress Subject Headings* (a four-volume work) in the reference section of your library. It can help you discover optional terms for your topic that you might not have thought of on your own.

Suppose you are investigating the way fashion reflects contemporary culture's preoccupation with technology. Looking up "fashion" in the *Library of Congress Subject Headings* would lead you to the terms "Manners and Customs" (the general heading) and "Costume," "Dress," "Materials and articles of clothing," and "Ornaments"—alternatives that might be more successful because they are more narrowly focused on your topic. Part of investigating a new subject is learning the language used by those who are experts in that field. Use the well-established subject categories of your library to help you identify the words that will call up the best information when you search (**see Figure 2.4**).

e-TIPS

Library of Congress Classifications

Your reference librarian can direct you to a list of Library of Congress subject categories, but you can also view these online. See *LC Classification Outline* at <http://www.loc.gov/catdir/cpso/lcco/lcco.html> or <http://www.itsmarc.com/crs/lcso0001.htm>.

Construct Boolean Search Phrases. I still remember the first time I was asked to conduct a *Boolean search.* The name alone seemed both ridiculous and intimidating. When the librarian (by way of explanation) distributed four or five handouts filled with confusing Venn diagrams, I thought that I would never be able to understand, much less construct, one. I've always been a bit math impaired, and this sounded and looked suspiciously similar to something I might have encountered in a statistics or calculus class. Imagine my surprise when I realized that the idea is not only very simple but very useful. In fact, if you do much surfing on the web, whether you know it or not, you have probably already done a Boolean search.

LC Classification Outline

R Medicine

R RA RB RC RD RE RF RG RJ RK RL RM RS RT RV RX RZ

R	5	-	920	**Medicine (General)**
	131	-	784	History of medicine
	735	-	847	Medical education
	895	-	920	Medical physics. Medical radiology. Nuclear medicine

RA	1	-	1270		**Public aspects of medicine**
	1	-	418	.5	Medicine and the state Including medical statistics, medical economics, provisions for medical care, medical sociology
	421	-	790	.85	Public health. Hygiene. Preventive medicine Including environmental health, disposal of the dead, transmission of disease, epidemics, quarantine, personal hygiene
	791	-	954		Medical geography. Medical climatology and meteorology
	960	-	999		Medical centers. Hospitals. Clinics
	1001	-	1171		Forensic medicine
	1190	-	1270		Toxicology

RB	1	-	214	**Pathology**

RC	31	-	1245		**Internal medicine. Practice of medicine** Including diagnosis, individual diseases and special types of diseases, diseases of systems or organs
	86	-	88	.9	First aid in illness and injury
	321	-	571		Neurology and psychiatry
	952	-	954	.6	Geriatrics
	955	-	962		Arctic and tropical medicine
	963	-	969		Industrial medicine
	970	-	1015		Military medicine
	1030	-	1160		Transportation medicine

FIGURE 2.4 The subject categories listed in the *LC Classification Outline* suggest narrowly focused terms under more general topics.

I became less frightened when I realized that the system's odd-sounding name was merely the result of having been created by George Boole. Even though Boole was a mathematician (thus the Venn diagrams), you don't have to be a rocket scientist to understand the process. A Boolean search refines your quest by linking keywords with **AND, OR,** or **NOT** to demonstrate the relationships between the terms. Most research projects have a narrow focus, and Boolean phrases allow you to pinpoint the types of documents that directly address your topic.

QUICK CHECK
A Brief Guide to Boolean Logic
Boolean **AND** *requires all terms to be in records retrieved.*
> *Example:* turtles AND salmonella

Boolean **OR** *allows either term.*
> *Example:* turtles OR reptiles

Boolean **NOT** *excludes terms.*
> *Example:* salmonella NOT "food poisoning"

Combine terms using parentheses (actions in parentheses will be performed first).
> *Example:* (turtle OR reptile) AND (salmonella NOT "food poisoning")

Enclose multiword search phrases in quotation marks.
> *Example:* "food poisoning"

A few years ago a student who worked in a pet store decided to investigate the federal law that forbids the sale of turtles less than four inches in size. The law was enacted to protect consumers from the threat of salmonella poisoning. Her argument was that the law, although well meaning, was illogical. Salmonella can be spread by any number of reptiles (not just turtles), and infection is not limited to small turtles. After compiling a simple list of keywords ("turtles," "reptiles," "salmonella"), she organized them into search phrases using the Boolean term **AND** (Boolean terms are always capitalized to distinguish them from the keywords), indicating that both terms in the following examples should appear in the document.

- turtles **AND** salmonella
- reptiles **AND** salmonella

However, when my student attempted to use these Boolean phrases in her school's online catalog, there were no matches. While these terms are clearly connected to the topic (and may prove productive in another search engine), they did not trigger the desired response in the online library catalog. Therefore, this researcher had to rethink her list of keywords. Her first strategy was to abandon the Boolean terms and conduct a simple keyword search using just the term "turtle."

However, this proved unfruitful **(see Figure 2.5)**. The solution to this problem is not to think more generally but to determine how the information you are looking for specifically differs from what you are finding.

A quick look at the results of the "turtle" keyword search reveals documents about sea turtles, fictional turtles, Ninja turtles, and by publishers with the word "turtle" in their name. When I asked this student how these "turtles" differed from what she was searching for, she readily answered that she was searching for "pet" turtles. She conducted two new Boolean searches:

- turtles **AND** pets
- reptiles **AND** pets

These searches returned documents that were more appropriate **(see Figure 2.6)**.

FIGURE 2.5 A search using the term "turtle" produces 410 hits, and the first 3 seem totally unrelated to the topic.

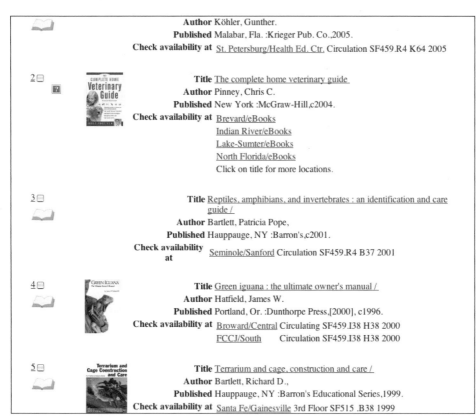

Combining phrases is a way to *refine* your search. By this I mean that a Boolean search weeds out unrelated documents and produces matches that directly address your topic. The two preceding searches could be combined into one by using the Boolean term **OR** (use parentheses to group search phrases).

- (turtles **OR** reptiles) **AND** pets

My student soon determined that she needed to learn more about salmonella (how it is transmitted, the symptoms, treatment, etc.). She conducted a simple search using the keyword "salmonella" and soon discovered that food poisoning, as well as reptiles, can cause salmonella. Therefore, she refined her search by excluding the terms "food poisoning" (multiword search terms should be enclosed in quotation marks) with the Boolean term **NOT**:

- salmonella **NOT** "food poisoning"

Electronic search tools vary. Some allow you to use complicated search phrases; others can't respond to more than one or two Boolean terms per search. It would be ideal if you could conduct a search such as the following:

- (turtles **OR** reptiles) **AND** (salmonella **NOT** "food poisoning")

Sometimes online search tools allow you to do such advanced searches **(see Figure 2.7)**. It will take a certain amount of trial and error to determine what works best in your library's system.

Boolean searches are simple if you remember four basic rules:

1. Use the Boolean terms **AND, OR,** or **NOT** to specify the relationships between keywords:
   - Use AND when you want both keywords to appear in the document: **turtles AND pets**. [Note: Some search tools require a plus sign (+) instead (e.g., turtles + pets).]
   - Use OR when either keyword can appear in the document: **turtles OR reptiles**.
   - Use NOT to exclude unwanted terms: **salmonella NOT "food poisoning."** [Note: Some search tools require a minus sign (–) instead (e.g., salmonella – "food poisoning").]

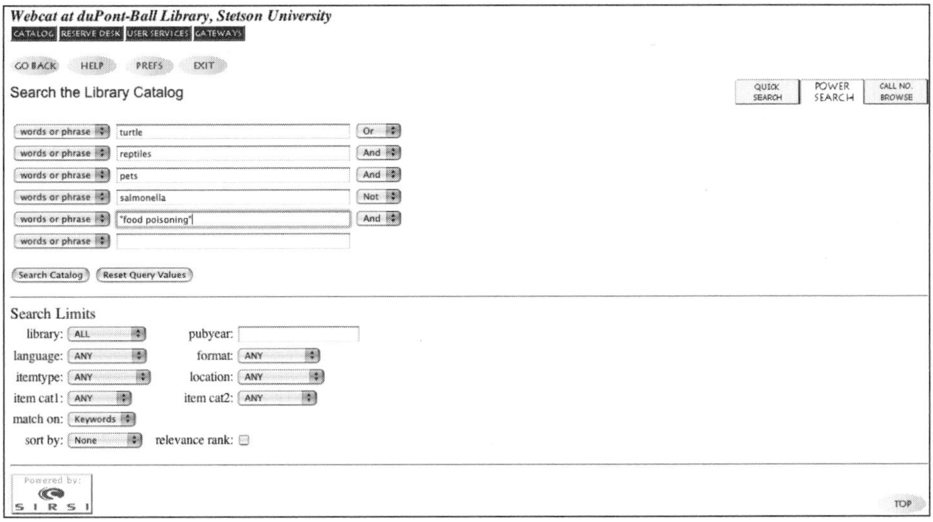

FIGURE 2.7 This online catalog offers a complex search that allows you to refine your query using up to five different Boolean terms.

2. Always capitalize Boolean search terms **(AND, OR, NOT)**.

3. Enclose groups of search terms in parenthesis to indicate which actions should occur first: **(turtles OR reptiles) AND salmonella**.

4. Enclose multiword search terms in quotation marks: **salmonella NOT "food poisoning."**

It may not be as exciting as finding that perfect someone, but you will probably feel a certain satisfaction when your keyword and Boolean searches turn up sources that contain just the information you need to get started on a well-documented research essay. As gratifying as this can be, it is only the starting point. The next chapter will discuss how to use your library's resources to continue to expand your search terms and refine your searches, connect with an even greater variety of sources, and evaluate which resources are best for your project.

QUICK CHECK
Identifying Keywords
Identify keywords that match your topic.
- Locate synonyms and alternative phrases for your topic.
- Discover the Library of Congress subject headings that address your topic.
- Combine your search terms into effective Boolean search phrases

Keep a running list of all search terms and phrases because different keywords will be successful in different research tools.

EXERCISES

1. Refer to the viable research topics you generated from the list of things that "tick you off" (Exercise 2 in Chapter 1). Work with a partner or a group of students to create a list of synonyms or alternative phrases for these topics.

2. The following topics frequently are the subject of student papers. For each of them, write as many synonyms or alternative phrases as you can discover.
   - School violence
   - Teen pregnancy
   - Domestic abuse
   - Antismoking laws
   - War on drugs

3. Using either the *Library of Congress Subject Headings* in your school library's reference section or an online guide (such as <http://lcweb.loc.gov/catdir/cpso/lcco/lcco.html>), locate all of the Library of Congress (LC) subject headings that are pertinent to ONE of the topics listed in Exercise 2.

   Enter your school's online catalog and use these subject headings as subject search phrases to locate and list four sources that directly address the topic.

   Print out the complete bibliographic information for these sources.

4. If you are using the InfoTrac College Edition database in your course, use the passcode provided with this textbook to access the database and conduct first a "Subject guide" search and then a "Keyword" search (click on the appropriate term in the menu on the left) for ONE of the topics listed in Exercise 2 (remember to enclose a multiword search term in quotation marks). Write a paragraph in which you describe the differences between the two search results and explain why these differences occur.

5. Combine the LC subject headings you identified in Exercise 3 with the synonyms and alternative phrases you discovered for that topic in Exercise 2 to create as many variant Boolean search phrases as you can (refer to the *Quick Check* on page 28 for help). Use the InfoTrac College Edition database and experiment with these search phrases to locate four sources that directly address the topic. (Note: Databases do not rely on LC subject headings in topic searches. Nevertheless, identifying the LC headings can help you refine your search.) Print out the complete bibliographic information for these sources.

If you are not using the Info-Trac database, exercises 4 and 5 could be adapted for your school's full-text databases.

3

Become a Research "Supersleuth"

As Plutarch so aptly noted, the search for relevant information requires a willingness to explore paths that may ultimately lead nowhere. This is especially likely when keywords result in numerous matches; in such cases it's very easy to feel overwhelmed by the sheer amount of information that seems to be available on a topic. Even more frustrating are the odds that many of these seemingly promising hits will not, on further exploration, prove so promising after all. No one wants to spend hours reading a book or article only to reach the conclusion that it isn't pertinent to his or her particular project. But how do you decide early on which sources deserve a closer look and which ones can be ignored? How do you minimize the blind alleys?

This chapter focuses on strategies that can help you zero in on the best leads. I like to compare what researchers do to how detectives work to solve a crime. When a crime is committed, detectives want to pursue only the most promising suspects. Like you, they want to avoid or at least minimize blind alleys or dead ends. Therefore, the first step in any criminal investigation is to develop the clearest and most accurate ideas about the crime, the suspect, and the motive. Expert detectives tirelessly question witnesses, comb the crime scene for clues, and assess possible motives. Taking the time to gather and evaluate evidence is time well spent; it will save valuable time later on. Once detectives have the most accurate picture possible of the crime, the suspect, and the motive, they can limit their search to the most productive leads. In the same way, if you take time at the beginning of a project to clarify your ideas about a topic, develop a working thesis, and then transform that

35

thesis into a series of research questions, you will be well on your way to determining the most direct route to the information you need. Even before you actually begin your "investigation," you will be able to identify whether the resources you discover are likely to be "hot tips" or merely "dead ends."

In short, it pays to know what you are looking for. Of course, in researching, as in sleuthing, sometimes the process is relatively simple and straightforward. Other times it can be more complex, and you will need to eliminate "red herrings," or false leads, before you find information that will provide the best answers to the questions at hand. In certain cases, what initially seemed irrelevant can even provide the thread that will unravel the mystery at the heart of the investigation. So you might not want to discard or dismiss anything too soon. At the same time, you'll need to avoid using flimsy or erroneous information—often the result of moving too quickly—to construct a false representation or flawed understanding of the subject. In sleuthing, that kind of error can lead to convicting the wrong person (or no conviction at all); in writing and research, it will result in a project that is fundamentally flawed because it ultimately does not establish what it sets out to prove.

Ask Questions

Most detectives begin their investigations by asking questions that will lead them to the perpetrator of the crime: Was anyone seen at or near the scene of the attack? Who would have benefited from the victim's death? Who knew or had access to where the jewelry was stored? You should do likewise, and compose questions that identify what kind of information you need and where you might locate it. What do you need to know before you can make a convincing claim? Which sources are reliable, accurate, and trustworthy? Using these questions to establish an accurate profile early in your investigation will transform your project from a "find a needle in the haystack" experience to a successful "pursuit and capture" of the information you require.

QUICK CHECK
Do *Effective* Research
- Transform your research topic into a series of research questions.
- Use research questions to identify new keywords and search phrases.
- Determine what type of information you need to locate.
- Remember that one good source can lead you to another.

What Are You Looking For?

Because all investigations involve locating information that will provide answers to questions, a good way to begin is by transforming your topic or thesis from a statement or assertion into a series of questions. To help you gain this focus, start by asking yourself, "What do I need to know to prove my point?"

For example, suppose (like Scott, one of my former students) you are interested in examining the ways federal financial aid programs favor traditional over nontraditional students. Scott had left a job with a good salary to return to school; however, he was shocked to discover that his previous income made him ineligible for financial aid (even though, as a full-time student, he was no longer employed). His experience led him to suspect that the financial aid system gives preference to students who are entering college directly from high school. But how could he be sure? His first attempts at searching in the online catalog produced an overwhelming number of prospective sources **(see Figure 3.1)**.

At this point, Scott realized he needed to determine more exactly what information he needed to support his theory. He composed a list of research questions that included the following:

- What are the criteria for financial aid?
- Why do these criteria exist?
- What is a "traditional" student?
- What is a "nontraditional" student?
- In what ways do the financial needs of traditional and nontraditional students differ?
- What assumptions are made by colleges, universities, and financial aid agencies about nontraditional students' needs?

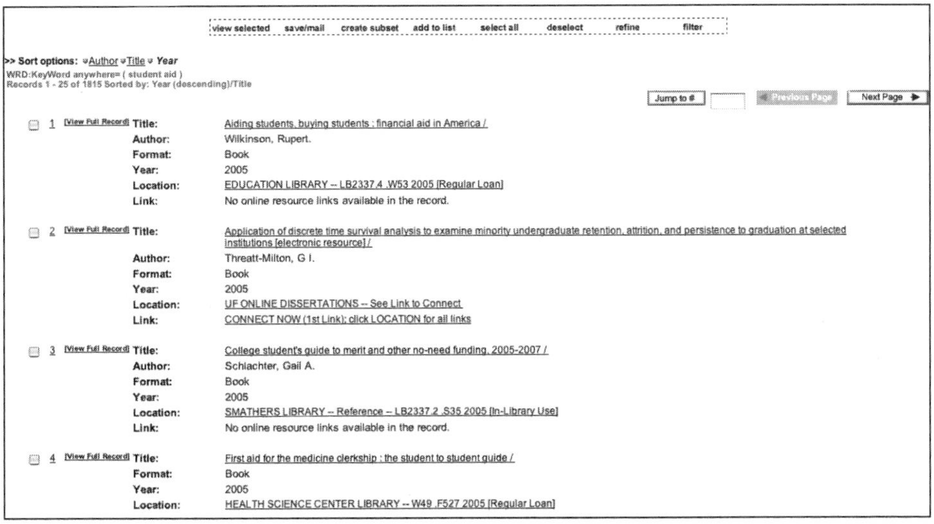
view selected save/mail create subset add to list select all deselect refine filter

>> Sort options: Author Title *Year*
WRD:KeyWord anywhere= (student aid)
Records 1 - 25 of 1815 Sorted by: Year (descending)/Title

Jump to # Previous Page Next Page

1 [View Full Record] **Title:** Aiding students, buying students : financial aid in America /
Author: Wilkinson, Rupert.
Format: Book
Year: 2005
Location: EDUCATION LIBRARY -- LB2337.4 .W53 2005 [Regular Loan]
Link: No online resource links available in the record.

2 [View Full Record] **Title:** Application of discrete time survival analysis to examine minority undergraduate retention, attrition, and persistence to graduation at selected institutions [electronic resource] /
Author: Threatt-Milton, G I.
Format: Book
Year: 2005
Location: UF ONLINE DISSERTATIONS -- See Link to Connect
Link: CONNECT NOW (1st Link); click LOCATION for all links

3 [View Full Record] **Title:** College student's guide to merit and other no-need funding, 2005-2007 /
Author: Schlachter, Gail A.
Format: Book
Year: 2005
Location: SMATHERS LIBRARY -- Reference -- LB2337.2 .S35 2005 [In-Library Use]
Link: No online resource links available in the record.

4 [View Full Record] **Title:** First aid for the medicine clerkship : the student to student guide /
Format: Book
Year: 2005
Location: HEALTH SCIENCE CENTER LIBRARY -- W49 .F527 2005 [Regular Loan]

FIGURE 3.1 A search of this online catalog using the keywords "student aid" returned an overwhelming number (1,815) of potential sources. Sifting through all of these possibilities without a clear agenda would take hours of research time.

Although he might have been able to give tentative answers to many of these questions before conducting any research, in order to construct a persuasive argument, Scott knew he needed to locate sources that would give him up-to-date information generated by people who had facts to back up their claims. Identifying the specific facts, statistics, definitions, and ideas he was looking for enabled him to sift through the long list of potential sources more selectively. By rephrasing his thesis into a series of questions, his research became *effective* (and by that I mean that he found the best resources available relatively quickly) because he was able to recognize whether the sources he found were trustworthy and whether they provided information relevant to his project **(see Figure 3.2)**.

Scott was on the right track. However, he soon discovered that an even more effective method of sleuthing was to use these research questions to identify the keywords and Boolean phrases that would quickly reduce the number of documents the catalog returned. Scott's first search used the keyword phrase "student aid," which produced 1,815 "hits"—too many to sift through! His research questions, however, suggested that he was most interested in a more specific issue: the distribution of financial aid for a particular kind of student. He first tried a Boolean search with the terms "student aid AND nontraditional student," but this did not match any of the library subject categories. (If you are unfamiliar with Boolean searches, see Chapter 2.)

☐ 10 [View Full Record]	**Title:**	Beyond the big test : noncognitive assessment in higher education /
	Author:	Sedlacek, William E.
	Format:	Book
	Year:	2004
	Location:	EDUCATION LIBRARY -- LB2351.2 .S43 2004 [Regular Loan]
	Link:	No online resource links available in the record.
☐ 11 [View Full Record]	**Title:**	Borrowing constraints, college aid, and intergenerational mobility /
	Author:	Hanushek, Eric Alan, 1943-
	Format:	Book
	Year:	2004
	Location:	LEGAL INFORMATION CENTER -- Tax Library -- HB1 .N37 no.10711 2004 [Regular Loan]
	Link:	CONNECT NOW (1st Link): click LOCATION for all links
☐ 12 [View Full Record]	**Title:**	College choices : the economics of where to go, when to go, and how to pay for it /
	Format:	Book
	Year:	2004
	Location:	Request Retrieval: -- WEST BOOK -- LB2350.5 .C647 2004 [Regular Loan]
	Link:	No online resource links available in the record.
☐ 13 [View Full Record]	**Title:**	Como reembolsar sus prestamos para estudiantes [electronic resource]
	Format:	Computer File
	Year:	2004
	Link:	CONNECT NOW (1st Link): click LOCATION for all links
☐ 14 [View Full Record]	**Title:**	Consolidation loans : what's best for past borrowers, future students, & U.S. taxpayers? : hearing before the Subcommittee on 21st Century Competitiveness of the Committee on Education and the Workforce, U.S. House of Representatives, One Hundred Eighth Congress, first session, July 22, 2003.
	Author:	United States. Congress. House. Committee on Education and the Workforce. Subcom
	Format:	Book
	Year:	2004
	Location:	SCIENCE LIBRARY, Documents -- (microfiche) -- Y 4.ED 8/1:108-28
		SCIENCE LIBRARY, Documents -- Y 4.ED 8/1:108-28 [Regular Loan (documents)]
		ONLINE -- See Link to Connect
	Link:	CONNECT NOW (1st Link): click LOCATION for all links
☐ 15 [View Full Record]	**Title:**	Evaluating the impact of the D.C. tuition assistance grant program /
	Author:	Kane, Thomas J.
	Format:	Book
	Year:	2004
	Location:	LEGAL INFORMATION CENTER -- Tax Library -- HB1 .N37 no.10658 2004 [Regular Loan]

FIGURE 3.2 When the topic is clearly defined, it takes only a quick look at many of these titles to determine whether the "hits" address the relevant issues. However, there are still almost 2,000 documents to "peruse."

Undaunted, Scott tried to think of synonyms for the type of student he considered "nontraditional." His subsequent search using the Boolean phrase "student aid AND adult" produced the results he sought **(see Figure 3.3)**.

As Scott's experience suggests, carefully composed questions and search terms will help you sift through extraneous information and locate the materials that address your subject directly. Like any good detective, the best researchers and writers are willing to change their minds if confronted with new information. Keep in mind, too, that as you work on the project, your strategies might shift or change as you discover new questions that you need to answer in order to address your subject more fully or successfully. You may even find that the evidence requires modifying your initial thesis. Still, if you don't maintain a clear sense of focus, you will probably feel overwhelmed when you begin to explore online library or Internet resources.

Where Should You Look?

Once investigators determine *whom* they are looking for, the next challenge is to ascertain *where* that individual can be found. Police are sometimes able to identify immediately a specific address, but often they have to settle for a more general location, such as an area of town or a neighborhood. Likewise, in this early stage of the research process, it is beneficial to think specifically about where you might find the kinds of information you will need to know to make your argument more convincing.

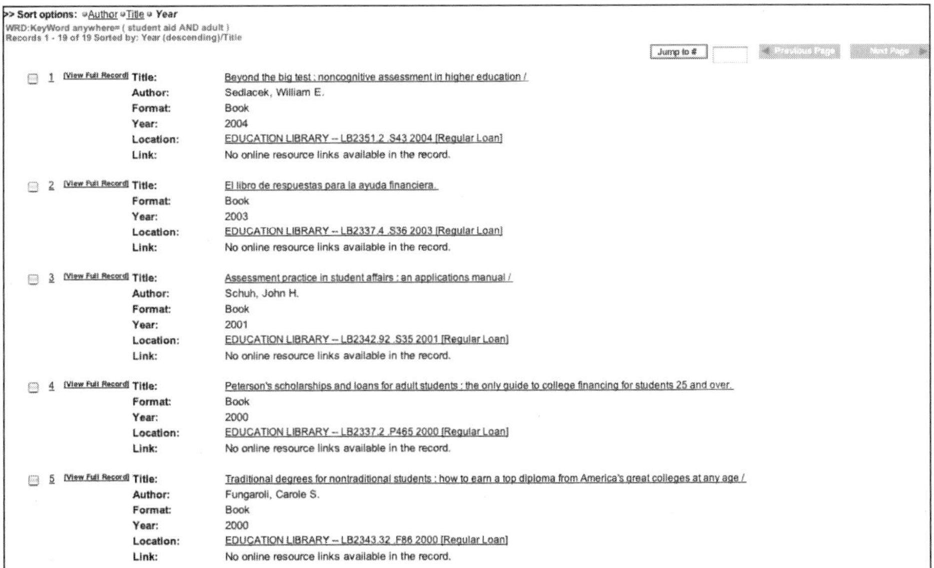

FIGURE 3.3 Refining a Boolean search so that it calls for a specific type of information (based on the student's research questions) reduces the number of "hits" from 1,815 to 19.

So far, we have only discussed the library online catalog to emphasize basic research strategies. However, there are many other resources to consider, both within the library and in the virtual and real spaces outside it. The next three chapters will discuss how to use databases, the Internet, and personal interviews and surveys to obtain information. You will be a much more effective academic "sleuth" if you take a few minutes before pursuing any of those options to consider very carefully and concretely what type of information you will need to convince a reader that what you are saying about your topic is valid. Is the purpose of your research to locate factual support for a position? To review opinions on a topic? To discover new ideas? To track down eyewitness accounts? To find reasonable arguments on a controversial issue in order to develop your own? If your project requires statistics and facts, the more current they are, the better. In such cases, you might want to use periodicals and/or the Internet to locate the most recent information. Does your project deal with local or regional issues? If it does, you might want to supplement information found in newspapers or government records with interviews or surveys. On the other hand, you may know that your topic has already generated considerable discussion in print. In this case you'll want to use databases and the library catalog to locate relevant texts. Given the nature of college-level writing assignments, most often your research will involve using some combination of these different sources.

Make Connections

Follow the Clues

Experienced detectives know that a successful investigation involves tracking down leads, eliminating red herrings, and following a trail of clues. A dropped matchbook cover leads to a nightclub, which leads to an observant bartender, which leads to a description of a suspect (which, of course, may or may not be accurate). Academic research is similar—one good source will lead you to another. A book might contain an excellent bibliography that yields five or six additional good sources. A periodical article might reference another source that proves even more fruitful than the original.

Like so many other aspects of research, the computer has greatly enhanced our ability to track these sorts of connections. We have already discussed how you can refine your keyword searches to maximize the number of profitable "hits," but what you might not realize is that online catalogs are designed expressly to help you track down promising leads. Because some entries in online catalogs are hyperlinks, a search under one key term will almost always lead to other pertinent sources (and potential keywords).

e-TIPS

One Good Source Leads to Another

Consider the example of the student who was interested in turtles and salmonella. Her most productive search phrase was "reptiles AND pets", which returned 22 titles. A quick glance at this list reveals one that seems particularly appropriate: *The Care of Reptiles and Amphibians in Captivity* by Chris Mattison. A click on that title brings up the full-display description that includes a list of subject categories under which this book has been cataloged **(see Figure 3.4)**. Two of the subject headings (the ones including the word "amphibian") broaden the search beyond turtles and reptiles. However, one of them ("captive reptiles") appears especially promising. "Captive" expands the search beyond "pets," but "reptiles" remains focused on the specific type of animals that are the subject of the project.

Format Book
Description 317 p., [16] p. of plates : ill. (some col.) ; 22 cm.

Notes Includes bibliographical references (p. 303-306) and indexes.
Contents General care -- Some biological considerations -- Thermoregulation; social behaviour -- Obtaining specimens and making a start -- Selecting species; legal aspects; selecting specimens; preparations -- Accommodation -- Cages; equipment -- Creating the right environment -- Temperature control; lighting control; humidity control; control of biological factors; the planted vivarium -- Foods and feeding -- Vegetable food; animal food; supplements; methods of feeding; water; overfeeding -- Breeding -- Sex determination; conditioning; stimuli; mating; pregnancy; parturition; egg-laying; incubation; rearing young; breeding programmes -- Diseases -- Controlling diseases; environmental diseases; nutritional diseases; bacterial infections; protozoan infections; endoparasites; ectoparasites; fungal infections; miscellaneous disorders -- Handling -- Descriptions of species and their maintenance -- Caudata: newts and salamanders -- Ambystomidae: Mole salamanders -- Salamandridae -- Plethodontidae: Woodland salamanders -- Anura: frogs and toads -- Pipidae: tongueless frogs.
(cont) Discoglossidae: fire-bellied toads, painted frog and midwife toad -- Pelobatidae: spadefoot toads -- Ranidae -- Raninae: true frogs -- Mantellinae -- Dendrobatidae: poison arrow frogs -- Rhacophoridae -- Microhylidae -- Bufonidae: true toads -- Hylidae: tree-frogs -- Leptodactylidae -- Crocodilia: crocodiles and alligators -- Chelonia: turtles and tortoises -- Pelomedusidae -- Chelidae: side-necked turtles -- Chelydridae: mud, musk and snapping turtles -- Emydidae: freshwater turtles -- Testudinidae: land tortoises -- Trionychidae: soft-shelled turtles -- Squamata: sub-order lacertilia: lizards -- Gekkonidae: geckos -- Eublepharinae -- Sphaerodactylinae -- Gekkoninae -- Xantusidae: night lizards -- Iguanidae: iguanas -- Agamidae: agamas -- Chamaeleontidae: chameleons -- Scincidae: skinks -- Cordylidae: zonures -- Gerrhosauridae: plated lizards -- Lacertidae -- Teiidae: tegus and whiptails -- Anguidae: slow-worms, glass lizards and alligator lizards -- Varanidae: monitors -- Amphisbaenidae -- Squamata: sub-order serpentes: snakes -- Typhlopidae and leptotyphlopidae: blind snakes.
(cont) Boidae: boas and pythons -- Colubridae: typical snakes -- Venomous snakes -- Colubridae -- Elapidae: cobras -- Viperidae: vipers -- Viperinae -- Crotalinae: pit vipers -- Laws pertaining to the keeping of reptiles and amphibians -- Herpetological societies.
ISBN 0713723386
Subject Captive reptiles.
Captive amphibians.
Pets Amphibians
Pets Reptiles

FIGURE 3.4 The subject hyperlinks reveal other Library of Congress categories under which this book is cataloged, providing easy access to additional sources that might contain pertinent information.

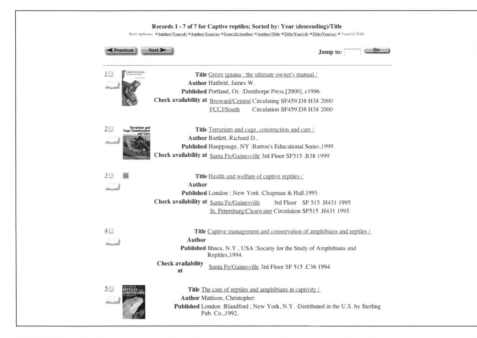

Records 1 - 7 of 7 for Captive reptiles; Sorted by: Year (descending)/Title

Sort options: *Author/Year(d)* *Author/Year(a)* *Year(d)/Author* *Author/Title* *Title/Year(d)* *Title/Year(a)* *Year(d)/Title*

◀ Previous   Next ▶   Jump to: [   ] Go

1☐   **Title** Green iguana : the ultimate owner's manual /
       Author Hatfield, James W.
       Published Portland, Or. :Dunthorpe Press,[2000], c1996.
       Check availability at Broward/Central Circulating SF459.I38 H38 2000
                             FCCJ/South   Circulation SF459.I38 H38 2000

2☐   **Title** Terrarium and cage, construction and care /
       Author Bartlett, Richard D..
       Published Hauppauge, NY :Barron's Educational Series,1999.
       Check availability at Santa Fe/Gainesville 3rd Floor SF515 .B38 1999

3☐   **Title** Health and welfare of captive reptiles /
       Author
       Published London ; New York :Chapman & Hall,1995.
       Check availability at Santa Fe/Gainesville   3rd Floor SF 515 .H431 1995
                             St. Petersburg/Clearwater Circulation SF515 .H431 1995

4☐   **Title** Captive management and conservation of amphibians and reptiles /
       Author
       Published Ithaca, N.Y., USA :Society for the Study of Amphibians and
                  Reptiles,1994.
       Check availability at Santa Fe/Gainesville 3rd Floor SF 515 .C36 1994

5☐   **Title** The care of reptiles and amphibians in captivity /
       Author Mattison, Christopher.
       Published London :Blandford ; New York, N.Y. :Distributed in the U.S. by Sterling
                  Pub. Co.,1992.

FIGURE 3.5 There are seven titles listed under the subject category "Captive reptiles"; several of them did not appear under the previous search phrase "reptiles AND pets."

Clicking on a subject hyperlink takes the researcher to a listing of all of the titles in that category (**see Figure 3.5**), revealing sources that haven't been located in previous searches. Even better, many of these texts seem more narrowly focused on diseases, medical treatments, and health issues of reptiles, indicating that they will likely provide the most useful information.

Depending on how specific your keyword terms are at the beginning of a search, you might repeat this narrowing-down process a number of times to locate your best sources.

Background Checks

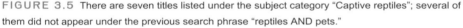

In addition to creating a profile of the suspect, working to determine where a suspect might be hiding, and pursuing promising leads, a good detective also runs background checks on people involved with the case. He or she does so to identify individuals with records of criminal activities and/or to determine their credibility. Likewise, academic researchers need to evaluate the "backgrounds" of potential sources to screen out unsuitable or untrustworthy sources and to identify those that are most appropriate and credible.

Evaluation Is an Art

A number of criteria are traditionally used to evaluate sources: purpose, reputation, intended audience, reliability, and timeliness, among others. You will no doubt quickly discover that applying these criteria involves skills that take time and experience to develop. In some ways, learning to evaluate sources is like developing a proficiency in the arts or athletics. A music teacher can instruct you in the basics of playing the clarinet—show you which holes to cover to produce certain notes and how to shape your mouth to accommodate the mouthpiece and reed—but you must practice diligently to learn the subtle control required to make music rather than squawks. A baseball coach can show you the proper stance and how to swing, but it will take much batting practice before you can step up to the plate with confidence. If you want to hit the ball to a particular spot on the field or play a musical composition with extremely high notes, you will need to learn to make minute adjustments and refine these skills to produce the desired result.

Evaluating sources is much the same. There is no single marker that demonstrates accuracy or appropriateness. Instead, you must analyze a variety of clues in relation to how you plan to use the information. If what you need are facts and statistics, then you will be especially concerned with accuracy, timeliness, and reliability, factors that gauge the quality of your source. If you need an opinion that supports a position, then you want to make sure the source is credible, reasonable, and authoritative. But if you are looking for firsthand experience that is persuasive because it is personal, then it might not matter if the author is renowned. Most research projects use a mix of all these types of sources. A former student who had worked in a day care center wanted to investigate how preschool children were affected by spending six to eight hours away from their parents. The final paper combined facts from recent psychological and sociological studies with the opinions of noted authorities on children and child care, as well as anecdotes from the students' own experiences.

As has already been mentioned, you can generally trust information housed in a library because it has undergone a great deal of evaluation. A number of controls ensure the quality of these sources. Textbooks, scholarly studies, and articles in specialized journals have been reviewed by the author's colleagues, editors, and publishers. On the other hand, you should never accept a library source as credible or appropriate just because it is in the library. Keep in mind that information exists in all sorts of forms (stories, reports, arguments, statistics) and is published for a variety of purposes (to express a belief, to entertain, to persuade); therefore, it is important to determine whether a source is suitable for your intended use. *Moby Dick* contains a great deal of information about whales, but you probably wouldn't want to use Melville's novel as a source for a research paper on marine biology.

Internet Sources Require Special Evaluation Skills

Nonetheless, even in the digital age, the library remains an excellent point of departure for the novice researcher because you can have confidence in the reliability of its resources. This is a point worth restating: The library is the best starting place for academic research. Also, library systems have been developed with evaluation in mind. The format of the online catalog provides you with much of the information you will need to determine the reliability of a text **(see Figure 3.6)**.

```
Webcat at duPont-Ball Library, Stetson University
CATALOG  RESERVE DESK  USER SERVICES  GATEWAYS

GO BACK   NEW      BACKWARD  FORWARD   CROSS       VIEW      PRINT    PREFS    EXIT
          SEARCH                       REFERENCE   OPTIONS   CAPTURE

Search Result -- Complex Search

Viewing record 30 of 61 from catalog words or phrase "gun control" . There are also cross references.
Jump to location/availability information
☐ Check here to mark this record for Print/Capture

HV7436 .G865 1997
The gun control debate : a documentary history
Bijlefeld, Marjolijn, 1960-

      Held by: MAIN
        Title: The gun control debate : a documentary history / edited by Marjolijn Bijlefeld.
Publication info: Westport, Conn. : Greenwood Press, 1997.
Physical descrip: xxxiii, 294 p. ; 24 cm.
  Series Title: (Primary documents in American history and contemporary issues)
Bibliography note: Includes bibliographical references and index.
     Contents: Historical background -- The Constitution and the Second Amendment -- State declarations of rights -- Modern views on the Second Amendment
               -- The Second Amendment goes to court -- The National Rifle Association -- Legislative responses to gun violence -- Gun Control Act of 1968 --
               The effectiveness of gun control legislation -- A nation divided -- Public opinion -- National statistics -- International comparisons -- Law
               enforcement's role -- The public health community enters the debate -- Guns in suicide -- Guns as self-defense security -- The 1990s-the debate
               takes center stage -- Kids, guns, and schools -- Guns, schools and the Supreme Court -- Court watch -- Are guns safe?
  Subject term: Gun control--United States--History--Sources.
  Subject term: Firearms--Law and legislation--United States--History--Sources.
 Added author: Bijlefeld, Marjolijn, 1960-
         ISBN: 031329903X (alk. paper)
          key: ocm36138391

                    Copy Material Location
Call Numbers for: MAIN
1) HV7436 .G865 1997      1 BOOK   REFERENCE (nocirc)
```

FIGURE 3.6   The listings in an online catalog provide much of the information you will need to evaluate it (i.e., author, publisher, copyright date, whether it contains references, and a summary of the contents).

The World Wide Web is an entirely different matter. Many novice researchers think that web pages must be reliable because they offer current information and are so easy to access. However, unlike more traditional forms of information media (books, magazines, journals, and government or organization documents), no one regulates information published on the web, and there is no standard method of cataloging information. Frequently the indicators needed for evaluation (authorship, date of publication, organizational affiliations) are missing. This poses unique problems for research that will be discussed more fully in Chapter 5. But before tackling those more complex situations, it makes sense to learn essential evaluation skills in the user-friendly online catalog. After all, it's necessary to master the basics before attempting to slam a line drive to the opposite field or hit a C above high G.

Key Factors of Source Evaluation

When detectives run background checks, they stipulate characteristics (things such as age, sex, race, home address, or even the type of car a person drives) to limit the pool of potential suspects. When it comes to academic research, there are similar indicators that can help you eliminate unlikely sources and locate valuable ones. Your research questions should help you determine whether the basic content matter of a source is relevant, but there are other factors to keep in mind.

When my student was trying to decide whether to use Chris Mattison's text on the care of reptiles for her research project, she had to evaluate whether it was a worthwhile source. The book is part of our school library's holdings—a good sign, but would it be a suitable resource that fulfilled the academic requirements for a scholarly research essay? Like a detective, she needed to be suspicious and not accept this information at face value. So she asked questions.

What Is Its Purpose? This is the first question you should ask when evaluating a potential source. Is it attempting to persuade you to adopt an idea or belief? Is it someone's opinion? Is it a report on facts or findings? Is it an advertisement? All information has a purpose or a goal, and an enormous amount of information in our culture professes to be unbiased but contains a hidden agenda intended to persuade the reader.

If you are trying to decide between buying a Mitsubishi Eclipse or a Ford Mustang, you might visit dealers and obtain brochures. However, unless you are extremely inexperienced, you wouldn't limit yourself to the information a salesperson supplies. The purpose of these brochures is to sell cars. Although the facts they contain might be accurate, they are intended to give you the most favorable impression of a vehicle. In fact, most of these publications are carefully contrived to leave you feeling as if your life would be wretched and empty if you did *not* purchase the vehicle. If you want a more accurate picture of how these two cars compare—one that takes limitations as well as advantages into account—you need to refer to *Consumer Reports* or some other less-biased source for information **(see Figure 3.7)**.

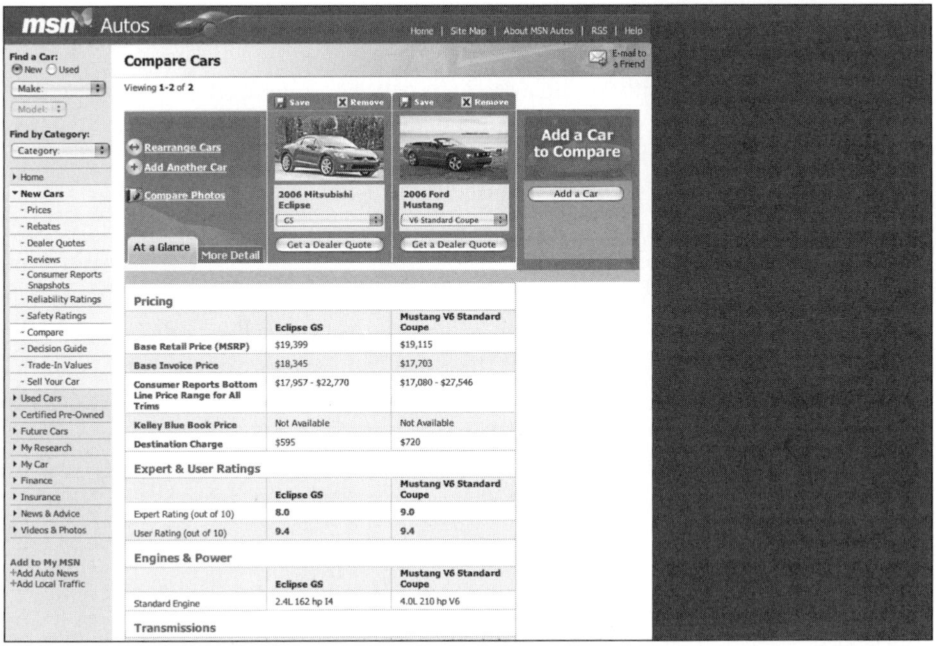

FIGURE 3.7 This website presents unbiased information that enables consumers to compare the price and features of two similar vehicles.

Even a biased source can be valuable to your research but only if you recognize its slant. Some writers (published authors as well as students!) are so intent on persuading readers to agree with their opinions that they misrepresent facts or ignore information that challenges their conclusions. Like the car dealer, they want to sell you on an idea without considering other options. To accept what these writers say as unequivocally true will only result in repeating their error.

Objectivity and balance are distinguishing features of academic research. A scholarly source will frequently present opinion, but intellectuals are committed to reasoned argumentation that considers (rather than ignores or withholds) conflicting viewpoints. Of course, some topics (such as abortion, capital punishment, and gay marriage) have elicited such extensive, heated, and polarized debate that the only way you will arrive at a balanced understanding is to read widely, becoming familiar with arguments on both sides of the divide.

A sarcastic or superior tone is frequently a sign of bias. Rather than draw on established facts and reasonable argument, writers with strong bias frequently resort to rude put-downs to discredit contradictory views. Television and radio talk shows have made us all too accustomed to this type of discourse. However, if the author of a source sounds like he or she could be a guest on a show hosted by Jerry Springer, Montel Williams, or Howard Stern, there is good reason to be skeptical. Scholarly writing relies on reason rather than ridicule to make its points. If you are already familiar with your topic, you might recognize serious omissions or distortions. But what if you are unsure whether the writer has been fair? The only way to allay your uncertainty is to run further background checks.

Where Does It Come From? One key to determining whether a source is taking a balanced, objective approach to the subject is to determine who has published it. One of my students recently wrote a research paper arguing against instituting any additional laws restricting the ownership or use of guns. His bibliography listed numerous publications, but the National Rifle Association (NRA) had published all of them. Because the NRA has invested millions of dollars attempting to block new gun legislation, it can hardly be expected to present all sides of this controversial issue. The information contained in its publications might be technically correct, but the organization's agenda will necessarily shape the argument in explicit and implicit ways. If the publisher is a university press, a well-established publishing company, or a government agency, then you can have greater confidence in the objectivity of the source **(see Figure 3.8)**. These organizations carefully examine and review information before affixing their names (and their reputations) to it. If the source is published by an organization, then you need to carefully review its goals and methods of "quality control."

FIGURE 3.8   The publisher of this document on gun laws is a subcommittee of the U.S. Senate. You can be reasonably confident in the accuracy and objectivity of this source because the information has been compiled and certified by a government agency rather than a commercial institution.

Blandford Press published the book about reptiles that my student was considering using for her research project. This publishing company was unfamiliar to both of us. Therefore, she conducted a quick search on the Internet using the search engine named *Google*.

e-TIPS

Search Engine Tip

Internet search engines are discussed at length in Chapter 5. *Google* is a good choice for this search because "Blandford Press" is a very distinctive search term. Notice that this multiword search term is enclosed in quotation marks to indicate that both words should appear as a phrase.

She wasn't able to locate a company website, but the search revealed numerous books published by Blandford (many of which dealt with reptiles and birds) that had been included in bibliographies compiled by reputable organizations (**see Figure 3.9**). This reassured her that the publisher was credible.

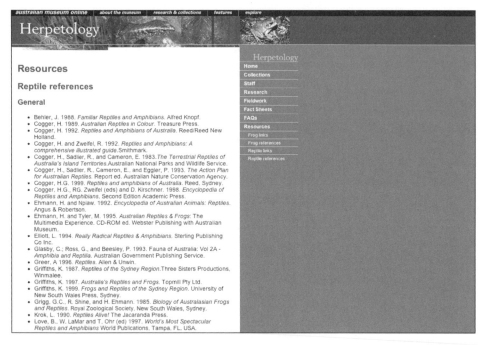

FIGURE 3.9 The results of an Internet search for "Blandford Press" included this site from the Australian Museum that includes a bibliography of credible and helpful sources about herpetology. Mattison's book is included in the list.

Even if you know that the publishing company is experienced and responsible, you still need to confirm that the author is an authority on the subject (i.e., has the necessary education and credentials). You can verify an author's qualifications by determining which organizations or institutions he or she is affiliated with. Often a brief biography is included in the publication itself. (Refer to *Who's Who in America* or the *Biography Index* if in doubt.) You might also conduct an author search in the online catalog to determine if he or she published other books or articles on the subject.

Determining the credentials of the author is especially important when you are evaluating articles in mainstream periodicals. Even though many reputable news magazines (e.g., *Time, Newsweek, U.S. News and World Report*) provide accurate information, they are usually not the best source of information for academic papers. This is because journalists write most of the articles in these magazines. They conduct research and interview experts, but they usually are not themselves authorities on the subject.

For instance, in her pet turtle research, my student located a newspaper article about how to prevent the spread of salmonella. However, when she did an Internet search of the author's name, she discovered that the reporter usually wrote restaurant and food reviews. The information in the article is probably accurate, but although the author might be an authority on the tastiest turtle soup in town, she is clearly not an expert on bacteriology. This is why you should locate scholarly journals that contain information written and reviewed by experts rather than reporters.

An author search using the online catalog revealed that the library owns 15 books on reptiles authored by Mattison. A subsequent Internet search revealed that he is a zoologist who has also published numerous journal articles and is an acknowledged expert on wildlife.

Who Is the Audience? Just as it is important to determine a publisher's and author's credentials, so too it is necessary to consider the intended audience of a source. In fact, many choices you make in everyday life are governed by this principle. When baby-sitting your four-year-old nephew, you might rent *Finding Nemo* to entertain him, but if you popped *Nemo* into the DVD player on a first date, you'd probably find you have a lot more Friday nights free for baby-sitting. When evaluating a source, the key principle is that the information must not be too simple (or too technical) for an educated adult audience.

For instance, the keyword search for "reptiles AND pets" produced a text that lists *Juvenile literature* as one of its subject categories (**see Figure 3.10**). Obviously this work was written for children. Once again, the full-display listing found in the online catalog provides clues that enable the astute researcher to eliminate inappropriate sources.

At the same time, you can't rely on receiving such obvious clues in all cases. For that reason, it is important to pay attention to the vocabulary of the source and its attention to detail. Encyclopedia articles generally provide information that is technically correct, but these articles are probably not suitable sources for college-level research papers. This is because encyclopedias target a very general (rather than a scholarly) audience, and they tend to summarize rather than elaborate on a topic.

On the other hand, you also need to eliminate sources that are too technical or specialized. For her "turtle law" project, my student realized she needed to understand more about the transmission and treatment of salmonella. One search uncovered a 40-page article that argued that "gram-negative bacteria do not 'secrete' proteins into their environment but only export proteins in their strategic periplasm."[1] There was no question about the accuracy and academic reliability of this source, but it was so full of medical jargon and technical information that she could hardly read it, much less understand it enough to incorporate it effectively in her own writing.

---

[1]Cornelis, Guy R., and Van Gijsegem, Frédérique. "Assembly and Function of Type III Secretory Systems." *Annual Review of Microbiology* 54 (2000): 735-74. *Academic Search Premier.* EBSCOHost. Seminole Community College Library. 3 Jan. 2006.

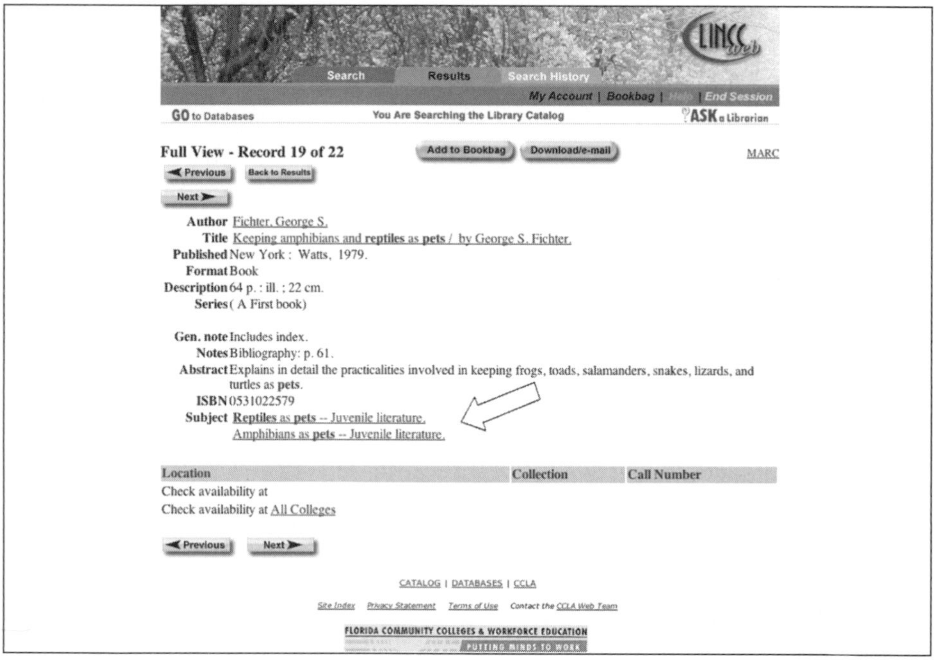

FIGURE 3.10 The online index clearly indicates that this book was written for children and would be too elementary for a college research project.

When Was It Produced? For many research projects, the more up-to-date the information is, the better. Because knowledge is constantly being created and revised, you must carefully note when information was created and determine if it is still valuable. Depending on your topic, you may want to limit your search to information produced in the past 5 or 10 years. If you are interested in some discipline in which information is quickly outdated (such as genetic research), information even a year old may be useless.

On the other hand, because something was produced many years ago doesn't necessarily mean it is irrelevant. Even if your topic deals with a rapidly changing field, such as technology, an older text might be valuable. If you were investigating the history of the development of artificial intelligence, you might be interested in reading a report by Thomas Watson, a former chairman of IBM. In 1943 Watson declared, "I think there is a world market for maybe five computers." Likewise, the proceedings of the 1977 Convention of the World Future Society might prove pertinent. At this gathering of forward-looking "techies" Kenneth H. Olson, president of DEC (a leader in computer sales that in the 1960s produced the first small computer to be sold on a retail basis), announced, "There is no reason for any individual to have a computer in his home." The expectations of these pioneers of the computer industry form a striking contrast with current attitudes and practices. Depending on your topic, even a text written in another century might prove valuable.

e-TIPS

Searching by Publication Date

Many library search tools allow you to limit your search to a particular time period. This allows you to refine your search even further to eliminate inappropriate sources. If your online catalog doesn't have a place in the search window to enter "year" or "publication year," check to see if there is an "advanced search" window that does.

Nonetheless, for many research topics the most current information is the most desirable. For this reason, you need to pay attention to copyright dates. Mattison's book was published in 1992. Because it is over 15 years old, it doesn't offer the most current knowledge on the topic. However, this doesn't mean it won't be a useful source. All the same, this student was cautious about her use of this text and made sure that she located other, more recently published resources to verify some of the scientific information.

What Does It Look Like? It is a well-known fact that the best way to learn to detect counterfeit money is to study the genuine article. Once you become familiar with the appearance, coloring, and texture of real bills, you will immediately spot a false one. For the same reason, starting in an academic library where so much of the information bears the marks of authenticity and reliability will help you recognize suitable sources.

Scholarly work looks serious. By this I mean that it may contain illustrations, graphs, or charts, but it will rarely have glossy, flashy photos designed to appeal to a mass audience. The language used assumes an educated readership. These sources don't "talk down" to the reader; instead, they employ the language used by experts in the field.

Most importantly, a scholarly work offers various forms of corroboration to confirm its credibility. It will support any claims made with statistics and information from other sources. Look for footnotes and parenthetical citations within the text as well as an index, works cited, or bibliography section in the back. Again, the full-text display of the online catalog often will help you determine whether your text has the proper "pedigree" required of a scholarly text. The catalog record of Mattison's book refers to a bibliography and an index **(see Figure 3.11)**. The proper documentation of supporting sources is fundamental to academic writing. (You should remember this when you produce your own research project!)

What Do Others Say About It? A recommendation is an important tool in evaluation. When Roger Ebert and Richard Roeper both give an enthusiastic "thumbs up" to a new movie, you are more likely to head to the theater. If a new restaurant gets a positive review in the local newspaper, you might take your significant other there to celebrate his or her birthday. Before buying a DVD player you will probably read what experts have to say about the performance and reliability of various models or brands.

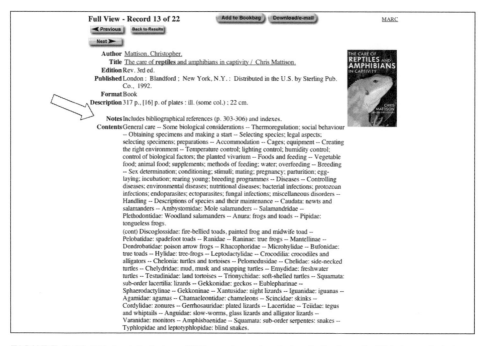

FIGURE 3.11 This book includes a bibliography and an index, indications that this is a scholarly work.

Reviews and recommendations are another way to evaluate the merit of a source. If it has been recommended by an instructor or cited in another reputable source, you can trust that it is credible. Frequently library search tools provide information about the text (a summary, abstract, or listing of the contents) that allows you to better assess whether a resource is appropriate. The full-text display of Mattison's book indicates that there is a bibliography and index. It also contains a very detailed listing of the contents of the book **(see Figure 3.11)**.

The Thrill of the Hunt

On most TV detective shows, a crime is committed, a suspect is identified, and the detectives make their arrest—all within an hour. (Sometimes there is even time for the trial and conviction.) In real life, however, the process involves a great deal of mental, as well as physical, "legwork." Some might consider research tedious, but when you begin to gain confidence because you know what you are looking for, where to look for it, and how to properly identify it when you "capture" it, you will begin to experience the "thrill of the hunt."

QUICK CHECK

Key Factors of Source Evaluation

- What is the purpose of the document?
  - ☐ Does it present fact, opinion, or both?
  - ☐ Does it maintain a fair, balanced, and reasonable perspective?
- Where does the document come from?
  - ☐ Who is the publisher?
  - ☐ Who is the author?
- For whom is the document intended?
  - ☐ Is it written for a scholarly, college-level audience?
  - ☐ Is it too technical or specific for your project?
- When was the document published?
  - ☐ Does it include the most up-to-date information available?
  - ☐ If dated, does it offer an interesting perspective or point of contrast?
- What does the document look like?
  - ☐ Does it look serious and scholarly?
  - ☐ Does it have footnotes, a bibliography, an index, and other signs of credibility?
- What do others say about the document?
  - ☐ Has it been recommended by an instructor or cited in another, credible source?
  - ☐ Is there a review of the source in an abstract or summary?

EXERCISES

1. Your sociology teacher has assigned a paper on "hate speech on the Internet." Compose a list of research questions that will help you focus this topic.

2. Review the research questions you composed in Exercise 1 and list the types of information (e.g., facts? statistics? opinions of experts? definitions? eyewitness or personal testimony? a combination of some or all of these?) you will need to fulfill this assignment. Indicate, as well, the types of sources (e.g., books, periodicals, surveys, interviews, websites) that you think might be fruitful places to look for this kind of information.

3. Access your school's online catalog, and conduct a *keyword* search (make sure you click on the appropriate "search type") using the phrase " 'hate speech' AND Internet" (remember to enclose multiword search terms in quotation marks and capitalize the Boolean "AND"). Choose two of the results that seem most relevant to the assignment, and list of all of the Library of Congress subject categories under which these sources are cataloged.

4. From the two sources you selected in Exercise 3, choose the one you consider to be the best match for this topic. Using the "Key Factors of Source Evaluation" listed in this chapter, write a paragraph in which you detail why this source is/is not a credible and appropriate source of information for the assignment mentioned in Exercise 1.

5. If you are using the InfoTrac College Edition database in your course, use the passcode provided with this textbook to access the database and conduct a "Keyword" search (check the appropriate term immediately under the

search phrase window) for the phrase " 'hate speech' AND Internet." Choose the result that appears most relevant. Using the "Key Factors of Source Evaluation" and the suggestions for determining the origins of a source listed in this chapter, write a paragraph in which you detail why this source is/is not a credible and appropriate source of information for the assignment mentioned in Exercise 1.

6. Using the same source you chose in Exercise 5, click on the box marked "Link" in the left margin and a list of related topics will appear. Choose two of these related topics and (in a sentence or two) explain how these topics are pertinent to the assignment outlined in Exercise 1.

If you are not using the Info-Trac database, exercises 5 and 6 could be adapted for your school's full-text databases.

4

Get Immediate Results: Databases

Although I am a bit troubled by his gendered language (Disraeli made his statement in an age less concerned with inclusiveness), for the researcher, his sentiment certainly holds true. Thus, the aim of this chapter is to help you become a successful researcher by showing you how to acquire the best information. Given that we live in "The Information Age," this might not seem to be such a difficult task. After all, as mentioned throughout this book, the Internet has made an enormous amount of information available to anyone with a dial-up or cable connection. But the operative word here is *best*. Note that Disraeli didn't link success to volume; he linked it to quality. The successful researcher is adept at rejecting unreliable and/or unverifiable information in favor of that which is "best"—trustworthy, reliable, and relevant.

For this reason, we initially focused our attention on the library. In fact, until now, the only research tool discussed at length has been the online catalog. Those of you who regularly surf the net may have experienced moments of frustration. You may even have been impatient enough to skip ahead. Compared to the split-second access of the web, the online catalog seems technologically challenged and a tedious, painfully slow way to get what you want. Although the catalog identifies potential sources, you still need to physically find the texts and check them out. If you are accustomed to the immediate gratification of the Internet, the online catalog might seem positively antiquated. Nowadays, if you are reading *Catcher in the Rye* and become curious about what the "J. D." stands for in author J. D. Salinger's name, you can *"Google"* (<http://www.google.com>) Salinger's name and get your answer (Jerome David) in seconds. Do you need to locate the hotel where your friend's wedding reception is taking place? Go to the online yellow pages, type in the hotel name, the city, and state and get not only an address but also a map to print out and take with you. Are you stumped about what to make for dinner? Visit *Betty's Kitchen* (<http://www.bettycrocker.com>), and in minutes find a recipe that matches the ingredients in your refrigerator. However, there is a library tool that provides immediate access to information in a way that is reminiscent of the World Wide Web. That tool is the full-text database. In fact, students sometimes confuse databases with web pages because the information they provide is so instantaneous. Databases are likely to be one of the most important resources you'll use as a researcher; through them you can acquire some of the *best* information available on your topic—information you'll need to become a successful researcher.

What Is a Database?

A database, simply put, is a collection of computer data that has been arranged so that it can be automatically retrieved. Computers are great organizers. In fact, you probably have used a computer at home or at work for just this purpose. Businesses usually keep information about customers in a database so they can access it in a number of different ways (according to last name, phone number, address, etc.). When used in reference to library research, however, the term "database" refers to a very specific tool.

Library databases come in two basic varieties: bibliographic and full-text. One way to understand the differences between the two is to consider that all-American institution: Denny's restaurant. Many of my international students tell me that when they first came to the United States, they frequently ate at Denny's. This wasn't because the food reminded them of their native cuisine, but because Denny's provides large full-color pictures of the meals in their menu. You don't need to know much English to order an Original Grand Slam from one of these. However, despite the better than real-life photos it offers, no one older than two would confuse the menu with the food itself. Bibliographic databases are like Denny's menus. They give you an excellent sense of what a source is like. On the other hand, full-text databases serve up the food, hot and mouthwatering, right to your table. They transmit not only information about a source but the actual document.

In recent years, many databases have been produced that are a combination of both bibliographic and full-text entries. A search will produce "hits" that include both full-text articles as well as bibliographic information about pertinent articles (often with abstracts) that you must locate elsewhere **(see Figure 4.1)**.

e-TIPS

Bibliographic Citations Versus Genuine Documents

The distinction between bibliographic material and the genuine document is important. Sometimes students will cite a bibliographic index or an abstract from a bibliography on their Works Cited pages. I tell my students that is like bringing me a picture from a Denny's menu rather than the bacon-cheddar burger and french fries I requested. In order to include a resource in your project, you must track down the actual article.

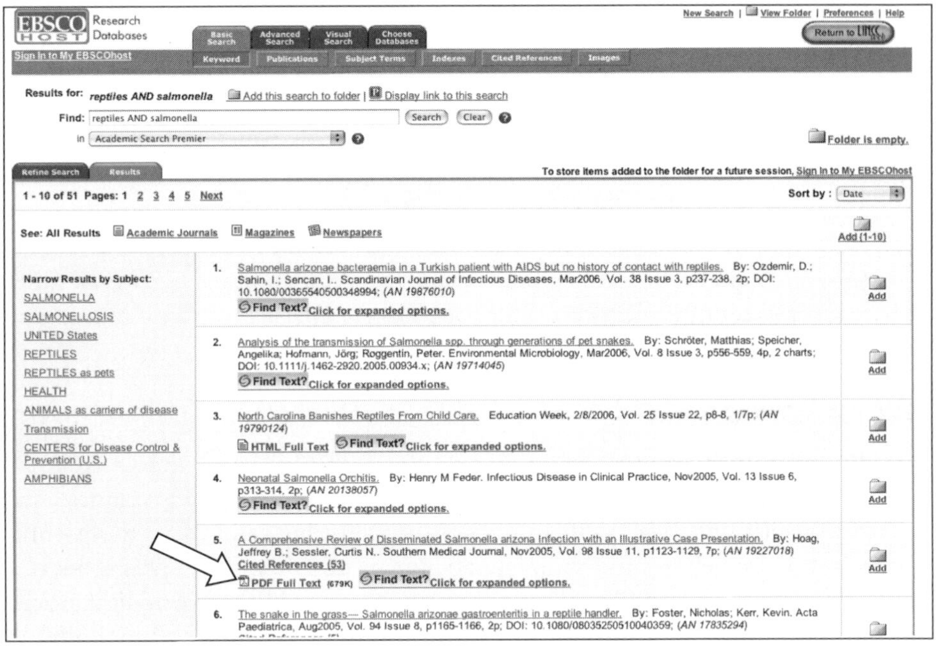

FIGURE 4.1 This database provides a combination of bibliographic/full-text results. Notice that entries that are available in full-text are indicated (e.g., PDF or HTML Full Text). The other "hits" in this list must be accessed by other means (e.g., interlibrary loan).

Bibliographic Databases

A bibliographic database is simply an electronic version of a bibliographic index. You are probably familiar with the bibliographies at the conclusion of a book or article (you even may have been required to include one at the conclusion of a term paper). In these instances, a bibliography is an alphabetical listing of all of the sources a writer has consulted or cited in his or her work. You may not realize, however, that there are many different types of bibliographies. (*The Readers' Guide to Periodical Literature* is one.) Although some of these bibliographies are general in nature (they index documents on a broad range of topics), many are devoted to specific disciplines. Print bibliographies, which you will find in the reference section of your library, are typically huge multivolume works with very small type and are usually published annually to catalog all of the documents published that year. To use these hard-copy versions, you must look up your key term or phrase in each volume—working year-by-year through the set. The electronic versions are much more user friendly. They allow you to search all of the records (regardless of the year of publication) simultaneously. Be advised, however, that most databases only go back as far as the mid-1970s, and some only to the mid-1980s. If you want to locate texts that were published earlier than this, you will usually have to use the printed volumes.

These bibliographic indices operate a lot like the library catalog. They help you discover documents (frequently articles in periodicals, but sometimes government documents, essays, or chapters in books, etc.), but you still need to locate the texts themselves to access this information. Because they are library tools, these bibliographic databases are designed with research in mind: They allow you to locate information according to subject, author, title, or publisher. Often they provide excellent "abstracts," or summaries, of the articles that permit you to evaluate the contents quickly without having to read the entire article **(see Figure 4.2)**.

Like their hard-copy cousins, bibliographic databases are usually organized according to specific disciplines or interests. For example, the *Arts & Humanities Citation Index* indexes articles in major arts and humanities journals as well as relevant items from leading science and social science periodicals. *GPO* is an index of U.S. government publications. The *Book Review Digest* provides citations and reviews of current English-language fiction and nonfiction books.

Full-Text Databases

The other type of database is the full-text database. The full-text database is similar in many ways to the bibliographic database. The search mechanism is identical, and it provides a citation as well as an abstract or summary, but (and this is the essential difference) it also delivers the complete document to you, online. This is because full-text databases are actually collections of previously published periodical articles that have been made available in a format that can be transmitted electronically.

FIGURE 4.2 This database provides bibliographic information as well as an extensive abstract, or summary, of the article. All of this information can help you evaluate, as well as locate, the text; however, it does *not* provide the full text of the article.

Because periodicals are frequently so important to academic research, full-text databases are the most revolutionary of all of the new electronic library tools. Full-text databases provide instantaneous access from one's home or office to numerous newspapers, magazines, and scholarly or professional journals—publications that are published on a daily, weekly, or monthly schedule. You'll recall that periodicals are vital to many research projects for a number of reasons. They are published more quickly than books, so the information in a journal article is often more current than what you will find on your library shelves. Articles that appear in academic and professional journals (as opposed to popular magazines) are frequently written by experts and reviewed by other experts in a field, making them very credible and authoritative sources. They also tend to be more focused than books, rarely exceeding 25 to 30 pages in length. Books, on the other hand, are frequently 200 pages (or more). Although books often provide indices in the back to help pinpoint specific pages for particular facts, you sometimes need to page through a lot of extraneous information to find what you need. In many instances, all you really require is one chapter. If you have limited the scope of your search by posing specific research questions (see Chapter 3), you have a definite idea of what you are looking for. For this reason, it often takes less time to locate what you are looking for in a periodical than in a book.

For those of us who did our undergraduate and graduate work some years ago, the seemingly limitless access to vital research materials provided by full-text databases can evoke a powerful emotional response. Despite years of teaching students to use these tools, I am still amazed by how easy it is to access publications using a database. Although most libraries (public as well as academic) subscribe to major news and popular interest periodicals (e.g., *Newsweek, Time, Sports Illustrated*), until now, only libraries at large universities could afford to subscribe to and house many of the academic journals available. This meant that if you were enrolled at a smaller school with limited holdings, the only way you could acquire an article from some journals was through a lengthy interlibrary loan process that often took four to six weeks. Today, almost all public and school libraries subscribe to numerous databases, some of them full text. As a result, no matter how limited a library's physical resources may be, it can now offer 24-hour access to journals and periodicals that were once available only at major research institutions.

Get to Know Your Databases

Because libraries make independent decisions about which databases they will purchase, it is impossible to predict what you will encounter at your particular school or public library. However, there are a number of databases that, like the chain stores you encounter in virtually every mall across America (The Gap, Aeropostale, Express, Foot Locker, etc.), are perennial favorites.

Often, libraries will purchase a package deal from a database provider. These are actually database "libraries" that feature numerous databases, some bibliographic, some full text. InfoTrac College Edition, OCLC, EBSCOHost, Gale and Lexis-Nexis are examples of database publishers that provide databases either singly or in groupings. Deciphering your library's holdings can be a bit confusing at first because some databases can be purchased as either bibliographic or full text. In fact, purchasing a database is a bit like buying a car—there are some things that are standard equipment, but there are a lot of options to choose from as well. For that reason, you might encounter similarly named databases in slightly altered forms in different libraries.

How Do Databases Work?

On-site or Website Access

The first thing you need to determine is how to access your library's databases. Libraries pay a lot of money to subscribe to a database, so they almost always limit access to patrons (enrolled students in the case of school libraries or cardholders in the case of public libraries). Some libraries limit access by making the databases available only through on-site terminals (sometimes called intranet or LAN connections). This means that you can only use a database if you are in the library or at a related school site (such as a tutoring or media center). Yet, an increasing number of libraries make it possible for students to access a database through a password-protected link to a library web page or special server. By making databases available via the Internet, these libraries have truly "gone virtual." If you are working on a paper at two in the morning (and many of my students swear they do their best work at that hour) and discover you need an additional source or further information, you can point your browser at your library's website and find what you need. You are no longer limited by library hours or physical access, for you can locate full-text academic articles from your home computer.

Systems vary from school to school, so you should contact your library or information technology department if you are unsure how to access your library's database collection. The most important first step is to discover what databases your school has subscribed to and how you can gain access to these important tools. Your library may have published this information on its homepage. Also, with this text you may have received a subscription to InfoTrac College Edition, a full-text database that is available 24/7 for your research needs.

Search Tips When Using Databases

All of the research strategies we have discussed so far *also* apply to using library databases. Like the online catalog, a full-text database is a "stocked pond." The documents you locate using a database are previously published (and therefore regulated and reviewed) articles. Because it uses an electronic search tool (like the online catalog), a database allows you to "find a perfect match" by using the keywords and phrases you have discovered while converting your topic into research questions (see Chapter 2) and following the leads revealed by your online catalog's subject category hyperlinks (see Chapter 3). However, understanding a few subtle differences will make your searches more effective.

As mentioned in Chapters 2 and 3, the online catalog uses Library of Congress subject categories for classifying texts. This means that the keywords and phrases that immediately come to mind might not be the most successful search words. (Remember the student who couldn't locate any documents using the search terms "turtles AND salmonella," but who found excellent resources when she used the terms "reptiles AND pets" and "captive reptiles"?) This is because the online catalog cannot electronically search word-by-word through all of the books on your library's shelves. Instead, when books are cataloged in the library, they are categorized according to established subject headings; you must identify these to access the best information on your topic. Bibliographic databases operate much the same way. When the information about a particular document is entered (such as author, title, publication information), it is also classified with relevant subject categories (often called "descriptors" or "identifiers") that help you locate the document using a subject or keyword search **(see Figure 4.3)**. Be advised that the categories in bibliographic databases are frequently different from Library of Congress terms. Sometimes it takes a little trial and error to discover which terms work best.

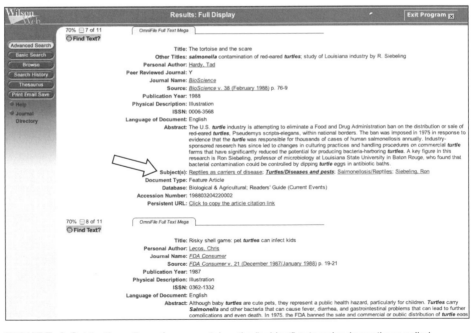

FIGURE 4.3 Like the online reference catalog, the "subject" categories (sometimes called "descriptors") are hyperlinks. If this article is a good resource, you might be able to link to other documents that address your topic.

e-TIPS

Keeping a List of Search Terms

Because the search engines of different online tools (e.g., the online catalog, databases, the World Wide Web) respond to different keyword phrases, it is important to keep a list of all possible search terms. Something that is unsuccessful in one system could produce excellent results in another.

However, because the documents in a full-text database are recorded electronically, database search engines can normally conduct a word-by-word search through each text. This may require that you use the "advanced search" option and/or check a special box before conducting a search **(see Figure 4.4)**.

Because a match is made if a keyword appears anywhere in the wording of the document, a search term that was unsuccessful in the online catalog or a bibliographic database might work in a full-text database. This may seem fairly simple, but it actually puts a great deal of pressure on you to be precise in how you phrase your searches (and spell your search terms). Remember the tips about multiword and Boolean search phrases (see Chapter 2)? For instance, a full-text database search using the phrase "school violence" returned only 24 hits (because the search engine was looking for the phrase "school violence"). On the other hand, a search using the same tool for "school AND violence" resulted in approximately 3,400 matches.

The advanced search mode also allows you to refine other aspects of your search, thus limiting your results to the most pertinent sources. If your research requires the most up-to-date sources, you can limit your search to the past year or two. Some instructors require that your research include different types of publications. The advanced search mode permits you to restrict your search to specific types of publications (e.g., articles from newspapers or journals). Most importantly, if you are looking for "instant gratification" and the database you are using includes both bibliographic and full-text entries, it is possible to limit your results to only full-text articles.

e-TIPS

Conduct an "Advanced Search"

Most databases offer the option of conducting either a "basic" or "advanced" search. The advanced search mode features alternatives for refining your search and limiting your results. Most advanced search modes permit you to search the entire text of the document, limit your results to full-text documents, narrow your search to certain types of publications (e.g., journals or newspapers), and restrict the date of publication to a particular time period **(see Figure 4.4)**.

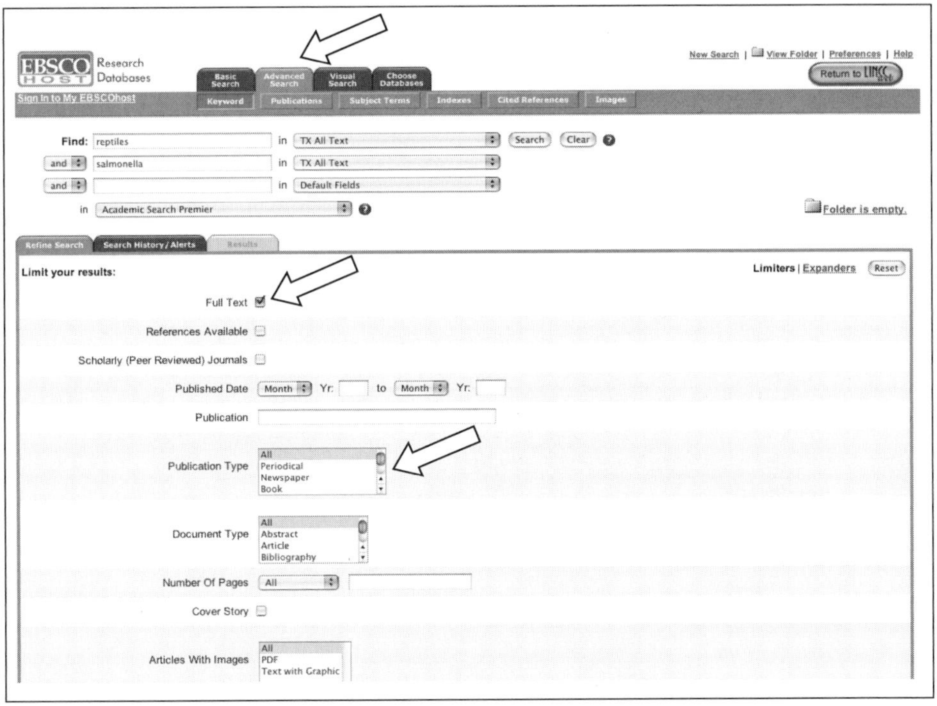

FIGURE 4.4 Using the "advanced search" mode, it is possible to search the entire text of a document for the search phrase and results can also be limited to full-text documents (if the database includes both bibliographic and full-text entries). You can further limit your search by publication type and date.

Like other electronic library tools, full-text databases enable you to be a "research sleuth," for they provide a way for you to connect with relevant resources (see Chapter 3). Once you locate a promising source, explore these possibilities by clicking on the identifiers or descriptors that hyperlink to lists of other related documents **(see Figure 4.5)**.

Of course, the beauty of full-text databases is that when you click on the hyperlink to view the "full text," up pops the complete article **(see Figure 4.6)**. You can print it out or read it online. One potential drawback to full-text databases is their limited coverage—most include articles printed only in the last 20 to 30 years, and none will include every article, no matter how relevant. However, the best databases continue to expand their coverage, increasing their holdings daily.

e-TIPS

Using Your "Sleuthing" Skills

If you get an overwhelming number of matches for a keyword(s) search in a database, use your "sleuthing" skills. Quickly scan the titles until you locate an article that appears relevant. Read the abstract or summary to confirm your hunch, and if the article proves promising, notice the descriptors or indicators listed. Click on these hyperlinks to locate more articles like the one you have chosen.

New Search | View Folder | Preferences | Help

EBSCO HOST Research Databases

Basic Search | Advanced Search | Visual Search | Choose Databases

Sign In to My EBSCOhost

Keyword | Publications | Subject Terms | Indexes | Cited References | Images

Return to LINCC

◄ 12 of 51 ► Result List | Refine Search Print E-mail Save Add to folder Folder is empty.

Formats: Citation PDF Full Text (2.6MB)

Title: Effect of Regulation and Education on Reptile-associated Salmonellosis.

Authors: De Jong, Birgitta[1,2] *Birgitta.de.Jong@smi.ki.se*
Andersson, Yvonne[1]
Ekdahl, Karl[1,2]

Source: Emerging Infectious Diseases; Mar2005, Vol. 11 Issue 3, p398-403, 6p, 3 charts, 2 graphs

Document Type: Article

Subject Terms: *ANIMALS as carriers of disease
*REPTILES -- Infections
*SALMONELLA
*SALMONELLOSIS

Geographic Terms: SWEDEN

Abstract: ***Reptiles*** have become increasingly common as domestic pets, and with them reptile-associated ***Salmonella*** Infections in humans. From 1990 to 2000, a total of 339 reptile-associated ***Salmonella*** cases were reported in Sweden. In 1996, as part of its efforts to adapt its import regulations to those of the European Union, Sweden no longer required certificates stating that imported animals were free of ***Salmonella***. A subsequent increase was noted in the incidence of reptile-associated cases from 0.15/100,000 in the period 1990-1994 to 0.79/100,000 in 1996 and 1997. After a public education campaign was begun through the news media, the incidence dropped to 0-46/100,000. Children were the most affected age group among patients (incidence 1.3/100,000). ***Salmonella*** enterica serotype Enteritidis was the most frequent serotype (24% of isolates), followed by S. Typhimurium (9% of isolates). Import restrictions and public information campaigns are effective public health measures against reptile-associated salmonellosis. [*ABSTRACT FROM AUTHOR*]

Author Affiliations: [1]Swedish Institute for Infectious Disease Control, Stockholm, Sweden
[2]Karolinska Institutet, Stockholm, Sweden

ISSN: 1080-6040

Accession Number: 16338999

Persistent link to this record: http://search.epnet.com/login.aspx?direct=true&db=aph&an=16338999

Database: Academic Search Premier

View Links: Find Text? Click for expanded options.

Formats: Citation PDF Full Text (2.6MB)

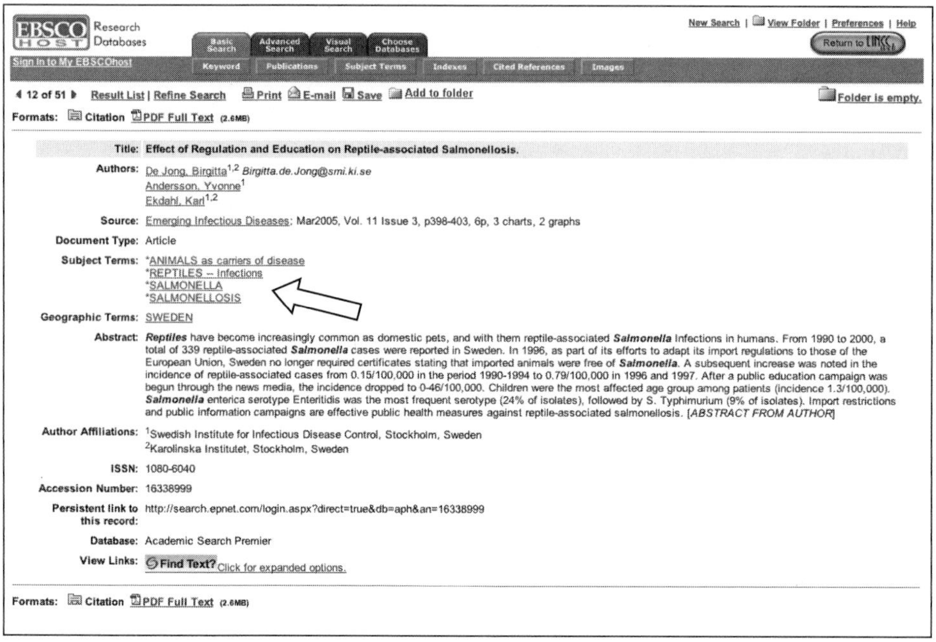

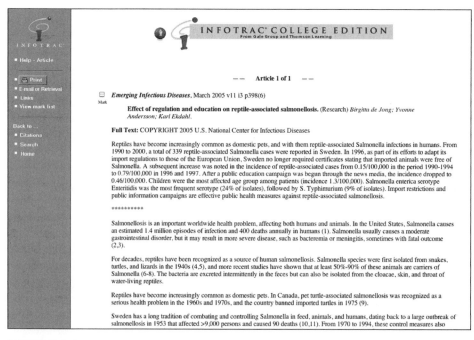

FIGURE 4.5 The abstract reveals that this is a pertinent source, and the "Subject Terms" hyperlinks indicate another search phrase ("REPTILES—infections") that could lead to more valuable resources.

INFOTRAC
- Help - Article
- Print
- E-mail or Retrieval
- Links
- View mark list

Back to ...
- Citations
- Search
- Home

INFOTRAC COLLEGE EDITION
From Gale Group and Thomson Learning

— — Article 1 of 1 — —

Mark *Emerging Infectious Diseases*, March 2005 v11 i3 p398(6)

Effect of regulation and education on reptile-associated salmonellosis. (Research) *Birgitta de Jong; Yvonne Andersson; Karl Ekdahl.*

Full Text: COPYRIGHT 2005 U.S. National Center for Infectious Diseases

Reptiles have become increasingly common as domestic pets, and with them reptile-associated Salmonella infections in humans. From 1990 to 2000, a total of 339 reptile-associated Salmonella cases were reported in Sweden. In 1996, as part of its efforts to adapt its import regulations to those of the European Union, Sweden no longer required certificates stating that imported animals were free of Salmonella. A subsequent increase was noted in the incidence of reptile-associated cases from 0.15/100,000 in the period 1990-1994 to 0.79/100,000 in 1996 and 1997. After a public education campaign was begun through the news media, the incidence dropped to 0.46/100,000. Children were the most affected age group among patients (incidence 1.3/100,000). Salmonella enterica serotype Enteritidis was the most frequent serotype (24% of isolates), followed by S. Typhimurium (9% of isolates). Import restrictions and public information campaigns are effective public health measures against reptile-associated salmonellosis.

****

Salmonellosis is an important worldwide health problem, affecting both humans and animals. In the United States, Salmonella causes an estimated 1.4 million episodes of infection and 400 deaths annually in humans (1). Salmonella usually causes a moderate gastrointestinal disorder, but it may result in more severe disease, such as bacteremia or meningitis, sometimes with fatal outcome (2,3).

For decades, reptiles have been recognized as a source of human salmonellosis. Salmonella species were first isolated from snakes, turtles, and lizards in the 1940s (4,5), and more recent studies have shown that at least 50%-90% of these animals are carriers of Salmonella (6-8). The bacteria are excreted intermittently in the feces but can also be isolated from the cloacae, skin, and throat of water-living reptiles.

Reptiles have become increasingly common as domestic pets. In Canada, pet turtle-associated salmonellosis was recognized as a serious health problem in the 1960s and 1970s, and the country banned imported turtles in 1975 (9).

Sweden has a long tradition of combating and controlling Salmonella in feed, animals, and humans, dating back to a large outbreak of salmonellosis in 1953 that affected >9,000 persons and caused 90 deaths (10,11). From 1970 to 1994, these control measures also

FIGURE 4.6 A full-text database provides you with a reprint of the complete article (including information about where it was previously published).

e-TIPS

Citations for Electronic Documents

The documents contained in a full-text database are reprints of previously published periodical articles that have been reissued digitally. As such, they require a special format for citation that indicates that you accessed them via a database. See Chapters 8 to 11 for more information.

EXERCISES

1. Locate the databases to which your school library subscribes. In a sentence or two, note how many of these databases provide full-text documents, and give the name of one or two general full-text databases that provide access to high-quality sources for a research project. In addition, note the name of a specialized bibliographic or full-text database that relates to your major or your educational interests.

2. Access one of the full-text databases you mentioned in Exercise 1 and conduct a keyword search for the phrase "salmonella AND reptiles." From the results list, choose the one you consider to be the most credible and appropriate source, and either print out or copy all of the bibliographic information (author, title of article, original source of publication, copyright date, page numbers) pertaining to it. Then write a paragraph explaining why you chose this source (based on your evaluation of the bibliographic information).

3. Because they contain electronic documents, full-text databases can search in a variety of ways, and this can produce different results. If you are using the InfoTrac College Edition database in your course, use the passcode provided with this text to access the database. From the menu on the left, select "Keyword search," type in the search phrase "salmonella AND reptiles"; click in the dot below the search phrase that states "in title, citation, abstract"; and click on "search." Write down the number of "hits" you receive. Conduct a second search with the same phrase, but this time click on the dot that states, "in entire article content." Write down the number of "hits" you obtain in this search, and then write a short explanation of why these numbers are different.

4. This chapter began with a quotation about how success is tied to acquiring the best information. The advanced search feature in InfoTrac College Edition can limit your search to only the best sources. In the menu on the left, click on "Start Over." Then click on "Advanced Search" (also on the left). From the drop-down menu that says "Select Index (Optional)," click on "Text Word (tx)," and enter the search phrase "salmonella AND reptiles." Then click on the box under the words "Limit the Current Search (Optional)" that states, "to refereed publications." (Refereed publications undergo a great deal of evaluation and thus are extremely credible.) Your results will appear when you click on the hyperlink "View" under "History." Write a brief comparison between these results and the results you received from the searches in Exercise 3.

If you are not using the Info-Trac database, exercises 3 and 4 could be adapted for your school's full-text databases.

PART

2

RESEARCH USING THE
WORLD WIDE WEB

5

Cast Your Net in Stocked Ponds

The printed word has a powerful allure. If you doubt this, then the next time you are in line at the grocery store, try *not* to read the headlines of the three or four tabloids that scream for your attention. It is as difficult as driving past a five-car pileup on the interstate without slowing down to sneak a glimpse at the bedlam. Even if you know that tabloids specialize in bizarre half-truths and fabrications, they are difficult to ignore. Not only do we all read these headlines (despite their dubious authority), many of us actually speculate whether there might be some truth to them. Is a certain multimillionaire addicted to painkillers? Could that TV actress be wasting away from anorexia? Did that dashing actor really murder his wife?

We hesitate to dismiss these trumped-up stories, in part because we have been trained to respect the printed word. Throughout our childhood we are taught to pay attention to books—to read, remember, and repeat what we find in them. Later, we learn that our society recognizes only written documents as legally binding. When we want to attest to the veracity of what we are saying, we "put it in writing." We know, intellectually, that the mere act of writing will not transform a false-hood into a truth. However, when we read a published document, there are powerful dynamics at work that can cause us to accept ideas that we might otherwise reject. These dynamics can, sometimes for good reasons and sometimes for bad, also lead us to think that published opinions and ideas are better than our own.

For this reason, the Internet, in spite of the enormous advances it has made in the transmission of information, can pose many problems for the novice researcher.

If the printed word is alluring, then the Internet (with text as well as graphics, moving images, and even sounds) is seductive. Like the tabloids, it can blur the distinction between truth and fiction, between information and entertainment. And, unlike articles published in credible sources, material published on the web may not have withstood the critical scrutiny of expert review.

Only a decade or so ago, student research was, for the most part, limited to printed media (books, newspapers, periodicals) that were carefully controlled. These controls determined who and what could be published. Today the World Wide Web has created a huge grab bag of potential sources. An Internet search might turn up precious sources of information, but it can just as likely lead you to cheap imitations of truth.

Nevertheless, despite its dangers and drawbacks, the WWW does allow access to information that may not be available through your school's library. Throughout this text I have cautioned you to be wary of the web, yet I spend many of my waking hours online. I use the web to locate information that aids me in my professional as well as personal life. To be frank, for some topics, unless you are attending a large research institution, the WWW might provide you with more current and extensive resources than your school library. If this is the case, the challenge you face is to locate sites from among the millions on the web that satisfy the rigorous requirements of verification and authentication required in academic research.

Academic Research on the Internet Must Be Authenticated

In everyday life, not all situations require the same level of precision or accuracy. For example, in some circumstances you can vouch for your own identity, whereas for others you are required to offer proof. When you show up for the first day of class, you normally only have to raise your hand or answer "Here!" when the professor calls your name. However, when you arrive to take the SAT, you had better have two forms of picture ID, or they won't let you take the test. In the first situation, you can vouch for yourself; in the second, the College Board demands legal confirmation that you are who you claim to be. Likewise, in most discussions, you can relate information you have read or heard, and (unless you have a reputation as a pathological liar or what you say defies common sense) most people will take you at your word. Academic research, on the other hand, has strict rules to establish the reliability of information. You must be able to demonstrate that your information is accurate, indicate where you found it, and establish that the source is credible. Once you grasp the more demanding standards of academic research, you can begin to comprehend—and overcome—the problems presented by the World Wide Web.

Because the standards for authenticating and documenting facts in academic research are more severe than those we employ in most everyday situations, library resources generally include only those sources that satisfy these more demanding standards. Online catalogs and subscription databases provide all of the information required to evaluate or verify the authority of a source **(see Figure 5.1)**. But unlike your library's digital resources, the web has no standardized system of organization or categorization. Internet search engines attempt to impose order on this chaos, but each has its own system of classification that affects the outcome of your search. In addition, no one checks the facts on web pages, so the sites you locate might contain deceptive, biased, or incorrect information. And even when you locate a resource that is both pertinent and credible, the web page editor(s) might not include all of the information necessary to adequately document or confirm the source.

For these reasons, it will take all of your research sleuthing skills to locate relevant and reliable sources on the Internet. It is critical that you:

- use search terms that will provide the best matches (see Chapter 2),
- explore the most promising locations, and
- evaluate (constantly) the quality of the information you find.

The previous chapters have focused on teaching basic research strategies using library tools for the same reason an instructor has a beginning driver practice in the relatively safe confines of an empty parking lot. New drivers need to become comfortable with the equipment and basic skills required before heading out to face the baffling challenges of the highway. Now that you understand basic research skills, you're ready for the unregulated information superhighway.

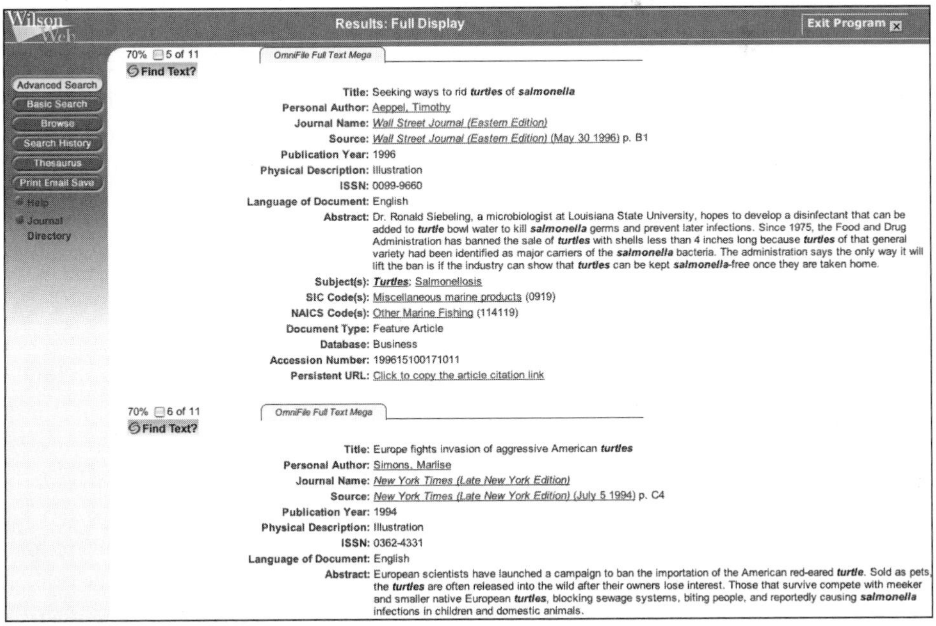

FIGURE 5.1 Library search tools include what you need to assess whether a source is credible and relevant. This entry from a database clearly indicates the author, publisher, date of publication, and a summary of the information contained in the article.

You might already be adept at navigating the web. And if you spend much time on the Internet, you have probably developed your own search strategies and a predisposition for certain search engines. It may seem to you that you already know enough to negotiate the demands of college research. Perhaps you do. You always need to keep in mind that when you are conducting research for an academic project, you must be *very selective.* When you are using the web, you must only cast your net into what I am calling "stocked ponds." Rather than using search tools that rely on computer robot programs to assign matches to your search terms, you need to use search guides that are highly evaluative and will lead you to web pages that fulfill the sophisticated requirements of academic research.

Academic Research on the Internet Must Be Done in "Stocked Ponds"

As Chapter 2 pointed out, most Internet search engines compile results by using computer "robots" or "spiders" that rank pages according to algorithmic programs. When you type in a search term, these robots look through the complete text of all of the web pages in their collection of sites (no search engine currently searches "all" of the WWW) to find pages that include your term. This type of search, which normally doesn't take the context of your term into account, almost always retrieves an unmanageable number of results—and these are not necessarily in the best order for your particular needs.

The most significant difference between regular search engines and subject guides or directories is that the former involve almost no human interaction, whereas the latter rely on a great deal of human selection and evaluation. Given the chaotic nature of the WWW, this assistance in evaluation can be invaluable. *Yahoo!,* one of the most widely used Internet guides, organizes its search mechanism around subject categories. Rather than simply matching terms, *Yahoo!* classifies the websites in its pool according to subject headings and returns results based on those headings. In fact, one of the reasons *Yahoo!* has become so popular is because searching by subject, rather than by exact terms, is—in many cases—more successful. When I was looking for a rocking chair for my front porch, I first tried a search engine that strictly relied on matching terms. My search phrase, "rocking chair" returned over 48,000 matches, and most of these pages had nothing to do with purchasing a rocker. In *Yahoo!,* I was able to narrow my quest by choosing *shopping,* then *furniture,* then *outdoor furniture,* until I finally refined my search to what I was really looking for. At this point, *Yahoo!* retrieved 62 sites for me to review **(see Figure 5.2).** Although these results are certainly more manageable, this experience illustrates another problem with Internet research: *Yahoo!*'s categories proved ultimately too limiting. Clearly, there are more than 62 online merchants that sell teak rocking chairs.

In the most basic sense, *Yahoo!*'s structure is similar to the classification system used in libraries. However, unlike the library, with its standardized Library of Congress subject headings, Internet subject guides adopt their own systems of

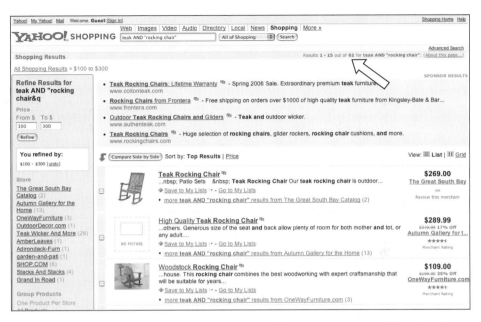

FIGURE 5.2 Using subject categories as a guide can help you narrow a search from almost 327,000 hits to 62.

categorization. *Yahoo!* is an all-purpose subject directory that attempts to address the most common uses of the Internet. It handles communication, everyday questions, and e-commerce rather well because the majority of WWW users are most concerned with these applications. But *Yahoo!* hasn't been designed with academic research specifically in mind. Therefore, its subject headings and web page selections frequently are not well suited for the topics and disciplines involved in most college-level research projects (**see Figure 5.3**).

Use Search or Subject Directories Most Conducive to Academic Research

It has become common practice for school libraries to create subject guides as part of their "virtual library" web pages. You would do well to check with a reference librarian about this, as librarians frequently consult with your professors when creating these subject guides. In fact, if your professor has a web page, he or she might have included a list of links that would be helpful in completing research assignments.

There are a number of subject guides that have been expressly designed for academic research. These tools are aptly named "guides" because they steer users to the most appropriate sites and help them avoid inaccurate and/or unverifiable web pages. Nevertheless, it is important to remember that the same qualities that make these guides so valuable—the fact that they are limited in scope and compiled with a great deal of human evaluation—can sometimes be their greatest liabilities (**see Figure 5.4**). The scope of some guides is limited and highly specialized and may reveal the limited perspective of individual human evaluators and compilers.

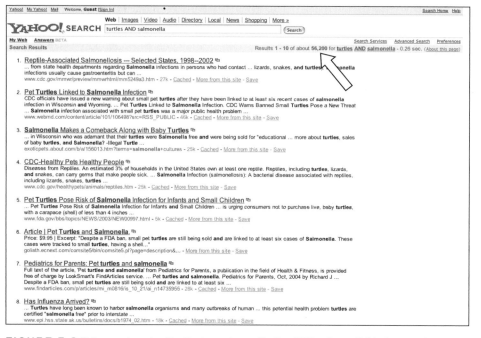

FIGURE 5.3 This search, using the Boolean phrase "turtles AND salmonella" in the popular search engine *Yahoo!* produced 56,200 hits. Reviewing this many web pages is an impossible task.

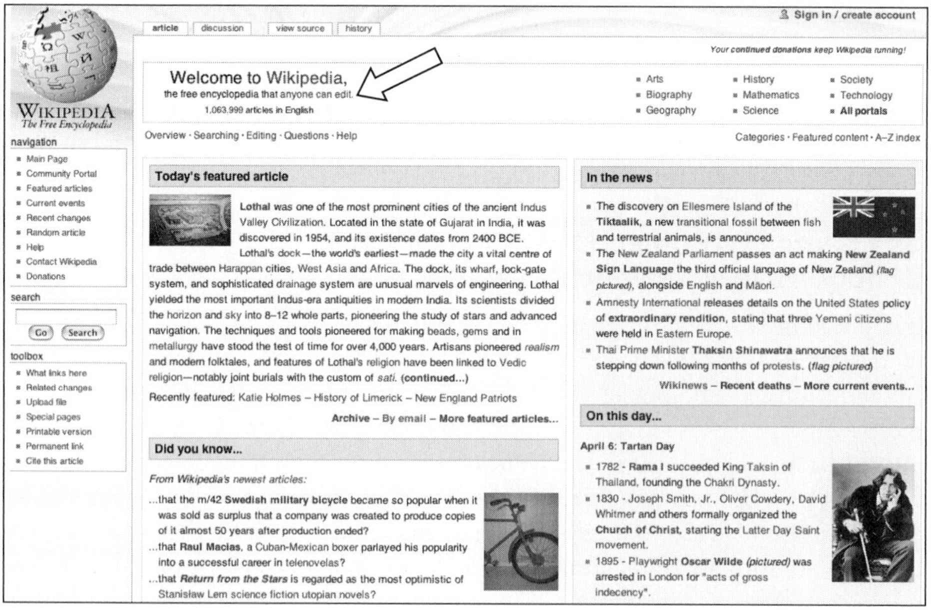

FIGURE 5.4 Frequently a *Google* search will take you to *Wikipedia*, an online encyclopedia. However, a disclaimer on the home page indicates that this site can be edited by *anyone*. Since information is only as credible as its source, I wouldn't recommend using this website in academic research.

A subject guide that has been compiled with scholarly research in mind—one that contains websites that take a careful and critical approach to academic subjects—is extremely valuable to the researcher who wants to use the Internet to locate resources. Such a guide provides access to a "stocked pond"—that is, to websites that have been appraised and judged current, credible, and relevant because they have been composed by reputable authors or organizations **(see Figure 5.5)**.

Moreover, because these guides are designed to be research tools, they often are modeled after library resources. Frequently the subject categories are similar to Library of Congress terms, and (unlike most commercial Internet tools) the initial list produced by a search will include the information necessary to evaluate the relevancy and credibility of a site (e.g., author/creator, date, descriptor hyperlinks, ratings, and a brief summary or abstract of the information) **(see Figure 5.6)**. And like an online library catalog, you might need to broaden your search (i.e., search the broader concept or what your topic is about) to locate the distinctive subject categories that will lead you to pages about your topic.

The following are some of the best subject guides currently available.

- *Librarians' Index to the Internet:* <http://www.lii.org/> One of the earliest, most diligently maintained, and well-ordered subject guides on the Internet. It contains tens of thousands of quality sites that have been compiled by public librarians into 14 main topics and 300 subcategories. Its scope is limited, but it has been organized to facilitate the academic researcher with brief abstracts and related subject category links.

- *Infomine:* <http://infomine.ucr.edu/> Compiled and maintained by academic librarians from a number of distinguished universities and colleges (including the University of California, Wake Forest University, California State University, and the University of Detroit—Mercy), this subject guide contains over 60,000 documents that are organized according to university-level subjects/disciplines.

- *U.C. Berkeley & Internet Resources by Academic Discipline:* <http://sunsite2.berkeley.edu:8088/ERF/servlet/ERFmain?cmd=allSubjects > Maintained by the University of California/Berkeley, this list of Internet resources on many academic disciplines has been selected by subject specialists.

- *Britannica's "Best of the Web":* <http://www.britannica.com/> Encyclopedia entries are only available to subscribers, but the "Best of the Web" category provides excellent summaries and reviews of web pages chosen by *Britannica* editors.

- *BUBL Information Service:* <http://bubl.ac.uk/link/> Funded by the United Kingdom, this very selective collection of Internet sources of mostly academic web resources is maintained by Strathclyde University in Scotland.

Web page property of the Florida Museum of Natural History

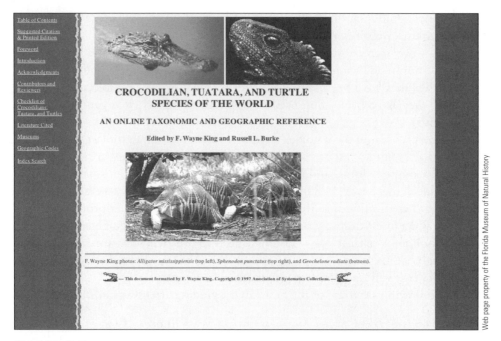

FIGURE 5.5 This excellent online resource (sources clearly documented) about reptiles was located by following related subject categories in the directory BUBL LINK 5:15. The category "Life Sciences" led to a page with more specialized terms, including "reptiles," which led to this annotated list of reptiles.

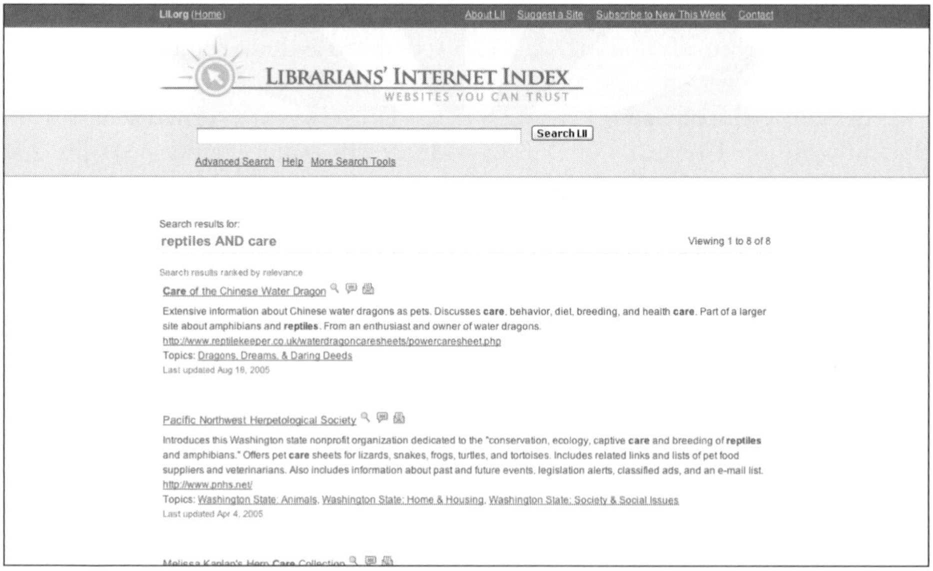

FIGURE 5.6 This list of returns for a search from "reptile care" in the *Librarians' Index to the Internet* illustrates all of the benefits of a search guide: a small number of returns (eight), information about the author or creator of the site, the date the page was last updated, hyperlinks to related topics, and a brief abstract of the contents.

- *The Internet Public Library:* < http://www.ipl.org/> The "Reference Center" and "Subject Collections" are limited, but this collection, maintained by the University of Michigan School of Information, is an effort by volunteer librarians and librarian students to provide access to credible academic resources on the web.

- *About.com:* <http://www.about.com/> This subject guide can be uneven because each topic is overseen by a different "guide," who determines the content. Some areas are very good, whereas others are disappointingly nonacademic in nature. However, with over a million documents cataloged, it deserves a try.

QUICK CHECK

Subject Directories and Search Engines Designed for Academic Use

Exceptional Subject Directories:

    Librarians' Index to the Internet: <http://www.lii.org/>

    Infomine: <http://infomine.ucr.edu/>

    U.C. Berkeley & Internet Resources by Academic Discipline:

    <http://sunsite2.berkeley.edu:8088/ERF/servlet/ERFmain?cmd=allSubjects>

    Britannica's Best of the Web: <http://www.britannica.com/>

    BUBL LINK 5:15: <http://bubl.ac.uk/link/>

    The Internet Public Library: <http://www.ipl.org>

    About.com: <http://www.about.com/>

Effective Search Engines:

    AltaVista Advanced: <http://www.altavista.com/web/adv>

    Google: <http://www.google.com/>

    Alltheweb Advanced: <http://www.alltheweb.com/advanced?advanced=1&cat=web&q=>

e-TIPS

Learning Search Engine Features

Whether you are using a subject directory or a regular search engine, always take a few moments to familiarize yourself with its features. Make sure the tool recognizes phrase searching (i.e., the use of quotation marks around multiword phrases—"affirmative action"), Boolean terms or has an advanced search mode that enables you to use these methods.

Use the Best Commercial Search Engines

It is best to begin with subject guides because they are designed with academic research in mind, and you can be confident that the web pages you find cataloged in them will be credible. Still, although they are reliable tools, they are not comprehensive. Certainly for some topics (such as ecological threats to the rain forests or critical interpretations of *Moby Dick*) you will find a number of relevant sources.

But for topics that are more regional in interest (such as local school bus regulations) or nonacademic in nature (such as waitstaff tipping protocol), you may have difficulty using these directories to locate the information you need.

In the latter case, or to locate additional web pages on your topic that were not cataloged in the academic subject guides that have just been discussed, you will need to use a search engine. Keep in mind, though, that not all search engines are created equal. Those that are best for shopping or travel (such as *Yahoo!*) are not usually the best for academic research. Here are some of the best search engines currently available for academic research, including some tips on how to use them effectively.

- *Alta Vista Advanced:* <http://www.altavista.com/web/adv> Perhaps one of the best search engines (because it is so large) for searching for distinctive exact terms or Boolean phrases, *Alta Vista* searches the complete text of documents. You must use the "advanced search" feature for Boolean searches; the "sort by" feature makes large lists of returns more manageable.

- *Google:* <http://www.google.com/> One of the biggest search engines, *Google* employs a unique method of ranking results based on page popularity. A site is given high ranking if a lot of other pages link to it. Sometimes this democratic approach really does result in locating the "best" pages (for instance, when shopping on the Internet), but it doesn't always ensure academic reliability. You will get the best results with *Google* if your search phrase is distinctive and technical. (At the time of publication, *Google Scholar* [<http://scholar.google.com/>] was still in the developmental stage. In the future this may prove a valuable tool. For now, the frequent changes in format and content make it too complex to describe or recommend.)

- *Alltheweb Advanced:* <http://www.alltheweb.com/advanced?advanced=1&&q=> Another large search engine, *Alltheweb's* advanced search feature allows you to conduct a variation on Boolean searches ("must include" = AND, "must not include" = NOT) and limit returns or "hits" according to domain (indicated by the last terms in the URL government [gov], education [edu], nonprofit organization [org], commercial [com], etc.) **(see Figure 5.7)**.

You may have used a metasearch engine (such as *Dogpile, Metafind,* or *MetaCrawler*) in the past. As the name suggests, a metasearch engine simultaneously searches many search engines to provide a collective list of results. Although this sounds like a time-saver, there are a number of problems with this approach. First, none of the metasearch engines include *Google,* one of the best search engines available for academic research. Second, most metasearch engines ignore quotation marks around multiword phrases and don't recognize Boolean search terms. Finally, none of the metasearch engines have advanced features that enable you to refine your search as you can with *Altavista* and *Alltheweb.*

℮-TIPS

Learning Advanced Search Engine Features

All of the search engines on the following page (except *Google*) have advanced search features. In the long run, you will save a great deal of time if you take a few minutes to learn how to use these features to limit your searches. A Boolean phrase in a standard search in most engines is interpreted as a "fuzzy AND" (which means that returns may have just one or both terms included). Most of the advanced search tools permit you to conduct a genuine Boolean search. In addition, these advanced features allow you to specify desired domains (the three letters of the URL that indicate the host address). Because many commercial and personal sites are biased or less credible, specifying domains that are government (gov), educational (edu), or nonprofit (org) can limit your results to more reliable websites. Advanced searches can also allow you to limit your results to web pages that have been updated in the last months or year, thus eliminating "stale" pages that might be out of date. Some even allow you to filter out offensive sites that might give "false" returns because words have been embedded in the page formatting.

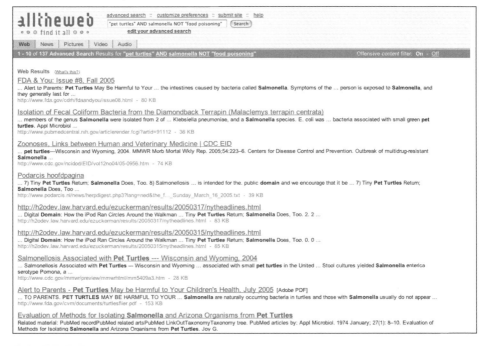

FIGURE 5.7 This search, using the advanced mode that eliminated commercial and personal web pages and required that the text include "turtles AND salmonella," not include "food poisoning," and be updated in the past three months, narrowed the return list to under 300 returns. (Compare this to a similar *Google* search that produced over 20,700 hits.)

Academic Research on the Internet Requires Careful Evaluation

When you locate a web page that is pertinent to your topic, you will need to evaluate the information carefully, using the criteria described more fully in Chapter 3 (purpose, reputation, intended audience, reliability, and timeliness). Because the WWW is not regulated like a library, the Internet researcher must assume even greater responsibility for conducting background checks to verify that the information on a web page is correct, credible, and properly documented. As always, the careful researcher is suspicious and never accepts information at face value. In addition to the tips on evaluation given in Chapter 3, asking the following questions about a website will help you determine its reliability:

What Is Its Purpose?

Although the Internet was developed primarily to enhance national security, its most common use today is e-commerce. The Internet makes it possible to circulate more information to more people than ever before. It has created a revolution in how goods are advertised, bought, and sold. Because so much on the WWW is intended to persuade you to buy something, it is especially important to evaluate the purpose of a website before including the information it contains in your research project. For example, you might think an article entitled "The Benefits of Ritalin" offers an objective analysis of how this drug has helped to treat children with attention deficit hyperactivity disorder (ADHD). However, if it appears on the website of the pharmaceutical company that produces the drug, the information will be part of a sales pitch or promotion. Even if a commercial web page contains accurate information, its undeniable bias makes it of questionable use in a scholarly project.

Where Does It Come From?

Because just about anyone can publish information on the WWW, determining the source of the information on a web page is especially important. Library sources prominently feature information about publishers and authors; however, on the Internet, authorship and organizational affiliation can be missing, misleading, or difficult to determine.

Be cautious about using an anonymous website in an academic research project. Remember that the source of the information you use determines its reliability, so anonymity will make your information suspect. If you know the name of the organization or author but have been unable to obtain any additional information, use the search engines *Google* or *AltaVista* and conduct a keyword search with the name enclosed in quotation marks. You might also see if an individual is listed at <http://www.whoswho-online.com/> or a site called "Whois" at <http://www.whois.net/>.

e-TIPS

Verifying the Website Author

It is often difficult to determine the author or organization responsible for a website (don't confuse a "webmaster" with the author—a webmaster may not create the text contained on a page). Look for the following to locate the name of an organization or an author:

- A header, footer, or page watermark that announces the name of an organization.
- The name of an organization or institution in the URL (this may indicate an official affiliation, but it may not). For instance, a tilde (~) before a name usually indicates a personal site linked to an institutional server. This is not an official page.
- A hyperlink at the bottom, top, or left side of the page to the "home page" (sometimes the link will be labeled "about us") or a hyperlink at bottom of the page to the author's home page.
- A link that allows you to e-mail the organization, the author, or the site webmaster (you can ask him/her about any affiliations).
- You can also try "backtracking" through the URL by systematically deleting each "layer" or section of the address located between slashes. This might lead you back to the home page.

On the other hand, websites that have been produced by known and respected organizations (whether educational, governmental, or nonprofit) will make excellent sources. In addition, articles in online journals that use peer review by editors or web pages with articles that have been digitally reprinted from books or journals give evidence of being reliable and truthful.

Who Is the Audience?

When used to support academic research, a source must be more than accurate: The subject must be investigated at a level of complexity appropriate for a college assignment. Much information on the Internet is designed for a general, rather than academic, audience. This is because the Internet has become a ready-reference tool for many people. Like the information in an encyclopedia or other general reference, web pages often provide succinct summaries and will be too basic to use as references for a college-level paper. Your professor undoubtedly will require that you go beyond encyclopedia entries in your search for information. This is why I recommend using a subject guide rather than a commercial search engine—it will direct you to pages that are scholarly as well as accurate.

Always compare the information you locate on the web with what you have found using library tools (the online catalog or full-text databases). Because the Internet is so unregulated, web authors are sometimes careless about acknowledging sources. But like the information found in books in your college library or in articles in scholarly journals, a website source can be well researched and documented. Be especially cautious if a site offers numbers or statistics without identifying any sources. An absence of documentation suggests sloppiness, distortion, or worse. One sure indicator of a valid academic resource—on the web as in your own work—is thorough documentation.

When Was It Produced?

Just as it is often hard to locate the name of the sponsoring organization or author of a web page, it can sometimes be difficult to determine the date it was created or updated. For many research projects, it is essential that information be up to date in order to be accurate. As noted previously, knowledge undergoes constant revision, and you want your research to be based on the best information available at the moment. So it is important to note when information was created and determine if it is still relevant. To determine the last update, enter the following: <javascript:alert(document.lastModified)> in the address field and then press "Enter". The last update information will appear in a window. Be cautious about using information from a web page that doesn't display a date or bears an old date, especially if it presents information that can change rapidly.

e-TIPS

Determine Last Update

For many projects, the best information is the most recent information. To determine when a website was last updated, enter <javascript:alert(document.lastModified)> in the address field and then press "Enter." The last update information will appear in a window.

What Does It Look Like?

You can often evaluate a web page by paying attention to the tone, style, or proficiency of the writing. For instance, a pattern of grammatical errors and spelling mistakes is a dead giveaway that a careful, reliable author has not produced the site. Most scholars carefully check their work for these kinds of errors. An occasional mistake in punctuation or spelling is to be expected, but consistent writing errors should raise an alarm.

What Do Others Say About It?

Subject guides often offer brief synopses and reliability ratings. Like the abstracts included in most library resources, these give the researcher a quick impression of the relevancy and validity of a source. Also, confirmation by other sources is important in academic research. Even for topics that are heavily disputed, if an argument is sound, there will be other learned people who agree with it. Beware of radical opinions or ideas that are not substantiated in other places. If you cannot find corroboration, then you should exercise caution in using that information.

To sum up then, the Internet has made innumerable sources available, but they vary in accuracy, reliability, and value. Train yourself to recognize a noteworthy resource by familiarizing yourself first with all your library offers on your topic. Then, when you are confident that you know enough to screen out information that is unreliable, unsupported, or poorly argued, venture out into the virtual world of the WWW. Researchers living in the digital age should never settle for unreliable information.

QUICK CHECK
Evaluate, Evaluate, Evaluate

Academic research on the Internet requires mastery in evaluating the credibility of sources. You must carefully appraise the web page to determine its purpose: Sarcasm and exaggeration reveal a biased opinion. Does the document present a well-reasoned, balanced approach to the topic?

Source: Anonymity destroys credibility. Who is the document written by, and is it affiliated with a reliable organization?

Intended Audience: Much on the Internet is designed for general consumption. Does the document acknowledge other sources and treat the topic with a certain amount of complexity?

Date of Publication: Good research requires up-to-date information. Has the page been updated regularly?

Appearance: You can tell something about a book by its cover. Is the website well written and grammatically correct, and does the general layout of the page (graphics, design, etc.) appear scholarly?

Reputation: Nothing speaks louder than a good referral. Has the website received good reviews or been recommended in a summary or abstract?

EXERCISES

1. Since September 11, 2001, there has been a great deal posted on the Internet about terrorism. To get an idea of just how much, go to the *Google* search engine (<http://www.google.com>) and enter the search term "terrorism." Note the number of "hits" you get. Next, go to the *Librarians' Index to the Internet* (<http://www.lii.org>), and record the number of the returns you get using the same search term ("terrorism"). Write a brief analysis that compares and contrasts these two search experiences.

2. Besides supplying information that is of publishable quality, databases also provide suggestions for additional search terms/phrases or ways to refine previous search attempts that you won't find in most web search tools. If you are using the InfoTrac College Edition database in your course, use the passcode provided with this text to access the database and conduct a "Subject Guide" search using the term "terrorism." Review the InfoTrac College Edition subjects that contain the word *terrorism* and choose three of the phrases that seem particularly interesting or relevant to you. Then access the search engine *Google* <http://www.google.com> and perform searches using these search phrases. In a brief paragraph, compare and contrast the results from these searches with the outcome of the *Google* search you conducted in Exercise 1.

3. The following two sites discuss the controversial issue of racial profiling: <http://www.domelights.com/racprof1.htm>; <http://www.racialprofiling-analysis.neu.edu/>. Write a brief evaluation (using the criteria presented in this chapter and in Chapter 3) analyzing why these websites would/would not be credible sources of information for a college research paper on this topic.

4. Now conduct a "Keyword" search in the InfoTrac College Edition database using the search phrase "racial profiling AND terrorism." Choose one of the results from this list and write a paragraph in which you compare/contrast the reliability and credibility of this source to the two websites in Exercise 3.

If you are not using the Info-Trac database, exercises 2 and 4 could be adapted for your school's full-text databases.

6

Field Research Online

For most topics, you will find all of the information you need to write your paper in books, reference works, databases, and on the Internet.

For others, you may need to conduct interviews with people who have expertise in the area or develop a survey that will enable you to understand the opinions of a particular population or group. When you interview or survey people to obtain their opinions, you are conducting fieldwork. Just as the value of any written source must be evaluated according to specific criteria (i.e., whether the source is up to date, pertinent, credible, and reasonably unbiased), so, too, is the value of fieldwork tied to how careful you are in choosing whom and how to query.

Conducting an Interview

Conducting an interview with an expert can make your research project more authentic; it can also give you an unexpected boost of interest or clarity of direction. Speaking to someone who has had firsthand or extensive experience with your topic is exciting. That excitement will often infuse your writing, making it more interesting for the reader as well. Of course, interviews alone can never replace the other forms of research we have already discussed in the first five chapters of this book. Don't assume that an expert will do your research for you or that speaking with an expert will substitute for thorough research. You will still need to conduct library research using the online catalog, databases, and select subject guides on the Internet. An interview is simply one more source of information.

Contact an Authority on Your Topic

The first question to consider when planning an interview is "Who?" As a student at a college or university, you have immediate access to experts in a wide range of fields. My former student who researched the turtle/salmonella law was able to interview a biology professor who had special training in herpetology and a nursing instructor who gave her firsthand information about the medical treatment of salmonella infection. As a citizen, you have access to local, and perhaps even national, government officials. Another student who was investigating the county school and bus scheduling system was able to interview the chair of the local school board. And as a member of the virtual community made possible by the World Wide Web, you have access to countless experts worldwide. A former student interested in the inequities of the financial aid system for nontraditional students was able to e-mail a state official with questions about student loan policies and received answers to his questions within a few days. The Information Superhighway gives you immediate access to innumerable experts who can provide vital, direct information about your subject—or point you in the direction of those who can.

If you're lucky, you might already have an expert in mind whom you would like to interview, but most times you will need to find someone who is an authority on your topic. One obvious source is the telephone book or an online telephone directory. Are you investigating the practices of day care providers? Consider contacting local day care centers. Are you examining stalking laws? Check an online "800" number phone book <http://www.inter800.com/> for the toll-free telephone numbers of specific associations that assist victims of domestic violence or sexual harassment. You might feel apprehensive about calling someone you don't know for an interview, but most people welcome the opportunity to discuss their work, either in person, by phone, or by e-mail. It's a good idea to suggest these different options because some people are more comfortable with e-mail or find it easier to fit an e-mail interview into their schedule. Be sure to call for an interview a few weeks in advance. Before you call, write out exactly why you want to speak to the person and what information you hope to obtain. Be as specific as you can about your research project, and be prepared to explain or give further details if necessary. If you sound knowledgeable and focused, the person you call will be more likely to agree to an interview.

Don't overlook the possibility of tracking down experts through the Internet. Many organizations have web pages with links that allow you to e-mail questions. If during the course of your research you locate an especially pertinent or noteworthy source published on the Internet, and an e-mail address is provided, then contact the author **(see Figure 6.1)**. Make sure that your questions extend beyond the information provided on the web page. You'll also want to allow enough time for a thoughtful reply; you might check your e-mail many times a day, but you can't expect everyone to respond so quickly.

E-mail is an excellent means of carrying out an interview. In fact, even if the authority you are consulting is located on your campus or in your town, you might want to consider conducting the interview via e-mail. There are a number of advantages to this approach. Sometimes it is difficult to coordinate schedules to meet face-to-face; by using e-mail to send your questions and responses, you can avoid this inconvenience. Receiving questions in writing that can be answered after careful consideration, rather than during a personal meeting with time limitations, enables more thoughtful responses. Finally, because you will receive your answers in writing, you will be less likely to forget information or misquote your expert.

FIGURE 6.1 This detail-rich website is a tremendous resource for information on school violence: it contains up-to-date statistics, pertinent legislation, current programs available, and a database of abstracts on relevant publications. At the bottom of the page a "related resources" link connects to another page with e-mail links and addresses to approximately 50 organizations and agencies that provide information on this subject.

e-TIPS

Using Online Discussions as Sources

You might be tempted to use a listserv (sometimes called a mailing group or discussion list) or newsgroup (often referred to as a discussion group) to gather personal opinions and ideas about your topic. There are, however, limitations to the usefulness of these forums. The discussions can be an excellent catalyst for stimulating your thinking, but the anonymity that surrounds most of the participants makes this an ineffective means of gathering authoritative information. Most of the people participating in these groups are interested novices, like yourself, rather than experts, and it is difficult to guarantee the credibility of anyone you meet online.

QUICK CHECK

Strategies for Locating an "Expert"

- *Consider your campus first:* Professors at your college are an excellent source of information, and they are usually willing to be interviewed for school projects.
- *Approach local officials and agencies:* Part of being a public servant is answering the public's questions. For example, government officials, police, fire, school, and hospital administrators (among others) in your community will often agree to meet with you.
- *Search the phone book:* Many organizations have toll-free numbers. Explore <http://www.inter800.com> for contact numbers of experts on your topic.
- *E-mail a noted expert:* Have you found a website with excellent information? See if there is a link that allows you to e-mail the author your questions.

Prepare Your Interview Questions

Once you have located an expert you would like to interview, take the time to develop good questions. Many novice researchers mistakenly think that once they locate an authority and set up an interview, the hard part is over, but composing thoughtful questions—questions that will elicit interesting responses—is equally demanding. In fact, preparing for an interview is an excellent way to refocus your project because it forces you to rethink the questions with which you began your research.

Avoid general questions that will elicit vague answers. Instead, do your homework. Read up on the topic (and the person you'll be interviewing, if possible) so that you can focus your questions and provide an opportunity for the expert you are interviewing to discuss his or her full range of knowledge. Ask for information that is not readily available from other sources. For instance, the student interested in reptiles asked her biology instructor what steps herpetologists took to protect themselves from exposure to the salmonella bacteria and whether he thought reptiles should be kept as pets. In her interview with a nursing instructor, she asked about the specifics of treating salmonella—what kinds of symptoms the patients suffered, how long the illness normally lasts, and what the therapy was like. She also asked if she would allow her children to keep a pet reptile, given the danger of infection.

Here are some additional suggestions to help you prepare for the interview:

- Prepare your questions in writing. Doing so will enable you to get the exact phrasing you want and arrange the questions in a logical order.

- Limit your questions to a few that are very specific. It is better to ask three or four pointed questions than eight ambiguous ones. This is especially true in e-mail interviews. Because your expert needs to type his or her replies, you are more likely to get thorough answers if you keep your questions to a minimum.

- Avoid questions that can be answered with a simple "yes" or "no." Instead, ask *who, what, when, where,* and—most important—*how* and *why* questions.

- Develop questions that are primarily interpretive or evaluative (e.g., "What is the biggest danger the salmonella bacteria pose to a patient?"), because they will elicit the most useful and interesting responses.

- Consider ending the interview with a question that leads to new information. For example, you might ask your expert to recommend other people to interview or specific books or articles to read.

The Interview and Follow-up

If you are conducting the interview face-to-face, it is important that you keep an accurate record of any and all answers. No one likes to be misquoted. In fact, because I have been misquoted so frequently, I no longer give face-to-face interviews with our school newspaper staff unless they agree to let me review any quotations they plan to use before the article is published.

Here are some suggestions for conducting the interview:

- To ensure accuracy, consider tape-recording the interview. If you do, be sure to obtain permission from the person being interviewed in advance.

- Take notes—even if you record the interview. Tape recordings have been known to fail.

- Put quotation marks around any statements in your notes that are direct quotations. Check these with the person being interviewed to make sure you have quoted him or her correctly.

- Be flexible. Sometimes a question will generate a response that inspires a follow-up question that you haven't prepared beforehand. If that happens, don't hesitate to add questions or let the interview take a slightly different direction.

- Before you end the interview, check your notes for accuracy. If (in the course of your conversation) your expert furnished you with explicit details or statistics, confirm them while you're still with the person.

- Immediately following the interview, jot down your impressions and complete any unfinished statements in your notes. Clearly mark information that might be most useful to your project.

- If you need to clarify a point or a quotation, make sure you contact the interviewee. To be courteous, you should follow up the interview by sending a short thank you to the person you interviewed.

Developing a Survey

If you have ever taken a statistics or methods course in psychology or sociology, you know that there is a science to gathering information. Unless you take time to learn the rules about how to compile a random, accurate sample; unless you compose forthright, revealing questions; and unless you correctly interpret the results, you cannot expect your fieldwork to fulfill the strict specifications of academic research. Informal surveys can be useful as long as you thoroughly describe your procedures and qualify your conclusions. In fact, information gleaned from surveys can sometimes lend an immediacy that can energize your project and your writing.

Composing an Effective Survey

Composing a survey is very different from conducting an interview. Interview questions are like essay questions—they are open-ended and attempt to draw out extended answers. A survey is more like an objective test—the questions should elicit short, yet revealing, responses. The questions should be phrased so people can answer quickly, and the responses must fit a pattern that enables results to be easily compiled and compared. Most questions should be answered as simply as "yes or no," "true or false," or with a ranking scale—say, from 1 to 5.

Like an interview, however, your survey questions should reflect your own understanding of the topic. You cannot devise a good survey unless you have already completed a good deal of research and are familiar with the most significant ideas related to your topic. A good survey will enable you to include people's views on specific questions you have already formulated: Are motorcycle helmet laws necessary? Does the college need to provide more student parking? Should talk shows that deal with controversial, adult subjects be aired only after 9 P.M.? You need to understand the purpose of the survey before you can create a series of questions that will help you gather the information necessary to respond to it.

Here are some general suggestions for preparing your survey questions:

- Ask no more than 8 to 10 questions.
- Use clear, concise, and unambiguous language. (Test your questions on friends, and simplify any phrasing they find unclear or confusing.)
- Phrase your questions so they can be answered with a "yes or no" or "true or false" response or a range of alternative choices (i.e., strongly disagree, disagree, no opinion, agree, strongly agree). Maintain a consistent response pattern to avoid confusion.
- A survey question may simply gather factual information or ask for opinion. In either case, make sure the question doesn't "lead" the respondent.

    Example:
    Leading: *Are you dissatisfied with the administration's failure to solve the parking problem on campus?*

Revised: *Do you think the administration has responded appropriately to the parking problem on campus?*

- Arrange your questions from easiest to hardest. Doing so allows your respondents a chance to warm up before being asked the most challenging queries.

- Prepare your surveys so they are easy to read and complete. Instructions should be brief and explicit. Limit the amount of writing required—instead, respondents should be able to circle or check responses.

- Don't ask for unnecessary or revealing personal information. The more anonymous the survey is, the more likely you will receive an honest response. (If a person's name, age, sex, religious affiliation, employment status, or race isn't relevant, don't ask. If you need personal information to properly interpret the results, then promise confidentiality and honor your pledge.)

Administering the Survey

Like an interview, whom you ask to answer your questionnaire is important. Determine in advance the nature of your target group, and think about ways to best administer the survey to reach representative members of that group. For example, if you want to know what parents think about an issue, then you need to distribute the survey to people with children. You want a random sampling (which means that you want a fair representation of varying opinions and ideas) that polls a cross section of your target group. Polling only your friends or people who agree with you will obviously skew your results.

Failure to identify your target group accurately or to distribute the survey to them effectively will skew your results. For example, I once served on a committee that met with student government officers to determine students' most pressing concerns for change on campus. They had surveyed a few hundred students who were asked to rank how important certain changes in student services or school policies were to them. Expanding the parking lots, improving the food service, and bringing better entertainment to campus ranked very high. But I was surprised to see that providing child care assistance was ranked last, since a large percentage of the students in my classes are single mothers who are struggling to balance parenting with their education. When I asked how the survey had been administered, I realized why the results were so curious. No effort had been made to poll men and women in equal numbers, and most of the surveys had been distributed at school functions (such as athletic and social events) that a busy student/mom would most likely not attend. It was clear to me that the results didn't accurately depict the concerns of our student body because the sampling didn't represent the diversity of our student population.

You should model your methods of survey on the professional model—have a random and broad spectrum of respondents.

Here are some general suggestions to help guide you in administering your survey:

- Administer the survey yourself to limit the variables and allow you to describe accurately how the survey was conducted.

- Give yourself enough time to administer the survey and tabulate and interpret the results.

- Keep the number of the sample realistic. You might think that the more questionnaires completed, the better. In reality, you can get an effective outcome from a fairly small number of results, as long as the sampling is random. Suggestion: It is reasonable to assume that your fellow classmates in a general requirement class (first-year English, math, psychology, history, etc.) represent a cross section of the students taking courses in your college. Of course, if the class meets in the evening or on Saturdays, they may not accurately indicate a random sampling of the student population.

- Use a standardized form to keep track of answers. (You might choose to administer the survey orally, but you should develop a set answer sheet on which to record responses.)

- Record when, where, and how your survey was conducted.

- Carefully tabulate your results.

e-TIPS

Conducting Surveys via E-Mail

Surveys, like personal interviews, can be conducted effectively via e-mail. Abide by the same rules concerning random sampling (don't just e-mail the survey to your friends or family—you must try for a cross sampling of opinion). Make sure that you specify a date of completion, and be prepared to remind people to return them to you on time.

When you report your results in your essay, present your findings in a manner that will make sense to your readers (i.e., use percentages or ratios). Always describe your methods as well. Indicate the date(s) on which you conducted the survey, where you questioned people, and the procedures you followed. Most importantly, specify the limits of your study. Note the number of people questioned, the general population they represented, and the techniques you used to ensure that this was a random sample.

Personally interviewing an authority on your subject or conducting a survey of opinions on your topic can be a useful research experience. Because people are such a great source of information, these methods can reveal ideas and attitudes not available from other sources. Nevertheless, be careful to qualify any conclusions you draw from this data and resist overstating the results.

EXERCISES

1. Your psychology teacher has assigned a research paper project, and you have chosen to write about eating disorders. Compose a list of potential experts (using the suggestions you received in this chapter) whom you might interview to help complete this assignment.

2. If you are using InfoTrac College Edition in your course, access the following article in the database [*hint:* conduct a "Title Search"]:

   Browne, Lorna, and Anthony Curtis. "Eat to live or love to eat? The paradox of eating disorders." *Psychology Review* 7.4 (2001): 20–25.

   Using the information contained in this article (and keeping in mind the suggestions made in this chapter), compose a list of five questions you could ask in an interview with one of the experts you identified in Exercise 1.

3. You decide to prepare a survey of the students at your school about eating disorders. Briefly describe in one paragraph what your target group would be and how you would administer the survey to ensure a random sampling of that group.

4. Access the following article in the InfoTrac College Edition database [*hint:* conduct a "Title Search"]:

   Kowalski, Kathiann M. "Body image: how do you see yourself? How you feel about your body has a big impact on your health. Learn to like the person you see in the mirror!" *Current Health 2* 29.7 (2003): 29–35.

   Using the information contained in this article (and keeping in mind the suggestions made in this chapter), compose a list of five survey questions you could ask of the group you identified in Exercise 3.

If you are not using the Info-Trac database, exercises 2 and 4 could be adapted for your school's full-text databases.

PART

3

RESEARCH

DOCUMENTATION

Documentation: General Rules

"The wisdom of

the wise and the

experience of

the ages are

perpetuated by

quotations."

BENJAMIN DISRAELI

If, like many people, you wait until you've written your paper before composing a Works Cited page, you're probably feeling exhausted. For that reason, it is unfortunate if you leave this very important part of the research project for the last minute. What you probably don't know is that many professors turn to the Works Cited page first, even before they read an essay, to obtain a general impression of the research that underpins the paper. (In fact, I know several instructors who will refuse to grade a paper if there are too many errors on the Works Cited page.) Indeed a research paper is only as good as its sources. If you think about that for a moment, you'll see that it makes sense. After all, what is a reasonable person going to trust more: an argument based on the best available evidence or one grounded in outdated, obscure, or unreliable information? Moreover, if you haven't accurately formatted this documentation page, it will betray (at best) that you are unfamiliar with academic "protocol" or (at worst) that you don't care about the quality of your work. If you don't care, why should your reader?

Properly documenting a research paper requires that you pay meticulous attention to detail. It requires that you accurately identify the nature of your source and that you distinguish and follow the proper format for citing that source, both in the text and on the Works Cited page. In a pre-electronic library, it was fairly easy to determine the type of source with which you were working. The most common were books, articles in periodicals, articles in reference works (i.e., dictionaries or encyclopedias), government documents, pamphlets, or interviews. With the advent of computers, and then the

Internet, new systems of delivery have made this task of identification more difficult. Now information also might be delivered by a CD-ROM, a database, a website, an online subscription service, or an e-mail. What makes documentation even
more complicated is that, as technology changes, these forms are continuously
morphing into new modes of data transmission. This makes it extremely challenging for even the most careful writer to remain up to date on the conventions
of documentation.

Nevertheless, because improper documentation can sometimes mean the difference between an A or a B, it is in your best interest to incorporate source material
into your research paper correctly. You make a strong impression, either positive
or negative, by how carefully you integrate material into your essay, acknowledge
your research within the text of the paper, and document your resources on the
Works Cited page.

A Few Words About Plagiarism: *DON'T DO IT!*

Many college students are understandably uncertain about what constitutes plagiarism. Their confusion stems from a number of causes. For one thing, beginning
writers often aren't taught to paraphrase properly and/or to acknowledge sources
when they begin writing "research" papers in elementary school. Thus, very early
on they develop the bad habit of plagiarizing throughout their academic careers—
often without fully realizing it. For another thing, the "cut and paste" nature of
the Internet has blurred the boundaries of intellectual property. But don't be
deceived—your professors expect you to respect the ideas and words of others and
to properly document any use you make of them.

Plagiarizers Are Not Born; They're Made

I remember when I wrote my first researched essay—it was on Texas. I consulted
the *Encyclopedia Britannica,* carefully copied, word for word, pertinent information from this reference work, and then skillfully wove in some of my own words
and phrases. Occasionally I enclosed significant sentences in quotation marks, but
there were many directly quoted words and phrases that I did not indicate as such,
and much of the rest of the essay was a thinly disguised facsimile of the encyclopedia article that I (incorrectly) considered a "paraphrase." I made a cover out of construction paper, crayoned a likeness of the Lone Star State on the front, and tied
the report together with a piece of brightly colored yarn. When I handed it in to
my fourth grade teacher, she praised my efforts and rewarded me with an A+.
Many students begin their careers as plagiarizers in just this way.

By the time they reach high school, they have become more ingenious. Instead
of relying on an encyclopedia alone, they use a variety of sources. They learn
to create Works Cited pages or bibliographies (although they might not follow a

specific format for this). They piece together sentences from various sources, change a phrase here and there, and skillfully disguise thoughts and phrases that are not their own. In order to better conceal their theft, some especially clever students might even borrow heavily from a "secret" source that they don't acknowledge in their bibliography or Works Cited page. I have known a number of students who have become very adept at making these plagiarized reports look like their own writing; in actuality, these papers are what I call "plagiarism quilts"—other people's words and ideas stitched together, more or less seamlessly.

The Truth About Plagiarism

Even if you haven't developed such bad habits, you might still be confused about what constitutes plagiarism. This confusion is exacerbated by the way images and content are often "borrowed" on the Internet without proper attribution. When you surf the web, you have probably encountered identical images or articles on different pages, and it is very easy to "cut and paste" graphics or text from the web. All of this might lead you to conclude that the Internet is a big "grab bag" from which you can freely take what you want. However, this is *not* true.

There is a great deal of misinformation about this subject circulating in the halls of academe. I have had students confidently assert that as long as they change at least 10 percent of the words in a sentence, it is no longer considered a direct quote, and there is no need to use quotation marks or document the source. Others believe that they need to attribute a direct quote to a source, but a paraphrase doesn't need to be acknowledged. Sometimes I have received papers with little or no direct quotation, but after every sentence there is a parenthetical citation. This is a sad attempt at making a "plagiarism quilt" legitimate. However—and this is the important point—in spite of the students' efforts at documentation, *these aren't really research papers.* They are the subtly altered words and ideas of others represented as original creations. Too many students define plagiarism only as copying a friend's term paper or downloading a paper off the Internet and submitting it, in total, as their own. The truth is, plagiarism takes many forms.

e-TIPS

Schools Get Tough on Plagiarizers

The Internet has made it easier to for students to plagiarize. There are millions of legitimate documents that can be copied as well as "paper mills" that offer thousands of essays (both free and for sale). At times the temptation to "borrow" writing or ideas and represent them as your own might seem overwhelming. After all, a lot of students are doing it. Statistics indicate that instances of academic dishonesty are on the rise. However, the web has also made it easier for professors to recognize plagiarism. Many schools are "fighting back" and enforcing tough policies to ensure that students do their own work as well as subscribing to plagiarism detection programs like Turnitin.com. Resist the urge to take these types of shortcuts. The consequences can be severe.

The Many Faces of Plagiarism

Broadly defined, plagiarism is failing to acknowledge the words or ideas of another, but this failure can occur in a number of different ways and be either deliberate or accidental. I often compare these gradations to the different classifications for murder in our legal system. Someone who walks into a fast-food restaurant with an Uzi and opens fire, killing 16 people, is a murderer. Likewise, a busy truck driver who is unable to stop when traffic suddenly slows and rear-ends a commuter, accidentally killing him, is also a murderer (although the trucker may not be legally guilty to the same degree). Whether students deliberately set out to deceive a professor and pass off someone else's words and ideas as their own, carelessly fail to place quotation marks around another writer's words, or neglect to place the proper citation at the end of a paraphrase, the end result is the same. *All of these examples constitute plagiarism*—it's just that some are more egregious than others.

The important thing to remember is that *whenever* you incorporate information from someone else's work into your own writing, regardless of whether it is a direct quote, a careful paraphrase, or a brief summary, *you must properly indicate the source.* The one exception to this rule is information that legitimately could be considered common knowledge.

However, determining what should be considered "common knowledge" can be a tricky task. Material is normally considered common knowledge if it's something most people already know or could be found easily in a general reference source. For example, Ronald Reagan's birthday (February 6, 1911), the number of stomachs a cow has (four), the capital of Malaysia (Kuala Lumpur), or the Aaron Copland composition that includes a Shaker hymn *(Appalachian Spring)* are all examples of common knowledge. But what is considered common knowledge can vary according to audience (since it is based on what you assume your reader will already know or be able to access quickly). Age, profession, and level of education are all variables that can affect your decision to document a fact or not. Most professors would agree that if you can find the information undocumented in several different sources, it is probably common knowledge. (Be careful—the cut-and-paste nature of the web has resulted in incredible abuse of intellectual property. The judgment of web authors should not serve as a guide to your own decision regarding what is common knowledge.) Most instructors would encourage you to err on the side of caution. In other words, if you are unsure whether something is common knowledge, it is better to go ahead and document it.

It is important to remember that if the information is the intellectual property of another writer—whether that information takes the form of statistical evidence, individual opinion, distinctive analysis, original inquiry, or especially compelling phrasing—you need to document the source. In such cases, you must always enclose exact words or unique phrasing in quotation marks and include a proper in-text citation as well as a corresponding entry on your Works Cited page. If you use the same ideas as your source—even if you paraphrase—then you must acknowledge the original in a parenthetical citation and on the Works Cited page.

Your instructor expects that as a member of an academic community, you will respect and uphold these basic rules of academic integrity.

QUICK CHECK
Types of Plagiarism
Students sometimes differentiate between "deliberate" and "accidental" plagiarism. But whether you deliberately set out to plagiarize or accidentally fail to acknowledge a source, it is STILL plagiarism.

- **Deliberate plagiarism** involves copying someone else's words and/or ideas and passing them off as your own. (This could be an entire paper, portions of a paper, or simply copying the language and sentence patterns of another person's work.)
- **Accidental plagiarism** involves failing to place quotation marks around another writer's words (even if you provide a source at the end of your essay) and failing to provide the proper citation when you rely on another person's ideas.

A Sure Way to Impress: Incorporate and Document with Skill

As I mentioned at the beginning of this chapter, how you handle research sources in your paper makes a powerful impact. The most significant reason for using direct quotations or paraphrasing is to provide support for your claims or add credibility to your writing. If you let this principle guide you, you will develop expertise as a writer. But it is not enough to avoid plagiarizing; if you want to incorporate information into your project effectively, you must manage your sources skillfully and accurately.

General Rules for Incorporating Direct Quotations

One error that betrays many novice writers is that their essays are too dependent on direct quotations. This error can be manifested in two ways, but both create the impression that the writer lacks confidence in his or her thinking or writing. The first mistake is to quote too often. When the bulk of an essay is the words of others, it seems as if the writer of the essay has "disappeared." The second is to allow quotations to make your points rather than citing the words or ideas of others to support your own assertions and opinions. Your words and ideas always should always dominate the essay. Here are some rules of thumb to help you avoid either error.

- **No more than 15 percent of your paper should be direct quotation.** Most of the writing should be your own. Use the words and opinions of others only to support your own points and ideas.
- **Keep quotations short.** Resist the temptation to quote long passages of text, even if it seems remarkable and strikingly worded. Instead, smoothly incorporate fragments of direct quotations into your own sentences, making certain that the sentence structure is correct and makes sense.

- **Clearly identify each quotation.** If the purpose of direct quotation is to lend credibility to your writing, then you should indicate the authority behind the words. Never simply plop quotations into your paper without specifying who is speaking. Instead, use a signal phrase (sometimes called an identifying tag) to set up the quotation properly.

- **Precede and follow quotations with your own commentary.** Don't use a direct quote to *make* your point. Instead, state your idea in your own words, and supplement that with a quotation from an expert.

- **Interweave your sources.** When quotations from the same source are all clustered in one portion of a paper, it can be a clear sign of a "plagiarism quilt." Instead, your paper should blend information from different sources to create your own analysis.

Example:

- *Original Source Material:*

  In the early 1970s, the FDA banned the distribution and sale of baby turtles with shells 4 inches in length or less after a quarter-million infants and small children were diagnosed with having turtle-associated salmonellosis.

  From: "The Fright of the Iguana" by Carol Lewis in the *FDA Consumer.*

  Approximately 93,000 (7%) cases per year of Salmonella infections are attributable to pet reptile or amphibian contact.

  From: "Reptile-Associated Salmonellosis-Selected States, 1996–1998" in *Morbidity & Mortality Weekly Report* by C. Levy et al.

- *Improper Incorporation of Quotations:*

  But has the law banning turtle sales been successful? "In the early 1970s, the FDA banned the distribution and sale of baby turtles with shells 4 inches in length or less after a quarter-million infants and small children were diagnosed with having turtle-associated salmonellosis" (Lewis 33). Nonetheless, "approximately 93,000 (7%) cases per year of salmonella infections are attributable to pet reptile or amphibian contact" (Levy 1009).

> **NOTE:** The use of a question, rather than a statement, to lead into the quoted information accentuates the tentativeness of the writer. The excessive length of the quotations and the fact that they are not introduced with a signal phrase amplifies this initial impression. Finally, the facts are presented, but there is no attempt to analyze the significance of the statistics.

- *Quotations Skillfully Incorporated:*

  Carol Lewis states that the sale of baby turtles was prohibited in the seventies when an outbreak of salmonella affected "a quarter-million infants and small children" (33). A recent article in *Morbidity & Mortality Weekly Report* notes that more than 20 years later, of all the cases of salmonella reported each year, "Approximately 93,000 (7%) . . . are attributable to pet reptile or amphibian contact" (Levy et al. 1009). Obviously, the law banning turtle sales has not accomplished its purpose.

> **NOTE:** Note how an introductory "signal phrase" clearly identifies the source, direct quotation is kept to a minimum, the significance of the research material is indicated, and different sources are combined in the analysis.

General Rules for Paraphrasing

To paraphrase is to rewrite someone else's ideas in your own words. This is a simple concept, but it is extremely difficult to execute. The challenge of paraphrasing is to relate accurately the sense of a text without duplicating the language. Here are some suggestions to help you paraphrase correctly.

- **Write your paraphrase from memory.** It is very difficult to paraphrase without plagiarizing; if you attempt to rephrase something while you are looking at the original, you are almost doomed to failure. Instead, write your paraphrase without consulting the source. Afterward, compare it to the original and check for accuracy.

- **Indicate any direct quotation.** Any words or phrases that appear in the original source are considered direct quotes. You must enclose those words with quotation marks.

- **Clearly identify your source.** Just like a direct quote, a paraphrase needs to be introduced to indicate the authority of the source. In fact, an introductory, or signal, phrase is even more important because there are no quotation marks to distinguish these ideas from your own.

> **NOTE:** Remember, whether it is a direct quote or a paraphrase, you must always indicate your source within the text and on a Works Cited page.

Example:

- *Original Source Material:*

  Roughly 90 percent of the scaly pets are carriers of salmonella bacteria, says Fred Angulo, a medical epidemiologist with the Centers for Disease Control and Prevention. He has collected evidence that human infections are rising sharply with the animals' increasing popularity. Last year, he says, there were as many as 100,000 cases of reptile-related salmonella poisoning in people nationally—up from about 20,000 just five years ago.

  From: "A Reptilian Pet Peeve" by Ingfei Chen and Deborah Franklin in *Health*.

- *Improper Paraphrase:*

  According to Fred Angulo, an epidemiologist with the CDC, approximately 9 out of every 10 reptilian pets carry the salmonella bacteria. Angulo has conducted a study that proves that infections in humans are increasing as ownership of pet reptiles increases in popularity. He concludes that last year approximately 100,000 cases of Salmonella poisoning were traced to reptiles in the U.S.A.—whereas five years ago there were only 80,000 (Chen and Franklin 24).

> **NOTE:** Even though a signal phrase and parenthetical citation indicate the information comes from another source, the wording and structure of the passage is too similar to the original, and there are words and phrases that are identical. This would be considered plagiarism.

- *Proper Paraphrase:*

  An article in *Health* magazine reports that recent studies by the CDC link increases in salmonella infections in humans to the growing trend of owning reptiles as pets. Epidemiologist Fred Angulo contends that "roughly 90 percent" of these reptile pets are hosts of the bacteria, and they have caused an 80 percent increase in salmonella infections in the previous five years (Chen and Franklin 24).

> **NOTE:** The source is clearly identified in the signal phrase, the main ideas are summarized in unique wording and sentence structure, and where exact wording from the original is used, it appears in quotation marks. The paraphrase ends with a properly formatted parenthetical citation.

General Rules for Citing Sources

Any time you directly quote or paraphrase a source, you must provide the information necessary for a reader to locate easily that document and the specific information you have just cited. Students sometimes complain that the rules concerning documentation are too difficult and arbitrary. Indeed, for both the in-text and Works Cited page documentation, there are strict rules about what information to include, in what order it should be given, and how it is to be punctuated. Although many students seem baffled by these rules, the reason for this "pickiness" is to reduce confusion by having everyone conform to the same conventions. Documentation rules establish a uniform, universal format so a reader can quickly determine what type of source is being cited and, if desired, track down the text.

e-TIPS

Format Citations as You Write

Many students make the mistake of leaving the task of documentation until after a paper is completely written. Then they must go back and locate all of the places where they have cited information and retrieve the required details to correctly document the source. They may overlook places in their paper where they need to cite their sources, forget where a quotation came from, or misplace the source they used. It is much better to format as you write a paper. Include a parenthetical citation after any direct quotation or paraphrase. Word processing programs make it very easy to keep a current Works Cited page as you work. Even if you are not sure of the format, you can type (or copy and paste, if you are using electronic sources) the necessary information (author[s], editor[s], title, place of publication, publisher, date of publication, page numbers, date of access, etc.) on the last page or keep a separate file with this information.

What many students don't realize until late in their academic careers (sometimes not until graduate school) is that there is a logic to documenting essays. In some ways, their problem is similar to the difficulties many students have who study organic chemistry. I once asked a friend of mine who teaches that subject why so many seemingly capable students wash out when they take this course. He explained that the course requires students to memorize an enormous amount of seemingly disconnected information before they can discern a pattern. Few students are able to see the interrelatedness of what they are studying until they are well into the semester. With no conceptual grid to help them make sense of the myriad of facts they are attempting to muster, many falter.

The rules for documenting sources can seem like that. When you look at a style handbook, it can appear that there is no rhyme or reason to formatting rules. However, there is method to the madness. The in-text citation directs a reader to the first piece of information listed in the entry on the Works Cited page. Normally, that is the author's last name. (If there is no author listed, then it will cue the reader to the next piece of information listed: the title of the work.)

There are two major styles of documentation: the MLA (Modern Language Association) style, which is commonly used in the humanities, and the APA (American Psychological Association) style, which is usually employed in the social sciences. Although there are some significant differences between these formats, they are similar. Both require the following information.

1. A signal phrase
- usually appears at the beginning of a quotation or paraphrase, but can appear midphrase
- includes the name(s) of the author(s) or the title of the book, article, periodical, or website from which the information originates
- can use a variety of "verbs of address," such as:

adds	compares	grants	refutes
admits	confirms	illustrates	rejects
agrees	contends	implies	reports
argues	declares	insists	responds
asserts	denies	notes	suggests
believes	disputes	observes	thinks
claims	emphasizes	points out	writes

2. A citation
- provides a brief reference to the source document in the text of the essay
- is located inside parentheses and appears in the same paragraph as the information it documents
- normally appears at the end of the sentence that features the information being cited
- may appear in midsentence, especially if information from more than one source appears in the same statement

3. A Works Cited reference

- appears on a Works Cited page at the conclusion of the paper
- includes all of the required bibliographic information

These three components (signal phrase, parenthetical citation, and Works Cited reference) work together; if you exclude one of them, you have compromised the accuracy of your documentation. If the purpose of direct quotation and paraphrase is to lend authority to your essay, then failing to identify the source seriously undercuts your efforts.

EXERCISES

1. Briefly (in two or three sentences), and in your own words, explain why it is important to include outside sources in a research paper. At some point in this paragraph, correctly incorporate any portion(s) of the text below as a direct quote. Follow the suggestions you received in this chapter to do this successfully.

   > Use quotations selectively to add clarity, emphasis, or interest to a research paper, not to pad its length. Overquoting reduces the effectiveness of a paper because it suggests overdependence on other people's ideas.

   > From page 108 of Perrin, Robert. *Handbook for College Research.* New York: Houghton Mifflin Company, 1997.

2. Write a proper paraphrase of the paragraph below according to the instructions in this chapter.

   > College students appear to judge cheating as a matter of degree, with plagiarism—perhaps sharing work with a friend or lifting a sentence from an Internet page—as relatively minor, according to a 1999 study of beginning psychology students at a public university. The results, reported by G. A. U. Overbey and S. F. Guilding in "Student Perception of Plagiarism and the Evaluation of Assignments," <u>Journal of Excellence in College Teaching</u>, 1999(3), found that more than 70 percent of students said they should be able to resubmit a paper prepared for a previous course. Nearly 65 percent said they should have a chance to redo a paper, rather than receive a zero and be referred for additional campus sanctions, if an instructor catches some plagiarism in the work. Only 3 percent thought "plagiarism" should lead to discipline outside the classroom, while 19 percent said that submission of a purchased paper (a more egregious form of plagiarism, but plagiarism nonetheless) should be referred for student affairs action. Forty-one percent said a zero grade is appropriate for fully copied work. But another 30 percent said that students submitting work with some copied materials should get at least 50 percent credit for "effort."

   > From page 4 of "How Students View Plagiarism: Implications for Student Services." *National On-Campus Report* 30.5 (2002).

3. If you are using InfoTrac College Edition in your course, access the following article in the database [*hint:* conduct a "Title Search"]:

Petress, Kenneth C. "Academic dishonesty: a plague on our profession." *Education* 123.3 (2003): 624–27.

Write a brief summary of this essay (4–6 sentences). If you directly quote, remember to enclose these words in quotation marks.

4. Using your passcode, access the InfoTrac College Edition database and conduct a "Keyword" search for the phrase "plagiarism AND college." Scan the titles and abstracts of the articles that appear on the results page, and then write a brief paragraph (4–5 sentences) that summarizes common themes, attitudes, and viewpoints of these writers.

Documentation: MLA Format

"Any activity

becomes creative

when the doer

cares about doing

it right, or doing it

better."

JOHN UPDIKE

A system of documentation is a very precise method of telling your reader where you got your ideas and how you know this information is correct. The Modern Language Association (MLA) style of documentation is used in scholarly publications and in the humanities. Unless your professor specifically instructs you to use a different style, you should use the MLA style of documentation in your essays.

MLA In-Text Citations

The format for in-text citations has been designed to identify source material while interrupting the flow of the essay as little as possible. All that the MLA style requires you to include within the text of your essay is the author's last name and the page number on which the information appears. The reader can use this to reference the author's name on the Works Cited page and obtain more complete information (title, publisher, date of publication, etc.) about the source. This seems rather simple, but because there is some variation in how information is circulated, there can be subtle differences in how the in-text citations might appear.

There are two elements to a correct in-text citation: the signal phrase and the parenthetical citation. How you introduce your information determines what appears in the parentheses.

Examples of MLA In-Text Citations

1. A Work by One Author

- Carol Lewis states that a midseventies outbreak of salmonella affected "a quarter million infants and small children" (33).

- The <u>FDA Consumer</u> notes that a midseventies outbreak of salmonella affected "a quarter million infants and small children" (Lewis 33).

If the author's name occurs in the signal phrase, then only the page number need appear in the parenthetical citation. If the author's name doesn't appear in the signal phrase, it must be included in the parentheses. If there is an editor instead of an author, the editor's last name should appear in the signal phrase or parenthetical citation.

WRITING TIP

It is important to notice how to punctuate in-text citations. The parenthetical citation appears after the closing quotation mark and before the final punctuation. If a quotation is longer than four typed lines (in your essay, not in the original work), indent the passage one inch (on the left, but not on the right), omit quotation marks, and place the final punctuation mark before the parenthetical citation. The left indentation substitutes for the quotation marks that you otherwise would include.

2. A Work by Two or Three Authors

- Chen and Franklin contend that "human infections are rising sharply with the animals' [reptiles'] increasing popularity" (24).

- A recent article in <u>Health</u> magazine declares that "human infections are rising sharply with the animals' [reptiles'] increasing popularity" (Chen and Franklin 24).

If there are two or three authors, list all the last names joined by "and" in the signal phrase or the parenthetical citation.

3. A Work by Four or More Authors

- "Approximately 93,000 (7 percent) cases per year of Salmonella infections," <u>Morbidity & Mortality Weekly Report</u> confirms, "are attributable to pet reptile or amphibian contact" (Levy et al. 1009).

If there are four or more authors, include only the first author's name followed by the Latin phrase *et al.* (an abbreviation for *et alii,* which means "and others").

4. A Work by an Unknown Author

Often articles in encyclopedias, newspapers, dictionaries, and magazines do not include the name of the author. In these cases, the title of the article, NOT the title of the encyclopedia, newspaper, dictionary, or magazine, should appear in the in-text citation.

- A recent article in <u>National Geographic World</u> points out, "Pet reptiles . . . aren't affected by the bacteria, so they don't show signs that they are carrying it" ("Warning" 5).

- In "Warning: Pets Pose Problems" the author claims, "Pet reptiles . . . aren't affected by the bacteria, so they don't show signs that they are carrying it" (5).

If the author's name is not given, then provide the title in the signal phrase or a shortened version of the title in the parenthetical citation.

5. A Quotation Within a Source (an indirect source)

- Stephanie Wong, a veterinarian for the Centers for Disease Control, insists, "There's no way to tell that a reptile is salmonella-free" (qtd. in "Warning" 5).

If your source has quoted someone else, identify the original speaker or writer in your signal phrase. In the parenthetical citation use the phrase "qtd. in" (quoted in), the author's last name (or title if no author is given), and the page numbers of your source.

6. A Work in a Collection or Anthology

An "anthology" is a collection of essays or works of literature by different authors. The name of the author of the essay or work (not the editor of the anthology) appears in the signal phrase or parenthetical citation.

- The narrator states that Sarty "feels the old fierce pull of blood" and is often times confused about how to react to his father's violent actions (Faulkner 178).

- In Faulkner's tale, the narrator identifies Sarty's uncertain loyalty to his father as "the old fierce pull of blood" (178).

These citations indicate that you are quoting from a section of William Faulkner's short story "Barn Burning." The passage appears on page 178 of an anthology of many different literary selections.

WRITING TIP

Note that the signal phrase correctly identifies the speaker of the quote as the narrator rather than the author (Faulkner). When writing about literature, be careful not to confuse the author (who writes the line) with the narrator, speaker, or character in the story who speaks the line in the work.

7. A Work by a Government Agency or Corporate Author

The name of the corporate author (or shortened version of the name) appears in the signal phrase or parenthetical citation.

- According to the American Red Cross, "Bleach is an effective means of disinfecting areas that have been infected with salmonella microorganisms" (17).

- Medical professionals maintain that "Bleach is an effective means of disinfecting areas that have been infected with salmonella microorganisms" (American Red Cross 17).

This citation indicates that the American Red Cross has produced the item from which you are quoting. The passage appears on page 17.

8. Two or More Works by the Same Author

Include the title (or a brief version of the title) as well as the author's name in the signal phrase or parenthetical citation.

- In Flannery O'Connor's "A Good Man Is Hard to Find," the grandmother tries to pressure the family into changing their vacation plans (77).

- Shiftlet cons his way into Lucynell's life in Flannery O'Connor's "The Life You Save May Be Your Own" (99).

- Both the grandmother (O'Connor, "Good Man" 77) and Shiftlet (O'Connor, "Life" 99) are manipulative and deceitful.

These citations indicate that you are quoting from two works by Flannery O'Connor, "A Good Man Is Hard to Find" and "The Life You Save May Be Your Own."

WRITING TIP

When writing about literature, it is conventional to write in the present tense. Note the use of "tries" and "are" (present tense verbs) to refer to the actions of the characters in the stories.

9. Works by Authors with the Same Last Name

Include the first name of the author you are citing in the signal phrase or parenthetical citation. You may choose to mention the author's full name in the signal phrase.

- Malcolm Smith notes that some Indian snakes have developed special ridges in their skin to release pheromones while courting (82).

- Hobart M. Smith proposes that the ridges in snakes' skins provide greater friction when climbing and moving (112).

- The ridges in snakes' skins may house special glands that release pheromones (M. Smith 82) or provide greater friction when climbing and moving (H. M. Smith 112).

These citations indicate that you are quoting from different works by authors who share the same last name.

10. A Work in an Electronic Source

- In 1996, the <u>Wall Street Journal</u> reported on attempts to "develop a disinfectant that can be added to turtle bowl water to kill salmonella germs and prevent later infections" (Aeppel).

If your source is an electronic document (e.g., website, online journal, article from a database), treat it as you would any print source—indicate the name of the author (if no author is supplied, give the title or a shortened version of the title) in the signal phrase or parenthetical citation. (If your document includes paragraph numbers [since there are seldom page numbers in electronic documents], then the parenthetical citation should include the author's last name, followed by a comma, the abbreviation "par.," and the number. However, use this method only if the document comes with an established system of numbered paragraphs. Don't create your own paragraph numbers.)

e-TIPS

Page Numbers and Electronic Sources

One problem with electronic sources is that they lack page numbers. Don't be deceived by hard-copy printouts of electronic documents. Because printers differ, the page numbers created in a printout cannot be considered accurate. If the author's last name (or the title, when no author is given) appears in the signal phrase, there is nothing to indicate in the parenthetical citation. However, parenthetical citations play an important role because they designate where source information ends and your writing (or information from another source) begins. This is especially true when you are paraphrasing (quotation marks indicate the end of a direct quotation). Therefore, although it isn't a rule of MLA formatting, I advise my students to find an alternative way to introduce their source in the signal phrase (see the example) so they can include a parenthetical citation that identifies the author (or title if no author is given).

MLA Works Cited Entries

At the conclusion of a research paper, you need to include a Works Cited page that lists all of the references used. If your instructor wants you to list all of the sources you read, whether you cited them or not, this list should be entitled "Works Consulted."

Every entry on a Works Cited page includes the same basic information—author (last name, first), title, and publication information. However, the format (arrangement, punctuation, and spacing) differs depending on the type of source you are listing. Most instructors place a high premium on correctly formatting a Works Cited page. If for no other reason, you need to pay special attention to detail so you can produce a Works Cited page that will boost, rather than reduce, your grade.

The following are a few general rules to follow in order to properly format your Works Cited page.

- Begin a new page for your Works Cited list after the last page of your essay, and center your title (Works Cited) one inch from the top of the page.
- Double-space *everything* on the page (between the title and the first entry, within each entry, and between entries).
- Alphabetize the list by the authors' last names. If no author is provided for an entry, alphabetize according to the *first major word* of the title. (Include words like "A," "An," and "The" but ignore them when alphabetizing.)

- Begin each entry at the left margin. Subsequent lines in that entry should be indented one-half inch.

- Capitalize each word within titles of articles, books, etc. except for articles (*a, the*), prepositions (*against, of*), coordinating conjunctions (*and, so*), and "to" in an infinitive, unless it is the first word in the title or subtitle.

- Although convention allows you to either underline or italicize titles of books, journals, websites, etc., the MLA prefers that you underline for greater clarity. Whatever your decision, make sure you use the same method (underlining or italicizing) consistently throughout your list. Consult your instructor for his or her preference.

- Use quotation marks around the titles of short stories, book chapters, poems, songs, and articles in journals, magazines, and newspapers.

- Skip one space after each period, comma, and colon. (If a period appears after a title in quotation marks, place the period *inside* the quotation mark.)

- In listing the publisher, follow these guidelines:
  □ Omit articles (*A, An,* and *The*).
  □ Omit business abbreviations (*Co., Corp., Inc.,* and *Ltd.*).
  □ Omit descriptive words (*Books, House, Press,* and *Publishers*).
  □ When citing a university press, abbreviate "University" and "Press" (Oxford UP; UP of Mississippi; U of Chicago P).
  □ If the publisher's name includes the name of one person (W. W. Norton; John Wiley), cite the surname alone (Norton; Wiley).
  □ If the publisher's name includes the names of more than one person, cite only the first surname (Harcourt = Harcourt, Brace, Jovanovich; Prentice = Prentice Hall).

- End every entry with a period.

Printed and Recorded Sources

In order to format your Works Cited page correctly, it is important to identify the type of source that you are documenting. Standard MLA format for print sources (as opposed to electronic documents) has remained virtually unchanged for years and is readily available in numerous print and online sources. In addition to the information on the pages that follow, you may have a guide to basic MLA format in a writing handbook, and there are numerous websites to help you determine the proper format for your sources. The following are two of the best.

Purdue Online Writing Lab (OWL) Handout on MLA Style
<http://owl.english.purdue.edu/handouts/research/r_mla.html>

MLA Style Guide: Capital Community College
See the menu on the left margin for quick reference.
<http://webster.commnet.edu/mla/index.shtml>

Books:

Obtain all information from the title page (and the reverse side of the title page), not from the cover.

1. A Book with One Author or Editor
Basic format:

> Author or editor (*last name, first*), ed. (*if there is an editor instead of an author*) Title. Edition and/or volume number. (*if there is one*) Place of publication: Publisher, date of publication.

Always list the city of publication; if the city is unfamiliar (or if it is the name of a city in more than one state), list the state as well, using the two-letter ZIP code abbreviation.

Examples:

> Fudge, Alan F., ed. Laboratory Medicine: Avian and Exotic Pets. Philadelphia: Saunders, 2000.
>
> Frye, Frederic L. Biomedical and Surgical Aspects of Captive Reptile Husbandry. 2nd ed. Malabar, FL: Krieger, 1991.

2. A Book with Two or Three Authors or Editors
Basic format:

> First author or editor, (*last name, first*), and subsequent authors or editors, (*first name, first*), eds. (*if there are editors instead of authors*) Title. Edition and/or volume number. (*if there is one*) Place of publication: Publisher, date of publication.

Examples:

> Wray, C., and A. Wray. Salmonella in Domestic Animals. New York: CABI, 2000.
>
> Johnson-Delaney, Kathy A., and Linda R. Harrison, eds. Exotic Companion Medicine Handbook for Veterinarians. Lake Worth, FL: Wingers, 1996.

3. A Book with More Than Three Authors or Editors
Basic format:

> First author or editor, (*last name, first*) et al., eds. (*if they are editors instead of authors*) Title. Edition and/or volume number. (*if there is one*) Place of publication: Publisher, date of publication.

Example:

>   Garbrisch, Karl, et al. <u>Atlas of Diagnostic Radiology of Exotic Pets: Small Mam-
>   mals, Birds, Reptiles and Amphibians</u>. London: Wolfe, 1991.

4. Two or More Books by the Same Author

List books in alphabetical order by title. The first entry appears in the format appropriate to the type of source. The second entry begins with three unspaced hyphens followed by a period instead of the author's name.

Basic format:

>   Author or editor (*last name, first*), ed. (*if there is an editor instead of an author*)
>   <u>Title</u>. Edition and/or volume number. (*if there is one*) Place of publication:
>   Publisher, date of publication.

>   ---. <u>Title</u>. Edition and/or volume number. (*if there is one*) Place of publication:
>   Publisher, date of publication.

Examples:

>   Frye, Frederic L. <u>Biomedical and Surgical Aspects of Captive Reptile Husbandry</u>.
>   2nd ed. Malabar, FL: Krieger, 1991.

>   ---. <u>Captive Invertebrates: A Guide to Their Biology and Husbandry</u>. Malabar, FL:
>   Krieger, 1992.

5. A Selection (such as an essay or literary text) from a Collection or Anthology

Basic format:

>   Author of anthologized work. (*last name, first*) "Title of Anthologized Work."
>   <u>Title of Anthology</u>. Ed. (*meaning "Edited by," not "Editor(s)"*) Editor's name.
>   (*first name, first*) Edition and/or volume number. (*if there is one*) Place of
>   publication: Publisher, date of publication. Page numbers.

Example:

>   Ryan, Kay. "Turtle." <u>Literature: An Introduction to Fiction, Poetry, and
>   Drama</u>. Ed. X. J. Kennedy and Dana Gioia. 9th ed. New York: Longman,
>   2005. 832-833.

6. More than One Selection (such as essays or literary texts) from the Same Collection or Anthology

List each work from the anthology separately (in proper alphabetical order), followed by a brief cross-reference (editor's or editors' last name(s) plus page number) to the anthology. Include a separate entry with complete documentation information for the anthology.

Basic format:

> Author of anthologized work. (*last name, first*) "Title of Anthologized Work."
> Last name of editor(s) plus page numbers.

> Editor of Anthology (*last name, first*), ed. <u>Title of Anthology</u>. Edition and/or
> volume number. (*if there is one*) Place of Publication: Publisher, date of
> publication.

Example:

> Belloc, Hilaire. "The Hippopotamus." Kennedy and Gioia 873.

> Kennedy, X. J., and Dana Gioia, eds. <u>Literature: An Introduction to Fiction,</u>
> <u>Poetry, and Drama</u>. 9th ed. New York: Longman, 2002.

> Ryan, Kay. "Turtle." Kennedy and Gioia 832-833.

7. The Foreword, Preface, or Afterword of a Book

Basic format:

> Author of foreword, preface, or afterword. (*last name, first*) Preface. (*or Foreword*
> *or Afterword as appropriate*) <u>Title</u>. By (*author's or editor's name, first name, first*).
> ed. (*if there is an editor instead of an author*) Edition and/or volume number. (*if*
> *there is one*) Place of publication: Publisher, date of publication. page numbers.

Example:

> Frazer, Nat B. Foreword. <u>Turtle Conservation</u>. By Michael W. Klemens.
> Washington, DC: Smithsonian, 2000. xi-xiv.

8. A Multivolume Work

Basic format:

> Author or editor (*last name, first*), ed. (*if there is an editor instead of an author*)
> <u>Title</u>. Volume number. Place of publication: Publisher, date of publication.

Example:

> Doty, Mark. <u>Turtle, Swan & Bethlehem in Broad Daylight</u>. Vol. 1. Urbana, IL:
> U of Illinois P, 2000.

If you cite from two or more volumes, cite the entire work.

Example:

> Doty, Mark. <u>Turtle, Swan & Bethlehem in Broad Daylight</u>. 2 vols. Urbana, IL:
> U of Illinois P, 2000.

9. A Book in a Series

Basic format:

> Author. (*last name, first*) <u>Title</u>. Series Name and number. Place of publication:
>
> Publisher, date of publication.

Example:

> Heatwole, Harold. <u>Reptile Ecology</u>. Australian Ecology Ser. 43. St. Lucia,
>
> Queensland: U of Queensland P, 1976.

10. A Translation

Basic format:

> Author. (*last name, first*) <u>Title</u>. Trans. (*name of translator, first name, first*) Ed.
>
> (*if there is an editor*) Name of editor. (*first name, first*) Edition and/or volume
>
> number. (*if there is one*) Place of publication: Publisher, date of publication.

Example:

> Capula, Massimo. <u>Simon & Schuster's Guide to Reptiles and Amphibians of</u>
>
> <u>the World</u>. Trans. John Gilbert. Ed. John L. Behler. New York: Simon, 1989.

11. An Entry in a Reference Book

Basic format:

> Author. (*last name, first*) "Article Title." <u>Title of Reference Work</u>. Ed. (*first name,*
>
> *last*) Edition and/or volume number. Place of publication: Publisher, date of
>
> publication.

Often a reference work does not include the author of individual entries. If no name is given, begin with the article title. Do not list the editor of the reference work as the author of the entry.

Example:

> Gaffney, Eugene S. "Testudines." <u>McGraw-Hill Encyclopedia of Science and</u>
>
> <u>Technology</u>. Ed. Laurence S. Moss 7th ed. New York: McGraw, 1992.

If articles are arranged alphabetically in the reference work, omit the volume and page numbers. When citing familiar encyclopedias or dictionaries, include only the author's name (if given), title of the entry, the title of the encyclopedia or dictionary, the edition, and the date of publication.

Example:

> "Turtle." <u>The New Encyclopedia Britannica</u>. 15th ed. 1987.

12. A Government Publication

Basic format:

> Author. (*last name, first*) Name of Government. Name of Agency. <u>Title</u>. Place of
> publication: Publisher, date of publication.

Often a government publication does not list an author. In that case, begin with the name of the government.

Example:

> United States. Food and Drug Administration. <u>Code of Federal Regulations—</u>
> <u>Title 21</u>. Washington, DC: GPO, 2005.

13. A Pamphlet

Basic format:

> Author. (*last name, first*) <u>Title</u>. Place of publication: Publisher, date of
> publication.

If no author is listed, begin the entry with the title of the pamphlet.

Example:

> Witherington, Blair. <u>Sea Turtles and Lights</u>. Tallahassee, FL: Florida Power and
> Light, 2005.

14. A Dissertation

Basic format (Published):

> Author. (*last name, first*) "Title." Diss. Degree-issuing University, year degree was
> issued. Place of Publication: Publisher, date of publication. Order number. [*If
> published by University Microfilms International (UMI) or Dissertations Abstracts
> International (DAI).*]

Example:

> Conway, Kristen Marie. "Human Use of Two Species of River Turtles (Podocnemis
> spp.) in Lowland Eastern Bolivia." Diss. U of Florida, 2004. Ann Arbor: UMI,
> 2005. AAT 3145384.

Basic format (Unpublished):

> Author, (last name, first) "Title" Diss. Degree-issuing University, year degree was
> issued.

Example:

>Tiwari, Manjula. "Density-Dependent Effects on Hatchling Production in the Green Turtle Nesting Population in Tortuguero, Costa Rica." Diss. U of Florida, 2004.

Periodicals:

15. A Journal Article

Basic format:

>Author. (*last name, first*) "Article Title." Journal Title Volume number.Issue number (year of publication): pages.

In a journal with continuous pagination, do not include the issue number. For a journal in which each issue begins with page 1, add a period and the issue number after the volume number. Except for *May, June,* and *July,* use three-letter abbreviations for the months (*Jan., Mar., Apr.,* and *Sep.*).

In a range of page numbers, provide the second number in full for numbers through ninety-nine (2-7; 19-24; 56-82). For numbers beyond ninety-nine, provide only the last two digits of the second number, except when additional numbers are essential (92-107; 567-82; 567-608; 1709-14; 4668-777).

Examples:

(A journal with continuous pagination)

>Meehan, Shannon K. "Swelling Popularity of Reptiles Leads to Increase in Reptile-Associated Salmonellosis." Journal of the American Veterinary Medical Association 209 (1996): 531-63.

(A journal in which each issue begins with page 1)

>Hardy, Tad. "The Tortoise and the Scare." BioScience 38.2 (1988): 76-79.

16. A Magazine Article

Basic format:

>Author. (*last name, first*) "Article Title." Magazine Title date of publication: pages.

For a magazine published monthly or every two months, indicate the month(s) and year. For a magazine published weekly, indicate the day, month (abbreviated), and year. Do NOT include volume and issue numbers for a magazine. If the page numbers of an article are not sequential, indicate the first page the article appears on along with a + sign.

Examples:

>Pritchard, Peter. "Tickled about Turtles." Time 28 Feb. 2000: 76-78.

>Williams, Ted. "The Terrible Turtle Trade." Audubon Mar.-Apr. 1999: 44+.

17. A Newspaper Article

Basic format:

> Author. (*last name, first*) "Article Title." <u>Newspaper title</u> (*leave out any introductory article ["The"]*) date, (*day month year*) edition: section pages.

Example:

> Aeppel, Timothy. "Seeking Ways to Rid Turtles of Salmonella." <u>Wall Street Journal</u> 30 May 1996, late ed.: B3.

18. An Editorial

Basic format:

> Author. (*last name, first*) "Title." Editorial. <u>Newspaper Title</u> (*leave out any introductory article ["The"]*) date, (*day month year*) edition: section pages.

If the editorial appears in a magazine or journal, follow the name of the periodical with the rest of the proper publication information (for a magazine see #16; for a journal see #15). If no author's name is provided, begin the entry with the title.

Examples:

> Campos, Paul. "Turtles All the Way Down." Editorial. <u>Rocky Mountain News</u> 9 Aug. 2005: A35.
>
> "The Sea Turtle's Warning." Editorial. <u>New York Times</u> 10 Apr. 1998: A18.

19. A Letter to the Editor

Basic format:

> Name of Letter Writer. (*last name, first*) Letter. <u>Newspaper Title</u> (*leave out any introductory article ["The"]*) date, edition: section pages.

If the letter to the editor appears in a magazine or journal, follow the name of the periodical with the rest of the proper publication information (for a magazine see #16; for a journal see #15).

Example:

> Israel, Doug. Letter. <u>New York Times</u> 13 May 2002, New England ed.: A16.

20. A Book Review

Basic format:

> Name of Reviewer. (*last name, first*) "Title of Review." Rev. of <u>Title of Book</u>, by Author's name. <u>Journal Title</u> Volume number. Issue number (year of publication): pages.

If the review appears in a newspaper or magazine, follow the name of the periodical with the rest of the proper publication information (for a newspaper see #17, for a magazine see #16).

Example:

> Pizzi, Romain. "Chelonian Medicine and Surgery." Rev. of <u>Medicine and Surgery</u>
> <u>of Tortoises and Turtles,</u> by S. McArthur, R. Wilkinson, and J. Meyer.
> <u>Veterinary Record: Journal of the British Veterinary Association</u>
> 155 (2004): 30-31.

Other Types of Sources:

21. A Lecture

Basic format:

> Speaker. (*last name, first*) "Lecture Title." <u>Conference or Seminar Title</u>. Sponsor.
> Location. Date of presentation (*day month year*).

Example:

> Srikantiah, Padmini. "An Outbreak of Salmonella Javiana Associated with Am-
> phibian Contact." International Conf. on Emerging Infectious Diseases.
> Centers for Disease Control. Atlanta, GA. 25 Mar. 2002.

22. A Personal Interview

Basic format:

> Interviewee. (*last name, first*) Personal interview. Date of interview (*day month*
> *year*).

Examples:

> Johnson, Tom. Personal interview. 15 Sep. 2005.
>
> Spotila, James. Telephone interview. 15 Sep. 2005.

23. A Published Interview

Basic format:

For an interview published in a journal, see #15 for basic format. For an interview published in a magazine, see #16 for basic format. For an interview published in a newspaper, see #17 for basic format.

Examples:

> Ritschel, Lorie. "Lessons in Teaching Hope: An Interview with C. R. Snyder."
> <u>Teaching of Psychology</u> 32.1 (2005): 74-78.

Regis, Ed. "Interview: Hans Moravec." <u>Omni</u> Aug. 1989: 74+.

Nocera, William. "Donaldson: The Exit Interview." <u>New York Times</u> 23 July
   2005, late ed.: C1.

24. A Personal Letter

Basic format:

Name of Letter Writer. (*last name, first*) Letter to the author. Date of letter (*day
   month year*).

Example:

McGee, Anne. Letter to the author. 7 Apr. 2004.

25. A Movie

Basic format:

<u>Movie Title</u>. Dir. Name of Director. Name of Distributor, year of release.

Example:

<u>The Turtle Diary</u>. Dir. John Irvin. Samuel Goldwyn, 1985.

26. A DVD or Videotape

Basic format:

<u>Movie Title</u>. Dir. Name of Director. Videocassette (or DVD). Name of Distribu-
   tor, year of release.

Example:

<u>Sea Turtles: Ancient Nomads</u>. Dir. Christopher N. Palmer. Videocassette. Vestron,
   1989.

27. A Radio or Television Program

Basic format:

"Title of the Episode or Segment." <u>Title of the Program</u>. Name of the Network.
   Call letters of the local station, (*if any*) City. Broadcast date (*day month year*).

Example:

"Green Turtle." <u>Crittercam</u>. Natl Geographic Channel. 19 Nov. 2005.

28. A CD or Audiocassette

Basic format:

Name of Artist. <u>Title of the Recording</u>. Recording Company, year of release.

Example:

> Sting. <u>Dream of the Blue Turtles</u>. A&M, 1985.

29. An Advertisement

Basic format:

> Name of the Product or Company being advertised. Advertisement Publication
>
> information appropriate to the medium used.

Example:

> Turtle Wax. Advertisement. <u>Car and Driver</u> Nov. 2005: 113-14.

Electronic Sources

The Internet has made it possible to transmit information in new ways, and these methods and modes are in a constant state of flux. The challenge confronting the research paper writer in the age of the World Wide Web is that the essential components of a Works Cited reference (author's name, title, publication information) may be missing from electronic documents or may be present in a form that must be converted into something that makes sense in the MLA formatting system. For example, a website may not indicate an author (or the author might use an alias). The layout of an online document might make it difficult to distinguish between two or three possible titles, or there might be no title. A URL and the date when a site was last updated might have to replace more standard publication information. Last, but not least, information that has been "reprinted" on the web might lack complete documentation about the original source.

e-TIPS

Tricks for Finding Citation Information

If some information (the creator of the website, when a site was last updated, a sponsoring organization or institution) isn't immediately available on a web page, you can sometimes locate these facts by clicking on a hyperlink that takes you to a home page (sometimes labeled "About Us"). Also, you can often discover a home page (and more information about the source) by "backtracking." Try deleting the last portions of a URL to get to previous pages. Remember that a reference is only as good as its source. If you cannot locate a credible author or organization, you may not want to include this reference in your research project.

Yet another obstacle to correctly formatting a Works Cited page is identifying the type of source being used. Doctors need to correctly diagnose a disease before they can begin effective treatment, and researchers must pinpoint the type of source they are using if they want to "match" it with the correct MLA format. When it comes to electronic sources, this can be difficult; there are numerous variations with minute, often difficult to distinguish, differences. You should always remember that the dual purpose of documentation is to give credit to the author *and* to enable a reader to find the material cited. Therefore, you need to determine first whether the source is available via the web (so it has a URL that can be accessed by anyone with a browser) *or* if it is delivered via computer but available only through a licensing agreement or password (such as a subscription database, subscription service like AOL, or CD-ROM). Works Cited entries in the former category will include a URL, whereas those in the latter group may not.

e-TIPS

Accurate URLs

It is extremely important that the URL is accurate (otherwise the reader cannot access the page). Because URLs are often confusing and difficult to reproduce, it is always a smart idea to copy and paste (rather than try to type them) into your Works Cited entry.

In addition to distinguishing how a text is delivered via computer, there are some general rules to follow when using MLA format to document electronic sources on a Works Cited page.

- If the information has appeared previously in print form, include print information with the other (electronic) information necessary to locate the source.
- If a URL is long and must "wrap" onto the next line, DO NOT insert any punctuation (such as a hyphen). Instead, divide the electronic address after a slash ("/").
- Enclose URLs in angle brackets < >.
- URLs should not appear as hyperlinks. Often word processing programs will automatically transform a web address into a hyperlink. A quick way to change it back to normal type is to click on "Edit" and "Undo."
- Occasionally, the last update is not provided on the web page. To determine the last update, enter the following in the address field and then press "Enter": javascript:alert(document.lastModified). The last update information will appear in a pop-up window.

e-TIPS

Determine Last Updates

Frequently web editors will not include the last update on a web page. To determine this, type <javascript:alert(document.lastModified)> in the address field of the web page and press "Enter." The last update information should appear in a window.

Electronic Documents Available on the Web. The following examples are for documents that are available to anyone with a browser. Complete information is not always available on web pages, but you should cite as much of the required information as you can reasonably obtain.

30. A Single Web Page

A single web page is complete in itself and is not connected to a larger professional (e.g., corporate, educational, organizational) web project.

Basic format:

> Author, creator, or editor. (*last name, first*) Title of Website. (*Use a descriptor such as* Home page *[neither underlined nor in quotation marks] if there is no title*) Date the site was last updated. Name of any organization or institution associated with the site. Access date <URL>.

Examples:

> Fife, Richard. Salmonella and Your Privilege to Keep Reptiles to be Reviewed by the FDA. 3 Mar. 2003. 7 July 2003 <http://personal.riverusers.com/~richardfife/page20.html>.
>
> Power, Tricia. Salmonella in Reptiles and Amphibians. 19 Feb. 2001. 12 Dec. 2001 <http://www.icomm.ca/dragon/salmonella.htm>.

31. A Secondary Web Page

A secondary web page is part of a larger web project. The page has a title but also features the name of the project as well.

Basic format:

> Author, creator, or editor. (*last name, first*) "Title of Article or Topic of Page." Title of Website. Date the site was last updated. Name of any organization or institution associated with the site. Access date <URL>.

Example:

> Kuhrt, Trudy. "Trachemys Scripta." Animal Diversity Web. 2 May 2001. U of Michigan Museum of Zoology. 2 Dec. 2001 <http://animaldiversity.ummz.umich.edu/accounts/trachemys/t._scripta$narrative.html>.

32. An Online Journal Article

Basic format for an article that has previously appeared in a print journal and is being "reprinted" online:

> Author. (*last name, first*) "Article Title." Journal Title Volume number.Issue number (Year of publication): pages. Access date <URL>.

Example:

> Levy, C., et al. "Reptile-Associated Salmonellosis—Selected States, 1996-1998."
> Morbidity and Mortality Weekly Report 48 (1999): 1009-13. 12 Dec. 2001
> <http://www.cdc.gov/epo/mmwrpreview/mmwrhtml/mm4844a1.htm>.

Basic format for an article that has never been published in print, but appears only in an online publication:

> Author. (*last name, first*) "Article Title." Journal Title Volume number.Issue
> number (Year of publication). Access date <URL>.

Example:

> Rosner, Elsie. "Salmonellosis from a Trip to the Zoo." Physician's Weekly 13.39
> (1996). 13 Dec. 2001 <http://www.physweekly.com/archive/96/
> 10_21_96/cu4.html>.

33. An Online Magazine Article

Basic format for an article that has previously appeared in a print magazine and is being "reprinted" online:

> Author. (*last name, first*) "Article Title." Magazine Title Day (*if published weekly*)
> Month Year: pages. Access date <URL>.

Example:

> Turk, Michelle Pullia. "New Food Rules for Pregnancy." Parents July 2001: 32-33.
> 13 Dec. 2001 <http://www.parents.com/articles/pregnancy/1186.jsp>.

Basic format for an article that has never been published in print, but appears only in an online publication:

> Author. (*last name, first*) "Article Title." Magazine Title Date. Access date
> <URL>.

Example:

> "Is Your Child Safe From Salmonella?" Medscape Health for Consumers Feb.
> 2000. 13 Dec. 2001 <http://cbshealthwatch.aol.com/cx/viewarticle/210245>.

34. An Online Newspaper Article

Basic format for an article that has previously appeared in a print newspaper and is being "reprinted" online:

> Author. (*last name, first*) "Article Title." Newspaper Title Day Month Year, edition
> (*if available*): pages and section. Access date <URL>.

Example:

> Hampson, Rick. "Tiny Turtle Has Friends and Foes." <u>USA Today</u> 30 Apr. 1999:
>
> 3A. 13 Dec. 2001 <http://pqasb.pqarchiver.com/USAToday/
>
> tinyturtle.htm>.

Basic format for an article that has never been published in print, but appears only in an online newspaper or newswire:

> Author. (*last name, first*) "Article Title." <u>Newspaper or Newswire Title</u> Date of
>
> electronic publication. Access date <URL>.

Example:

> Ripley, Austin. "Salmonella and Reptile Pets." <u>Earth Times News Service</u>
>
> 17 Sep. 2001. 12 Dec. 2001 <http://earthtimes.org/sep/
>
> healthsalmonellafromsep17_01.htm>.

35. An Online Encyclopedia Article

Basic format:

> Author. (*last name, first*) "Title of Article." <u>Title of Reference Book</u>. Year of publi-
>
> cation. Sponsoring institution. Access date <URL>.

Often a reference work does not include the author of individual entries. If no name is given, begin with the article title. Do not list editor or web designer as the author of the entry.

Example:

> "Salmonellosis." <u>Encyclopedia Britannica</u>. 2003. Encyclopedia Britannica
>
> Premium Service. 10 July 2003 <http://www.britannica.com/eb/
>
> article?eu=667947>.

36. An Online Government Publication

Basic format:

> Name of the government. Name of the government agency. <u>Title of</u>
>
> <u>Publication</u>. Publication city: Publisher, year of publication.
>
> Access date <URL>.

Example:

> Utah. Dept. of Health. <u>Reptile-Associated Salmonellosis</u>. Salt Lake City: Bureau
>
> of Epidemiology, 2001. 13 Dec. 2001 <http://health.utah.gov/els/
>
> epidemiology/epifacts/reptile.html>.

37. A Chapter from an Online Book
Basic format:

>Author. (*last name, first*) "Chapter." <u>Book Title</u>. City of publication: Publisher,
>copyright year. Access date <URL>.

Example:

>King, F. Wayne, and Russell L. Burke. "Checklist of Crocodilians, Tuatara, and
>Turtles." <u>Crocodilian, Tuatara, and Turtle: An Online Taxonomic and
>Geographic Reference</u>. Washington, DC: Assn. of Systematics Collections,
>1989. 15 Dec. 2001 <http://www.flmnh.ufl.edu/natsci/herpetology/
>turtcroclist/chklst1/.htm>.

38. An Online Forum Posting
Basic format:

>Author. (*last name, first*) "Title of Document." Online posting. Date of posting.
>Name of forum. Access date <URL>.

Example:

>Peteralbrian. "Treating Parasites without Fecals." Online posting. 23 Apr. 2003.
>The Herpetological Health Forum. 7 July 2003 <http://
>forum.kingsnake.com/health/messages/5960.html>.

Electronic Documents with Restricted Access. These sources require a subscription or password to access them. Cite as much of the required information as you
can reasonably obtain.

Databases:

39. A Journal Article from a Database
Basic Format:

>Author. (*last name, first*) "Article Title." <u>Journal Title</u> Volume.Issue (Year of publica-
>tion): pages. <u>Name of database</u>. Name of service. Name of library. (*If accessed via
>a library system*) Access date URL of service (*If accessed via personal subscription*).

Examples:

>Lewis, Carol. "The Fright of the Iguana." <u>FDA Consumer</u> 31.7 (1997): 33-36.
><u>Academic Search Elite</u>. EBSCOHost. Seminole Community College Library.
>13 Dec. 2002.

Lecos, Chris W. "Risky Shell Game: Pet Turtles Can Infect Kids." <u>FDA Consumer</u>

21.10 (1987): 19-21. <u>InfoTrac College Edition</u>. Gale. 27 Nov. 2003

<http://www.infotrac-college.com>.

40. A Magazine Article from a Database

Basic Format:

Author. (*last name, first*) "Article Title." <u>Magazine Title</u> Day Month Year: pages.

<u>Name of Database</u>. Name of service. Name of Library. (*if accessed via a library*

system) Access date URL of service (*If accessed via personal subscription*).

Examples:

Williams, Ted. "The Terrible Turtle Trade." <u>Audubon</u> Mar. 1999: 44+.

<u>SIRSResearcher</u>. FirstSearch. Seminole Community College Library.

13 Dec. 2003.

Pritchard, Peter. "Tickled About Turtles." <u>Time</u> 28 Feb. 2000: 76-77.

<u>InfoTrac College Edition</u>. Gale. 27 Nov. 2003

<http://www.infotrac-college.com>.

41. A Newspaper Article from a Database

Basic Format:

Author. (*last name, first*) "Article Title." <u>Newspaper Title</u> Day Month Year:

pages. <u>Name of Database</u>. Name of Service. Name of Library. (*If accessed via a*

library system) Access date URL of service (*If accessed via personal subscription*).

Examples:

Webb, Tom. "New Weapon Against Salmonella." <u>Philadelphia Inquirer</u>

20 Mar. 1998. <u>SIRSResearcher</u>. FirstSearch. Seminole Community College

Library. 13 Dec. 2002.

"Resorts Bid to Save Turtles." <u>New Strait's Times</u> 4 July 2001: 17. <u>InfoTrac</u>

<u>College Edition</u>. Gale. 27 Nov. 2003 <http://www.infotrac-college.com>.

e-TIPS

Databases: Library Subscription or Personal Subscription?

To correctly complete your Works Cited entry for an article from a database, you must
determine whether you accessed the database via a library system (your school or local public library) or if you personally subscribe to the database (like the InfoTrac College Edition
subscription that may accompany this text). If access is via a library system, then you include
the name of the library after the name of the service.

42. An E-Book from a Database

Basic Format:

> Author or editor (*last name, first*), ed. (*if there is an editor instead of an author*) <u>Title</u>. Edition and/or volume number. (*if there is one*) Place of publication: Publisher, date of publication. <u>Name of database</u>. Name of Service. Name of Library. (*If accessed via a library system*) Access date URL of service. (*If accessed via personal subscription*)

Example:

> Torrey, E. Fuller and Robert H. Yolken. <u>Beasts of the Earth: Animals, Humans, and Disease</u>. New Brunswick, N.J: Rutgers UP, 2005. <u>NetLibrary</u>. OCLC. Seminole Community College Library. 22 Mar. 2007.

43. A Magazine Article from an Online Subscription Service (e.g., AOL)

Basic Format:

> Author. (*last name, first*) "Article Title." <u>Magazine Title</u> Day Month Year: page. Name of service. Access date. Keyword: search phrase.

Example:

> Hogan, Dan. "Rage for Reptiles." <u>Current Science</u> 14 Nov. 1997: 8. America Online. 15 Dec. 2001. Keyword: reptiles AND salmonella.

44. An Encyclopedia Article from a CD-ROM

Basic Format:

> Author. (*if given*) "Title of Article." <u>Title of Encyclopedia</u>. Edition or version. CD-ROM. Place of publication: Publisher, Date of publication.

Example:

> "Salmonella." <u>Compton's Interactive Encyclopedia</u>. CD-ROM. Vers. 2000Dlx. Carlsbad, CA: Compton's NewMedia, 2000.

45. An E-Mail Message

Basic Format:

> Sender. "Subject of Message." E-mail to recipient. Message date.

Example:

> Peppers, Janice. "Salmonellosis in Turtles." E-mail to the author. 10 May 2000.

Sample Research Paper Using MLA Style

The following paper uses MLA documentation style and provides an example of how to correctly incorporate both print and electronic documents into the text and the Works Cited page of a research paper. Annotations are provided to comment on some of the more complicated aspects of documentation.

MLA format doesn't require a title page. Place heading in the upper left corner and double-space everything.

Indicate an indirect source (someone quoted within your reference work) by the phrase "qtd. in" in the parenthetical citation.

MLA style dictates a one-inch margin at the top, bottom, and sides of each page.

Last name and page number should be flush with the right-hand margin and appear one-half inch from the top of the page.

Center title and double-space between title and body of paper.

Vary signal phrase by placing it at the end of a direct quotation.

No page number is used when referring to a one-page source.

Introduce any abbreviations you intend to use by providing the full title the first time.

Midori Sato

Professor Tensen

English 1101

November 24, 2002

Sato 1

How Not to Burn the House

While Roasting the Pig

"If we cannot protect our children from the obscenity on websites, the only solution is to protect them when they use the Internet," said Ernest Istook, a Republican, who introduced the Child Protection Act of 1999 in July (qtd. in Flagg). It's a challenge to preserve First Amendment rights while protecting minors from websites with adult content. I believe politicians should not enact temporary laws that protect minors but limit the First Amendment. Instead, they should focus on a long-term solution. Rather than working to regulate the Internet, we should educate parents about the safeguards available to ensure that their children are protected from what they feel is inappropriate material on the Internet.

During the past decade, Congress has struggled with the increasing problem of adult material being accessed by minors. In February 1996, Congress passed the Communications Decency Act (CDA). The CDA made it a crime to use a computer to show obscene materials to minors. However, the CDA did not solve the problem. After the CDA was enacted, the battle between those

Sato   2

fighting to protect freedom of speech and those working to censor

websites with adult content became even more heated. As one

lawyer has pointed out, the primary problem with the CDA is that

it "criminalizes the transmission of far more than obscenity"

(Sobel). Not all websites that contain adult content are

entertainment websites. Kiyoshi Kuromiya operates the Critical

Path AIDS Project website. His site includes safe sex

information that uses street language with explicit diagrams to

try and reach teenagers. Under the CDA, this website would be

censored, even though it is educational. This is because the

proposed CDA self-rating systems were similar to television or

movie ratings in that they excluded certain websites based on

specific words without considering the general subject matter or

purpose (Strossen 156). Other sex education websites might

also be censored; however, teenagers need them. It became

clear that while the CDA was intended to protect minors, it

restricted forms of speech that might actually benefit them. For

this reason, on June 26, 1997, the U.S. Supreme Court struck

down the CDA as unconstitutional. In his response, Justice

Stevens wrote that the CDA is like "burning the house to roast

the pig" (qtd. in Cate 56).

  In an attempt to follow this call for moderation, Congress

passed the Child Online Protection Act (COPA) the following year.

COPA attempted to correct the errors of the CDA by limiting the

---

Because web pages don't have pagination, all that appears in the parenthetical citation is the author's name.

This information from a web page is introduced by the author's name, so it doesn't include a parenthetical citation. The signal phrase contains all the information required to locate the entry in the Works Cited page.

This signal phrase introduces information that has been paraphrased as well as recognizing the authority of the source.

Paraphrase, as well as direct quotation, must be acknowledged by a parenthetical citation.

Limit the amount of direct quotation by smoothly incorporating remarkable or striking phrases into your own sentences.

Sato 3

This paragraph includes summarized material from two different sources—a government report and a book that offers a historical overview of the act. Both sources are acknowledged with an in-text citation in the appropriate place in the text.

persons subject to criminal enforcement of the CDA to commercial web authors. Under COPA, commercial web authors were subject to daily fines and even jail time for knowingly placing material on the Internet that was harmful to minors ("Recommendations"). However, like the CDA, the basic premise of COPA was found to be unconstitutional, and the law is currently awaiting review by the Supreme Court (Lewis 92). The Supreme Court most likely will follow the decision made concerning the CDA case. In that decision, the majority of the Court argued that the Internet should receive the same level of protection as the print media. In other words, website publishers are entitled to unfiltered discretion in free speech. The theory behind the Court's reasoning is the age-old argument that the government cannot engage in "prior restraint" of speech. What this means is that if government "restricts speech before it happens," people will be afraid to express themselves (Schmidt, Shelley, and Bardes 114). This would be against our democratic principles.

In citations with 2 to 3 authors, list all the names, separated by commas, with "and" between the last two.

Its deficiencies aside, COPA is an improvement on the CDA. Placing the responsibility on commercial websites is the first step in the solution to the problem of children's online access to adult materials. For example, some adult-entertainment Internet sites provide an Age Verification Service (AVS). This only allows access to users with a special ID. Customers pay a $19.95 annual fee for their ID that allows them access to over 58,000

The writer has chosen an alternative way to introduce the source in the signal phrase so she can include a parenthetical citation that identifies the author.

Sato   4

The name of the author or creator of this web page is unknown, so the title (underlined) is placed in the parenthetical citation.

adult websites (<u>CyberAge.com</u>). In a perfect world, all websites with adult content would require an AVS service to prevent access by minors. Once a solid foundation of AVS-backed sites is in place, the Internet will become a safer place for children.

This paragraph, and the one that follows, have no documentation because they represent the student's own ideas.

A similar type of commercial cooperation has occurred in other media industries. Thanks to the regulation of the FCC, television broadcasts have little problem with adult material. When families watch network television they usually do not have to worry about scenes with explicit adult content. Cable and satellite channels carry adult content programming, but as long as parents do not subscribe to these channels, adult content will not reach minors. Like network television stations, website authors should take responsibility for protecting minors.

No matter what regulations are in force, parents should be responsible enough to protect their children by educating them about the Internet. Unfortunately, children often know more about cyberspace than their parents. Nevertheless, parents should know what is on the Internet, especially about the prevalence of websites with adult content. Specifically, parents should be aware of how easy it is for a child to accidentally stumble upon inappropriate websites; illicit materials are as close as a click-of-the-mouse away from children.

Sato   5

The best way for parents to learn online safety is to go directly to the source. For instance, CyberAngels, the largest Internet safety organization founded by the Guardian Angels street organization, provides parents with the <u>Parent's Guide</u>. This is a beginner's guide to the Internet that can help parents instruct their children how to:

> develop a set of rules to govern their behavior online and to guide them into safer waters. [These] rules should be designed to help them understand proper netiquette, know what to expect from others online, how to behave when something unexpected occurs and how to protect themselves from getting hurt in cyberspace. (Aftab 4)

To conclude, the rapid growth of personal-computer and Internet use has challenged the U.S. government to pass laws to control the Internet. However, these laws have been held unconstitutional by the U.S. Supreme Court, which has given the Internet as much protection as print media. Therefore, the responsibility to protect minors lies with their parents. There are a number of ways parents can protect their children from inappropriate materials on the Internet. The first thing parents must do is learn about the Internet and the various safeguards available. Most importantly, parents must oversee their children's journey into cyberspace.

If you must alter the exact wording of a quotation in order to integrate it into your sentence structure properly, indicate any change by enclosing it in brackets.

A quotation of more than four lines should be indented ten spaces and double-spaced, with no quotation marks. The parenthetical citation is placed *after* the end punctuation.

Alphabetize your Works Cited list.

The first line of each entry is flush with the left margin. Indent subsequent lines.

If the author's name is not available, begin the entry with the title of the web page.

Always double-space everything on your Works Cited page (both within each entry and between each entry).

Works Cited

Aftab, Parry. <u>The Parent's Guide to Protecting Your Children in</u>
<u>Cyberspace</u>. New York: McGraw, 2000.

Cate, Fred H. <u>The Internet and the First Amendment</u>. Bloomington,
IN: Phi Delta Kappa International, 1998.

<u>CyberAge.com</u>. 25 Aug. 2002. 6 Jan. 2003.
<http://www.donsworld.com/verify.htm>.

Flagg, Gordon. "Filtering Mandate Introduced in House." <u>American</u>
<u>Libraries</u> 30.8 (1999): 12. <u>Academic Search Premier</u>.
EBSCOHost. Seminole Community College Library. 8 Nov.
2002.

Kuromiya, Kiyoshi. <u>Critical Path AIDS Project</u>. 8 Nov. 2002. 6 Jan.
2003. <http://www.critpath.org/>.

Lewis, Anne. "There Oughta Be a Law . . . ." <u>FamilyPC</u> Mar. 2000:
92-95.

"Recommendations." <u>COPA Commission</u>. 20 Oct. 2000. 5 Mar.
2000 <http://www.copacommission.org/
report/recommendations.shtml>.

If a URL is long and must "wrap" onto the next line, divide the electronic address at a slash ("/").

Schmidt, Steffen W., Mack C. Shelley II, and Barbara A. Bardes.
<u>American Government and Politics Today</u>. Belmont, MA:
Wadsworth, 1997.

This is an online version of a journal article (not a simple web page), so include previous publication information.

Sobel, David L. "The Constitutionality of the Communications
Decency Act: Censorship on the Internet." <u>Journal of</u>

Sato   7

Technology Law and Policy 1.1 (1996). 3 Mar. 2000

    <http://journal.law.ufl.edu/~techlaw/1/sobel.html>.

Strossen, Nadine. "Should Pornography on the Internet Be

    Regulated?" Mass Media—Opposing Viewpoints. San Diego:

    Greenhaven, 1997. 156-193.

Sample Literary Analysis Research Paper Using MLA Style

Research papers on literary topics adhere to all of the same rules that govern papers written in MLA format, but there are a number of conventions unique to writing about literature. For instance, when directly quoting, it is important to correctly attribute the passage to the character or narrator who "speaks" it (instead of attributing it to the author of the work). You should also use the present tense when discussing works of literature (except when discussing events that occur prior to the time of the text's main actions). The sample paper that follows illustrates these (and other) conventions peculiar to writing about fiction and demonstrates how to proficiently incorporate quotation (from both a literary text and secondary sources of literary criticism).

MLA format doesn't require a title page. Place heading in the upper left corner and double-space everything.

Center title and double-space between title and body of paper.

Short story titles are enclosed in quotation marks.

The introduction of a literary analysis should include the title of the literary work, the author's full name, and conclude with the thesis sentence.

The first mention of an author should use his/her *full* name. Subsequent mention should be by *last* name, only.

When quoting from a fictional source, correctly attribute it to the "speaker" of the quotation (either the narrator or one of the characters) rather than the author.

Helmick   1

Blaine Helmick

Professor Tensen

English 1102

November 29, 2005

Further Into a Deep, Complex Thing

In short stories, narrators both regulate what a reader knows and provide the means by which an author's vision is realized. "A Small, Good Thing," by Raymond Carver, is no different: in this story, the narrator guides the reader through a tale of suffering and redemption. Through a distinctive minimalist style, Carver selectively reveals the characters' inner thoughts and feelings through the narrator's limited omniscient perspective, leading to a powerful vision of human connection.

This writing style, so stripped of extraneous detail that it can be hard for a reader to follow, is characteristic of Carver's work. Carver removes all redundancy, leaving only the bare minimum. For example, near the beginning, the narrator describes how the baker (a central character) had "just come to work and he'd be there all night, baking, and he was in no real hurry" (Carver 2586). Here, as in the rest of this story, the narrator doesn't use fluff or filler: he rarely uses adjectives at all. This bare style is well suited to

Student's last name and page number should appear in the upper right corner (including the first page).

Helmick   2

the tough characters we find in Carver's texts. Gadi Taub suggests

that "it is hard to empathize with [Carver's] protagonists and

narrators. They are usually insensitive, hardened, and inarticulate"

(103). Taub is right to suggest that they are insensitive and hard,

but they certainly are not inarticulate. I would describe them as

"terse." They say what needs to be said and nothing more.

The terse quality of Carver's method extends beyond the

narrator. Throughout the text Carver relies upon what has been

termed "implicit communication" (Gearhart). With implicit

communication, readers must interpret the more subtle shades

of meaning in the context of the story's action. Take the following

exchange between Howard and the doctor:

"You said before he's not in a coma. You wouldn't call this

a coma, then—would you, doctor?"

Howard waited. He looked at the doctor. (Carver 2591)

The dialogue asks the obvious question: Is Scotty – the young boy

who was hit by a car and is Howard's son – suffering from a

coma? The father's agony, only implied by his question, is

highlighted in the mere act of looking.

Howard's pause and subsequent gaze communicates the

suspended hope and wishful thinking of a parent experiencing

extreme trauma. As readers, we hold our breath as Howard waits.

Marginal notes:

Student's last name and page number should appear in the upper right corner (including the first page).

A quotation of more than four lines is indented. (Normally, it would not be enclosed in quotation marks, but this contains dialogue.)

If you must alter the exact wording of a quotation (in order to integrate it into your sentence structure properly or provide clarification), indicate any change by enclosing it in brackets.

This quote is from an article in an electronic database (so there is no pagination). Only the author's name appears in the parenthetical citation.

When a larger quotation is indented, the parenthetical citation is placed *after* the end punctuation.

Helmick   3

The electronic document being quoted here has no pagination, and the author's name appears in the signal phrase; therefore, there is no need to use a parenthetical citation.

This is a wonderful example of the "implicit communication" to which Gearhart refers. Gearhart points, as well, to the self-conscious quality of such moments: "this substitution of implicit communication for verbal inarticulateness becomes a self-conscious act on the part of the characters."

When repeating significant terms that have been employed by your sources, enclose them in quotation marks to distinguish them.

The "implicit communication" of the characters (and of the narrator) in Carver's stories is the product of careful crafting. In an interview on Dan Swaim's <u>Book Talk</u>, Carver states that he enjoys rewriting stories more than writing them. He may begin with forty pages, only to pare it down to twenty before being satisfied. In "Raymond Carver and Postmodern Humanism," Carver points out that in his works, "words are linked together to make up the visible action of the story. But it's also the things that are left out, that are implied" (qtd. in Brown). His style works by implication.

Web site titles are underlined.

Indicate an indirect source (someone quoted within your reference work) by the phrase "qtd. in" in the parenthetical citation.

Indeed, Carver's style leads to remarkable results in "A Small, Good Thing," a reworking of an earlier story entitled "The Bath." Identical in plot, "A Small, Good Thing" is, ironically, significantly longer. It also includes a new ending in which Ann and Howard confront the baker. Adam Meyer, in "Now You See Him, Now You Don't," summarizes the new ending by remarking how it "now ends on a note of communion, of shared understanding and grief," unlike the earlier version.

Like the Gearhart article, this source is an electronic document (and has no pagination). Mention of the author's name in the signal phrase is all that is required to locate the source on the Works Cited page.

Punctuation falls inside the quotation marks.

Helmick   4

This story appears in an anthology. The parenthetical citation should include the name of the author of the story (not the editor of the anthology) and the page number.

Use present tense verbs when discussing literary works.

In "A Small, Good Thing," the baker is clearly at odds with himself. He tells Ann and Howard, "I'm not an evil man, I don't think" (Carver 2600). He feels responsible for Howard's and Ann's pain. He begs their forgiveness and offers them food and a forum to discuss their feelings. It is almost as if he takes Howard and Ann's loss as his own, suggesting a subconscious attempt at redeeming himself for his hard-heartedness or cynicism. "More significant, perhaps," notes Gearhart, "is the salvation of Ann and Howard Weiss, for they win a self-conscious battle with inarticulateness and, in so doing, provide for the redemption of the baker." In this case, the use of "inarticulateness" is fitting since Howard and Ann have difficulty expressing themselves to the baker. Gearhart points out that "the Weisses do not gain their epiphany through words, but through their ability to empathize with another's pain in the time of their own sorrow." Ann's revelation of Scotty's death to the baker provides an outlet of emotion that acts as her own absolution. The narrator reveals this, stating, "Just as suddenly as it had welled in her, the anger dwindled, gave way to something else, a dizzy feeling of nausea" (2599). It is at this moment that Ann's redemption begins.

This new ending, pitting the baker against Howard and Ann, is a significant departure from "The Bath." Carver himself notes that "it's different in conception and different in execution than

Vary the position of signal phrases—they can appear in the middle or at the end of direction quotation, as well as in the beginning.

"Sandwich" direct quotation from the text between your claim (that it is supporting) and a follow-up clarification of significance.

Because the previous citation is from the same source, there is no need to repeat the author's name. All that is required is the page number.

Use present tense verbs in signal phrases.

Use an ellipsis to indicate words that have been omitted in order to shorten the quotation.

Web pages do not have pagination, so only the author's name appears in the parenthetical citation.

Helmick 5

the earlier stories ... It's a much fuller story and if you look at the last paragraphs ... I think it's opening up to something entirely different" (Swaim). The difference signals a shift in Carver's philosophy. Much of his earlier work was influenced by his persistent battle with alcoholism. However, this later rewrite is much more optimistic. The new version is not really about the tragedy that occurs to Scotty; it's about Howard, Ann, and the baker and how they transcend their problems.

This philosophical shift is made obvious via the method by which the narrator in "A Small, Good Thing" reveals the story. The narrator's limited omniscience is a direct reflection of what Taub calls Carver's "moral vision." For Taub, Carver's narrators do not "usurp his protagonist's feelings, amplify them, or try to create a drama in the text apart from their own sense of what is happening to them" (103). In other words, the narrator's point of view resists sentimentality while creating real empathy for Ann and Howard. Although the narrator's "inarticulateness" or terseness might appear to create a distance or gap between text and reader, what it really accomplishes (in a quiet, still way) is a human bond that lives up to Carver's new sense of optimism.

Ultimately, Carver is a difficult writer to follow for someone who is unfamiliar with his work. However, a careful study of his narrator's complex point of view reveals the mastery of his vision

The author's last name appears in the signal phrase, so only the page number appears in the parenthetical citation.

Don't depend on direct quotation to make your point (it is meant to support). Always follow quotation with an explanation of its significance.

in "A Small, Good Thing." The death of Scotty is a tragedy, but the essence of the story is the redemption and absolution achieved by Howard, Ann, and the baker. Taub sums it up well: "What is offering hot rolls with butter in the face of the loss of a child? But it is a small good thing" (115). Indeed it is.

Although this article was accessed via an electronic database, it is a PDF file, so it is possible to indicate page numbers.

Always double-space everything on your Works Cited page (both within and between entries).

Alphabetize your works cited list.

The short story appears in an anthology. Notice that the entry begins with the author's name (matching the in-text parenthetical citation).

MLA format requires a hanging indent (first line at the left margin, subsequent lines indented).

Helmick   7

Works Cited ←

Brown, Arthur A. "Raymond Carver and Postmodern Humanism."

  Critique 31.2 (1990): 125-36. Literature Resource Center.

  Gale Group. Seminole Community College Library. 13 Nov.

  2005.

Carver, Raymond. "A Small, Good Thing." The Heath Anthology of

  American Literature. 5th ed. Vol. E. Ed. Paul Lauter. Boston:

  Houghton 2006. 2586-2601. ←

Gearhart, Michael Wm. "Breaking the Ties That Bind: Inarticulation

  in the Fiction of Raymond Carver." Studies in Short Fiction

  26.4 (1989): 439-46. Literature Resource Center. Gale

  Group. Seminole Community College Library. 13 Nov. 2005.

Meyer, Adam. "Now You See Him, Now You Don't, Now You Do

  Again: The Evolution of Raymond Carver's Minimalism."

  Critique 30.4 (1989): 239-51. Academic Search Premiere.

  EBSCOHost Seminole Community College Library.

  13 Nov. 2005. ←

Swaim, Don. "Interview with Raymond Carver: 1983." Wired for

  Books. Ohio University. 22 Nov. 2005.

  <http://wiredforbooks.org/raymondcarver/>. ←

Taub, Gadi. "On Small, Good Things: Raymond Carver's Modest

  Existentialism." Raritan 22.2 (2002): 102-18. Academic

  Search Premiere. EBSCOHost. Seminole Community College

  Library. 13 Nov. 2005.

Begin the Works Cited page on a new page, numbered like the others, with a heading (centered) at the top of the page.

Include all of the pages on which the story appears.

Articles from electronic databases must include original publication information as well as where *you* located it.

End every entry with a period.

Enclose URLs in brackets (don't include hyperlinks in your works cited entries).

If you access an article from a school database, indicate the name of the library and do *not* include a URL.

BOOKS

PERIODI-CALS

OTHER TYPES OF SOURCES

ELECTRONIC SOURCES

9

Documentation: APA Format

A system of documentation is a very precise method of telling your reader where you got your ideas and how you know this information is correct. The APA (American Psychological Association) style of documentation is used in many of the social sciences (e.g., anthropology, economics, political science, psychology, sociology). Nevertheless, you should always check with your instructor to make sure which style he or she prefers. The APA style is similar in many ways to the MLA format. Both use the threefold system of signal phrase, parenthetical citation, and reference list entry to indicate a source. However, the APA style emphasizes the date of publication, both in the parenthetical citation and the reference list entry.

APA In-Text Citations

The format for in-text citations has been designed to identify source material while interrupting the flow of the essay as little as possible. APA format follows an author-date method of citation. This means that the author's last name, the year of publication for the source, and—for direct quotation only—the page number should appear in the text separated by commas. If no author is indicated, use an abbreviated version of the title to substitute for the name of the author. The reader can use this in-text information to obtain more complete information (title, publisher, date of publication, etc.) about the source from the reference list at the end of the essay. This seems rather simple, but because there is some variation in how information is circulated, there can be subtle differences in how the in-text citations might appear. There are two elements to correct in-text APA citation: the signal phrase and the parenthetical citation. *How you introduce your information determines what appears in the parentheses.*

Examples of APA In-Text Citations

Some basic rules for in-text citation in the APA style are as follows:

- The **preferred** method for APA style is to include the author's name and the date (in parentheses) in the signal phrase. If you include a direct quote, then follow this with the page number (or other designation) in parentheses. Example: According to Kurtzweil (1997), in the 1970s, "15 million baby turtles were sold yearly in the United States" (p. 39).

- Commas should separate each element of the parenthetical citation. Example: (author, year, p. #) or (author, year).

- If you are directly quoting from a specific part of the text, use the appropriate abbreviation to indicate it. Example: *page* (p.), *paragraph* (par.), *chapter* (chap.) or *section* (sec.).

- When citing multiple authors in the in-text parenthetical citation, use an ampersand (&) between the final two names listed.

- If you are listing more than one source within the same parenthetical reference (because they appear within the same sentence), list them in alphabetical order.

- Italicize titles of periodicals, books, and reports in the text of the essay. (The APA style differs from the MLA style on this detail. The MLA style prefers underlining.)

1. A Work by One Author

- Lewis (1997) states that a mid-1970s outbreak of salmonella affected "a quarter-million infants and small children" (p. 33).

- A mid-1970s outbreak of salmonella affected "a quarter-million infants and small children" (Lewis, 1997, p. 33).

If the author's name and the date of the publication occur in the signal phrase, then only the page number need appear in the parenthetical citation. If the author's name doesn't appear in the signal phrase, it must be included in the parentheses. If there is an editor instead of an author, the editor's last name should appear in the signal phrase or parenthetical citation.

WRITING TIP

It is important to notice how to punctuate in-text citations. The parenthetical citation appears after the closing quotation mark and before the final punctuation. If a quotation is longer than 39 words, indent the passage one-half inch from the left margin, omit quotation marks, and place the final punctuation mark before the parenthetical citation.

2. A Work by Two Authors

- Chen and Franklin (1995) contend that "human infections are rising sharply with the animals' [reptiles'] increasing popularity" (p. 24).
- A recent article in *Health* magazine declares that "human infections are rising sharply with the animals' [reptiles'] increasing popularity" (Chen & Franklin, 1995, p. 24).

If there are two authors, join their names by *and* in the signal phrase and an ampersand (&) in the parenthetical citation.

WRITING TIP

Use brackets to indicate any words that are not in the original wording but have been added or modified to clarify meaning or blend more readily into your sentence structure.

3. A Work by Three to Five Authors

The first time you mention the source in your essay:

- This study concludes that "livestock are the main reservoir for human salmonellosis in industrialized countries" (Davis, Hancock, & Besser, 1999, p. 804).

Any subsequent mention in your essay:

- (Davis et al., 1999)

4. A Work by Six or More Authors

- (Ezell et al., 2001, p. 965)

Include only the first author's name followed by the Latin phrase "et al." (an abbreviation for *et alii,* which means "and others").

5. A Work by a Corporate Author

If the name of the corporate author is long, abbreviate it after the first reference.

First text citation:

- (American Veterinary Medical Association [AMVA], 1996)

Any subsequent mention in your essay:

- (AMVA, 1996)

6. A Work by an Unknown Author

Often articles in encyclopedias, newspapers, dictionaries, and magazines do not include the name of the author. In these cases, the title of the article, NOT the title of the encyclopedia, newspaper, dictionary, or magazine, should appear in the in-text citation.

- A recent article in *National Geographic World* points out, "Pet reptiles . . . aren't affected by the bacteria, so they don't show signs that they are carrying it" ("Warning," 2000, p. 5).

- In "Warning: Pets Pose Problems" (2000) the author claims, "Pet reptiles . . . aren't affected by the bacteria, so they don't show signs that they are carrying it" (p. 5).

If the author's name is not given, give the title in the signal phrase or a short-ened version of the title in the parenthetical citation.

WRITING TIP

When you omit unnecessary words to shorten your quotation, indicate this change by using an ellipsis (three periods). An ellipsis never appears at the beginning or the end of a quotation—only in the middle.

7. A Quotation Within a Source (an indirect source)

- Stephanie Wong, a veterinarian for the Centers for Disease Control, insists, "There's no way to tell that a reptile is salmonella-free" (as cited in Barber & Bolding, 2005).

If a source has quoted someone else and you want to use *that* information or wording in your own essay, you must identify the source *you* used. This source (Barber & Bolding) should appear in the reference list.

8. A Personal Communication

- During a private interview, a local pet store owner stated, "Many buyers are unaware that the reptile they are bringing home could carry salmonella" (J. Catphur, personal communication, November 15, 2005).

- In response to an inquiry, a doctor from Johns Hopkins e-mailed, "Over 50% of the salmonella cases we see at our hospital are the direct result of contaminated reptilian pets" (J. A. Zinck, personal communication, July 26, 2005).

Cite letters, telephone conversations, e-mail messages, personal interviews, class lecture notes, and messages from electronic bulletin boards or forums only in the text. These types of communication will not appear in the reference list.

9. A Work in an Electronic Source

- An article in the *Wall Street Journal* reported on attempts to "develop a disinfectant that can be added to turtle bowl water to kill salmonella germs and prevent later infections" (Aeppel, 1996).

If your source is an electronic document (e.g., a website, online journal, or article from a database), treat it as you would any print source—indicate the name of the author (if no author is supplied, give the title or a shortened version of the title) and the date of publication in the signal phrase or parenthetical citation. (If no date is given, insert "n.d." after the author's name.)

APA Reference List Entries

At the conclusion of a research paper, you need to provide a reference list that includes all of the references used. If your instructor wants you to list all of the sources you read, whether you cited them or not, this list is considered a bibliography.

Every entry on a reference list includes the same basic information—author (last name, first), year of publication, title, and publication information. However, the format (arrangement, punctuation, and spacing) differs depending on the type of source you are listing. Most instructors place a high premium on correctly formatting a reference list, so pay special attention to detail so you can produce a page that will boost, rather than reduce, your grade.

The following are a few *general rules* to follow to properly format your reference list.

- Begin a new page for your reference list after the last page of your essay, and center your title (References or Bibliography) one inch from the top of the page.

- Double-space *everything* on the page (between the title and the first entry, within each entry, and between entries).

- Authors' (or editors') names should always appear last name first. Indicate first and middle initials (if given).

- If the author's name is not available, the title of the source appears first, followed by the date of publication.

- Alphabetize the list by the authors' last names. If no author is provided for an entry, alphabetize according to the *first major word* of the title. (Include words like *A, An,* and *The* in the title, but ignore them when alphabetizing.)

- If you have more than one work by a particular author, order them by publication date, oldest to newest (e.g., a 1991 article would appear before a 1996 article).

- When an author appears both as a sole author and, in another citation, as the first author of a group, list the one-author entries first.

- Each entry must have a hanging indent (i.e., the first line should be flush with the left margin, and subsequent lines must be indented one-half inch).

- For the **titles of books**, italicize and use "sentence-style" capitalization; capitalize only the first word, all proper nouns, and the first word of the subtitle. Example: *Reptile care: An atlas of diseases and treatments.*

- For **titles of magazines and journals**, italicize and use "headline" style capitalization; capitalize the first letter of each important word. Example: *U.S. News & World Report.*

- For the **titles of book *chapters* or magazine and journal *articles*** use "sentence-style" capitalization, and *do not* use underlining, italics, or quotation marks. Example: A trail of tiny turtles.

- For the publisher's name, omit terms unnecessary to convey your meaning (e.g., Publishers, Co., and Inc.).

- Skip one space after each period, comma, and colon.

- End every entry with a period, except when a URL appears as the last item in the entry.

Printed and Recorded Sources

In order to correctly format your reference list, it is important to identify the type of source that you are documenting. Standard APA format for print sources (as opposed to electronic documents) has remained virtually unchanged for years and is readily available in numerous print and online sources. There are numerous websites to help you determine the proper format for your sources. The following are two of the best.

Purdue Online Writing Lab (OWL) Handout on APA Style
<http://owl.english.purdue.edu/handouts/research/r_apa.html>

APA Style Guide: Capital Community College
<http://www.ccc.commnet.edu/apa/index.htm>

Books:

1. A Book with One Author or Editor

Basic format:

> Author (*last name, first initial*). (Ed.). (*if there is an editor instead of an author*)
>
> (Year of publication). *Title.* (volume and/or edition number). (*if there is one*)
>
> Place of publication: Publisher.

Always list the city of publication; if the city is unfamiliar (or if it is the name of a city in more than one state), list the state as well using the two-letter ZIP code abbreviation.

Examples:

> Ackerman, L. (Ed.). (1997). *The biology, husbandry and health care of reptiles.* Neptune City, NJ: Tropical Fish Hobbyist.
>
> Frye, F. L. (1991). *Biomedical and surgical aspects of captive reptile husbandry.* (Vols. 1-2). Malabar, FL: Krieger.

2. A Book with More than One Author or Editor

Basic format:

> Authors. (*last name, first initial, with comma and ampersand before last author*).
>
> (Eds.). (*if there are editors instead of authors*) (Year of publication). *Title.*
>
> (volume and/or edition number). (*if there is one*) Place of publication: Publisher.

Examples:

> Bartlett, R. D., & Bartlett, P. P. (1999). *Terrarium and cage construction and care.* Hauppauge, NY: Barron's Educational Series.
>
> Warwick, C., Frye, F. L., & Murphy, J. B. (Eds.). (1995). *Health and welfare of captive reptiles.* New York: Chapman & Hall.

If there are more than six authors or editors, list the first six (as directed above) followed by "et al." (an abbreviation that means "and others").

3. A Book with No Listed Author or Editor

Basic format:

> *Title.* (volume and/or edition number). (*if there is one*) (Year of publication). Place of publication: Publisher.

Example:

> *A global action plan for conservation of tortoise and freshwater turtles.* (2002). Washington, DC: Conservation International and Chelonian Research Foundation.

4. A Selection from an Anthology

Basic format:

> Author(s) of the selection (*last name, first initial, with comma and ampersand*
> *before last author*). (Year of publication). Title of Anthologized Work. In Editor
> of the anthology (*first initial followed by last name*) (Ed.) *Title of anthology*
> (pp. *include all pages on which the selection appears*). Place of publication:
> Publisher.

Example:

> Auffenburg, W., & Iverson, J. B. (1979). Demography of terrestrial turtles.
> In M. Harless & H. Morlock (Eds.), *Turtles: perspectives and research*
> (pp. 541-596). New York: Wiley.

5. The Foreword, Preface, or Afterword of a Book

Basic format:

> Author of Foreword, Preface, or Afterword. (*last name, first initial*) (Year of
> publication). Foreword. (*or Preface or Afterword*) In Author of book,
> (*first initial last name*) *Book Title* (pp. *pages on which Foreword, Preface, or*
> *Afterword appears*). Place of publication: Publisher.

Example:

> Frazer, N. B. (2000). Foreword. In M. W. Klemens, *Turtle conservation*
> (pp. xi-xiv). Washington, DC: Smithsonian Institution Press.

6. A Multivolume Work

To refer to a single volume, include only the date and volume number
for *that* volume. When referring to more than one volume (see example),
include all the relevant volume numbers and the full range of years
of publication.

Basic format:

> Authors. (*last name, first initial, with comma and ampersand before last author*).
> (Eds.). (*if there are editors instead of authors*) (Year of publication). *Title*
> (Volume numbers). Place of publication: Publisher.

Example:

> Lutz, P. L., Musick, J. A., & Wyneken, J. (Eds.). (1995). *The biology of sea turtles*
> (Vols. 1-2). Boca Raton, FL: CRC Press.

7. An Entry in a Reference Book

Basic format:

> Author. (*last name, first initial*) (Year of publication). Article title. In *Book Title* (Vol. #, pp. #s). Place of publication: Publisher.

Example:

> Rouf, M. A. (1991). Salmonella. In *The encyclopedia of human biology* (Vol. 6, pp. 701-714). New York: Academic Press.

8. A Government Publication

Basic format:

> Name of Agency. (Year of publication). *Title* (Agency Publication No.). (*if there is one*) Place of publication: Publisher.

Example:

> Senate Committee on Foreign Relations. (2000). *Inter-American convention on sea turtles: Report* (DOCID: f:er.018.106). Washington, DC: U.S. Government Printing Office.

9. A Work with a Corporate Author

If a corporation or organization is both the publisher and the author, include the word "Author" at the end of the citation rather than repeating the publisher's name.

Basic format:

> Name of Corporation or Organization. (Year of publication). *Title*. Place of publication: Author.

Example:

> Sea Turtle Survival League. (2003). *Florida sea turtle and coastal habitation program: An educator's guide*. Gainesville, FL: Author.

10. A Pamphlet or Brochure

If the author's name is not given, begin entry with the title.

Basic format:

> Author. (*last name, first initial*) (Year of publication). *Title*. Place of publication: Publisher.

Example:

> Witherington, B. (2005). *Sea turtles and lights*. Tallahassee, FL: Florida Power and
>
> Light.

11. A Dissertation

Basic format:

For dissertations obtained from the shelves of the degree-granting university (or through interlibrary loan), the entry is formatted in the following manner:

> Author. (*last name, first initial*) (Year). *Title*. Unpublished doctoral dissertation,
>
> Degree-issuing University, Place.

For dissertations published on microfilm by University Microfilms International (UMI), or Dissertations Abstract International (DAI), include that information as well as the volume number, page numbers, and microfilm (number in parentheses).

Examples:

> Tiwari, M. (2004). *Density-dependent effects on hatchling production in the green*
>
> *turtle nesting population in Tortuguero, Costa Rica*. Unpublished doctoral
>
> dissertation, University of Florida, Gainesville.
>
> Conway, K. M. (2004). Human use of two species of river turtles (Podocnemis
>
> spp.) in lowland eastern Bolivia. *Dissertation Abstracts International, 65*(01),
>
> 1037A. (UMI No. 3145384).

Periodicals:

12. A Journal Article

Each year of a scholarly journal's publications is known as a "volume," but most journals are published more than once a year (each is an "issue" of that year's "volume"). If each issue of the volume begins with page 1, the issue is said to have "separate pagination" and you must include the issue number in your reference list. However, some volumes have "continuous pagination" (an issue begins with the next page number from where the previous one ended); for these journals, you do NOT include the issue number. Notice that the journal title and volume number are italicized and that major words in journal and magazine titles are capitalized.

Basic format:

> Author(s). (*last name, first initial, with comma and ampersand before last*
>
> *author*) (Year of publication). Article title. *Journal Title, volume number*
>
> (issue number), (*if there is separate pagination*), pages on which the article
>
> appears.

Examples:

For a scholarly journal with separate pagination:

> Barsimantov, J. (2004). Balancing on a turtle's back. *Earth Island Journal, 18*(4),
> 42-43.

For a scholarly journal with continuous pagination:

> Pasmans, F., De Herdt, P., & Haesebrouck, F. (2002). The presence of salmonella
> infections in freshwater turtles. *Veterinary Record, 150,* 692-693.

13. A Magazine Article

Basic format:

> Author(s). (*last name, first initial, with comma and ampersand before last author*)
> (Year, month day). Article title. *Magazine Title, volume number,* pages on which
> the article appears.

Example:

> Adler, T. (1999, November). Turtles in trouble. *National Geographic World,* 78,
> 17-22.

14. A Newspaper Article

If the article begins on one page and continues on a nonconsecutive page, give all page numbers, separated by commas. If no page numbers are given, indicate this with "n.p."

Basic format:

> Author. (*last name, first initial*) (Year, month day). Article title. *Newspaper Title,*
> pp. #s.

Example:

> Grady, D. (2005, March 15). Tiny pet turtles return; salmonella does, too.
> *New York Times,* p. F9.

15. A Letter to the Editor

Basic format:

> Letter writer. (*last name, first initial*) (Year, month day of publication). Letter
> title [Letter to the editor]. *Newspaper Title,* p. #.

Example:

> Israel, D. (2002, May 13). Eat pike, save turtle [Letter to the editor].
> *New York Times,* p. A16.

Other Types of Sources:

16. A Published Letter

Basic format:

> Letter writer. (*last name, first initial*) (Year of publication). Letter to Name of recipient. In Author's or Editor's full name, *Book title* (p. #). Place of publication: Publisher.

Example:

> White, G. (1946). Letter to Thomas Pennant. In P. Parkinson (Ed.), *The portrait of a tortoise, extracted from the journals & letters of Gilbert White* (p. 14). London: Chatto & Windus.

17. A Motion Picture

Basic format:

> Name of Director or Producer (*last name, first initial*) (Director or Producer). (Year of release). *Title* [Motion picture]. Country of origin: Production company.

Example:

> Irvin, J. (Director). (1985). *The turtle diary* [Motion picture]. United States: Samuel Goldwyn.

18. A Television Broadcast

Basic format:

> Name of Producer (*last name, first initial*) (Executive Producer). (Year, month day of broadcast). *Title of Show* [Television broadcast]. Place of production: Production company.

Example:

> Boyce, S. (Executive Producer). (2005, November 14). *Explorer* [Television broadcast]. Washington, DC: National Geographic Television and Film Production.

19. A DVD or Videotape

Basic format:

> Name of Director or Producer(s). (*last name, first initial*) (Director or Producer). (Year of release). *Title* [Motion picture] (*Distributor's name and complete address, if limited circulation*).

Example:

> Palmer, C. N., De Nixon, R., & Kelly, K. (1989). *Sea turtles: ancient nomads*
> [Motion picture] (Available from Vestron Video, 320 Park Street, Stamford,
> CT 06518).

20. A CD or Audiocassette

Basic format:

> Speaker or performer. (*last name, first initial*) (Year of publication). *Title* [CD or
> Audiocassette]. Place of Production: Production company.

Example:

> Sting. (1985). *Dream of the blue turtles* [CD]. Los Angeles: A&M Records.

Electronic Sources

The Internet has made it possible to transmit information in new ways, and these methods and modes are in a constant state of flux. The challenge confronting the research paper writer in the age of the Internet is that the essential components of a reference list entry (author's name, year of publication, title, publication information) may be missing from electronic documents, or they might be present in a form that must be converted into something that makes sense in the APA formatting system. For example, a website may not indicate an author (or the author might use an alias). The layout of an online document might make it difficult to distinguish between two or three possible titles, or there might be no title. A URL and the date when a site was last updated might have to replace more standard publication information. Last, but not least, information that has been "reprinted" on the web might lack complete documentation about the original source (**see Figure 9.1**).

Yet another obstacle to correctly formatting a reference list is identifying the type of source being used. Doctors need to correctly diagnose a disease before they can begin effective treatment, and researchers must pinpoint the type of source they are using if they want to "match" it with the correct APA format. When it comes to electronic sources, this can be difficult; there are numerous variations with minute, often difficult to distinguish, differences. You should always remember that the dual purpose of documentation is to give credit to the author *and* to enable a reader to find the material cited. Therefore, you need to determine first whether the source is available via the web (so it has a URL that can be accessed by anyone with a browser) *or* if it is delivered via a computer but available only through a licensing agreement or password (such as a subscription database, subscription service like AOL, or a CD-ROM). Reference list entries in the former category will include a URL, whereas those in the latter group will not.

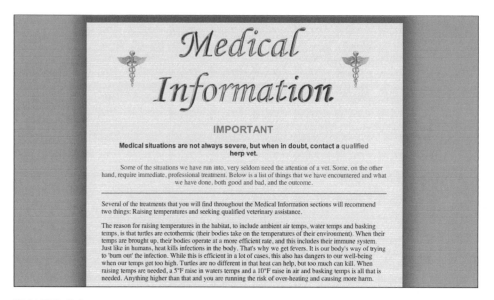

Medical Information

IMPORTANT

Medical situations are not always severe, but when in doubt, contact a qualified herp vet.

Some of the situations we have run into, very seldom need the attention of a vet. Some, on the other hand, require immediate, professional treatment. Below is a list of things that we have encountered and what we have done, both good and bad, and the outcome.

Several of the treatments that you will find throughout the Medical Information sections will recommend two things: Raising temperatures and seeking qualified veterinary assistance.

The reason for raising temperatures in the habitat, to include ambient air temps, water temps and basking temps, is that turtles are ectothermic (their bodies take on the temperatures of their environment). When their temps are brought up, their bodies operate at a more efficient rate, and this includes their immune system. Just like in humans, heat kills infections in the body. That's why we get fevers. It is our body's way of trying to 'burn out' the infection. While this is efficient in a lot of cases, this also has dangers to our well-being when our temps get too high. Turtles are no different in that heat can help, but too much can kill. When raising temps are needed, a 5°F raise in waters temps and a 10°F raise in air and basking temps is all that is needed. Anything higher than that and you are running the risk of over-heating and causing more harm.

FIGURE 9.1 Here is an example of how difficult it is to correctly evaluate web documents. This page looks impressive and is part of a larger project entitled *ATP: Austin's Turtle Page* (backtracking through the URL—as described in Chapter 8—reveals this). It would appear to be part of a larger "professional project." However, the site never reveals exactly who "Austin" is (or whether he has training in herpetology or medicine). The lack of authoritative authorship should sound a strong warning against using this site as a source in an academic paper.

In addition to distinguishing how text is delivered via a computer, there are some general rules to follow when using APA format to document electronic sources on a References page.

- If the information has appeared previously in print form, include print information with the other (electronic) information necessary to locate a source.
- If a URL is long and must "wrap" onto the next line, DO NOT insert any punctuation (such as a hyphen). Instead, divide the electronic address after a slash ("/") or before a period.
- APA style recommends referring to specific website documents rather than home or menu pages.
- URLs should not appear as hyperlinks. (Often word processing programs will automatically transform a web address into a hyperlink. A quick way to change it back to normal type is to click on "Edit" and "Undo.")
- Occasionally, the last update is not provided on the home page. To determine the last update, enter the following in the address field and then press "Enter": javascript:alert(document.lastModified). The last update information will appear in a window.

-TIPS

APA Style for Web Documents

A special problem confronting anyone who wants to document electronic documents using APA style is that although the association has issued directions concerning previously published texts that have been reprinted online, they have been slow to develop formatting rules for web documents. In this text I have attempted to use the principles of APA documentation style to extrapolate a format for web pages that agrees with the official rules of the APA's *Publication Manual.*

Electronic Documents Available on the Web. The following examples are for documents that are available to anyone with a browser. Complete information is not always available on web pages, but you should cite as much of the required information as you can reasonably obtain.

21. A Web Page

Basic format:

> Author. (*last name, first initial*) (Year, month day of last update). *Title.* Retrieved
>
> Month Day, Year, from URL

Notice that the URL is not followed by a period, contrary to what is customary in other APA-style entries.

Examples:

> Funk, R. S. (2001). *Health alert for reptile owners: Salmonellosis.* Retrieved
>
> December 13, 2001, from http://mesavet.com/library/salmonella.htm
>
> Power, T. (2002, October 30). *Salmonella in reptiles and amphibians.* Retrieved
>
> November 27, 2002, from http://www.icomm.ca/dragon/salmonella.htm

22. A Web Page with No Author or Date

Basic Format:

> *Document title or Name of web page.* (n.d.). Retrieved Month Day, Year, from URL

Example:

> *Salmonella bacteria and reptiles.* (n.d.). Retrieved December 2, 2001, from
>
> http://www.hilltopanimalhospital.com/salmonella.htm

23. An Online Journal Article

Basic format for an article that has previously appeared in a print journal or magazine and is being "reprinted" online:

> Author. (*last name, first initial*) (Year). Article title [Electronic version]. *Magazine*
>
> *or Journal Title, volume*(issue), pages. Retrieved Month Day, Year, from URL

Example:

> Levy, C., et al. (1999). Reptile-associated salmonellosis—selected states,
>
> 1996–1998 [Electronic version]. *Morbidity and Mortality Weekly Report,*
>
> *48*(44), 1009-1013. Retrieved December 12, 2001, from
>
> http://www.cdc.gov/epo/mmwrpreview/mmwrhtml/mm4844a1.htm

Basic format for an article that has never been published in print, but appears only in an online publication:

> Author. (*last name, first initial*) (Year). Article Title. *Magazine or Journal Title,*
>
> *volume*(issue). Retrieved Month Day, Year, from URL

Example:

> Rosner, E. (1996). Salmonellosis from a trip to the zoo. *Physician's Weekly, 13*(39).
>
> Retrieved December 13, 2001, from http://www.physweekly.com/
>
> archive/96/10_21_96/cu4.html

24. An Online Magazine Article

Basic format for an article that has previously appeared in a print magazine and is being "reprinted" online:

> Author. (*last name, first initial*) (Year, month day). Article title [Electronic
>
> version]. *Magazine Title,* pages. Retrieved Month Day, Year, from URL

Example:

> Turk, M. P. (2001, July). New food rules for pregnancy [Electronic version].
>
> *Parents,* 32-33. Retrieved December 13, 2001, from http://www.parents.com/
>
> articles/pregnancy/1186.jsp

Basic format for an article that has never been published in print, but appears only in an online publication:

> Author. (*last name, first initial*) (Year, month day). Article title. *Magazine Title.*
>
> Retrieved Month Day, Year, from URL

Example:

> Is your child safe from salmonella? (2000, February). *Medscape Health*
>
> *for Consumers.* Retrieved November 16, 2001, from http://
>
> cbshealthwatch.aol.com/cx/viewarticle/210245

Notice that the author's name is not available, so the title of the article appears first, followed by the date of publication.

25. An Online Newspaper Article

Basic format:

> Author. (*last name, first initial*) (Year, month day). Article Title. *Newspaper Title.*
> Retrieved Month Day, Year, from URL

Example:

> Ripley, A. (2001, September 17). Salmonella and reptile pets. *The Earth Times*
> *News Service.* Retrieved December 12, 2001, from http://earthtimes.org/
> sep/healthsalmonellafromsep17_01.htm

26. An Online Encyclopedia Article

Basic format:

> Author. (*last name, first initial*) (Year). Article Title. In *Title of Encyclopedia.* [On-
> line]. Retrieved Month Day, Year, from URL

Often a reference work does not include the author of individual entries. If
no name is given, begin with the article title (and list date immediately
following). Do not list editor or web designer as the author of the entry.

Example:

> Salmonellosis. (2003). *Encyclopedia Britannica.* [Online]. Retrieved
> July 10, 2003, from http://www.britannica.com/eb/article?eu=667947

27. An Online Government Publication

Basic format:

> Sponsoring Agency. (Year, month day). *Title* (Publication No. #).
> Retrieved Month Day, Year, from Name of Organization via Access
> Mode: URL

Example:

> U.S. Food and Drug Administration, Dept. of Health and Human Services.
> (2001, April 1). *Chapter 1, part 1240: Control of communicable diseases*
> (Publication No. 21CFR1240). Retrieved September 18, 2001,
> from the U.S. Government Printing Office via GPO Access:
> http://frwebgate3.access.gpo.gov/cgi-bin/
> waisgate.cgi?WAISdocID=4628754938+4+0+0&WAISaction=retrieve

28. A Chapter from an Online Book

Basic Format:

> Author. (*last name, first initial*) (Ed.). (*if there is an editor instead of
> an author*) (Year, month day). Chapter title. In *Book title* (chap. #). Retrieved
> Month Day, Year, from URL

Example:

> King, F. W., & Burke, R. L. (Eds.). (2002, February 12). Checklist of crocodilians,
> tuatara, and turtles. In *Crocodilian, tuatara, and turtle: An online taxonomic
> and geographic reference* (chap. 14). Retrieved November 1, 2002, from http://
> www.flmnh.ufl.edu/natsci/herpetology/turtcroclist/chklst1.htm

29. An Online Forum Posting

Basic Format:

> Author. (*last name, first initial*) (Year, month day). Message subject line [Msg. ID].
> (*if available*) Message posted to group URL

Example:

> East, B. (2001, May 25). Can't you get salmonella from reptiles? [Msg. 7.5].
> Message posted to http://www.landfield.com/faqs/pets/herp-faq/part3/
> section-5.html

Electronic Documents with Restricted Access. These entries usually will NOT
include a URL because they require a subscription, password, or CD-ROM to access them. Cite as much of the required information as you can reasonably obtain.

30. A Journal Article from a Database

Basic format:

> Author. (*last name, first initial*) (Ed.). (*if there is an editor instead of an author*)
> (Date). Article title. *Journal Title, volume* (issue), pages. Retrieved Month Day,
> Year, from Database (Article No.) (*if given*).

Notice that the journal title and volume number are italicized.

Example:

> Lewis, C. (1997). The fright of the iguana. *FDA Consumer, 31*(7), 33-36.
> Retrieved November 18, 2001, from Academic Search Elite database
> (Article No. 9711226176).

31. A Magazine Article from a Database

Basic Format:

> Author. (*last name, first initial*) (Year, month day). Article title. *Magazine Title.* Retrieved Month Day, Year, from Database (Article No.) (*if given*).

Example:

> Williams, T. (1999, March). The terrible turtle trade. *Audubon.* Retrieved October 8, 2001, from SIRSResearcher database (Article No. 098216).

32. A Newspaper Article from a Database

Basic format:

> Author. (*last name, first initial*) (Year, month day). Article title. *Newspaper Title.* Retrieved Month Day, Year, from Database (Article No.) (*if given*).

Example:

> Webb, T. (1998, March 20). New weapon against salmonella. *Philadelphia Inquirer.* Retrieved September 6, 2001, from SIRSResearcher database (Article No. 021062).

33. An E-Book from a Database

Basic format:

> Author. (*last name, first initial*) (Ed.). (*if there is an editor instead of an author*) (year of publication). *Title.* (volume and/or edition number). (*if there is one*) Place of publication: Publisher. Retrieved Month Day, Year, from Database.

Example:

> Torrey, E. F., & Yolken, R. H. (2005). *Beasts of the earth: Animals, humans, and disease.* New Brunswick, N.J: Rutgers UP. Retrieved March 22, 2007, from NetLibrary database.

34. A Magazine Article from an Online Subscription Service (such as AOL)

Basic format:

> Author. (*last name, first initial*) (Year, month day). Article title. *Magazine Title,* page. Retrieved Month Day, Year, from Subscription Service, Keyword: search phrase.

Example:

> Hogan, D. (1997, November 14). Rage for reptiles. *Current Science,* 8. Retrieved September 19, 2001, from America Online. Keyword: reptiles AND salmonella.

Sample Research Paper
Using APA Style

The following paper uses APA documentation style and provides an example of
how to correctly incorporate both print and electronic documents into the text
and reference list of a research paper. Annotations are provided to comment on
some of the more complicated aspects of documentation.

Sheconomy.com   1

Center
everything on
title page

Use a short title
and page
number in
upper right
corner of every
page (use
pagination
feature in word
processing
programs to
standardize
this).

Full title of essay

Sheconomy.com:
Women and E-Business Opportunities

Writer's name

Midori Sato

Economics 1101. Section 0435

Name of
instructor

Professor Johnson

October 11, 2002

Name and
section number
of course

Due date of
assignment

APA style requires
double spacing all
parts of the paper.

Sheconomy.com:

Women and E-Business Opportunities

When the modern women's liberation movement gained

momentum in the 1960s, many American women secured greater

social freedom. However, over 40 years later most women still do

not have complete social equality with men, and this inequity is

most evident in today's economy. According to Newcomb et al.

(2000), there are only 46 women on *Forbes'* list of the "400

Richest in America." This indicates that men continue to control

American economics, and the "glass ceiling" that has prevented

women from ascending to the top of the business ladder still exists.

Even though women aren't at the top, they are playing a

significant role in economic growth. Haynes and Haynes (2000)

report that recent government projections indicated that by the

close of the year 2000, women will own half of all U.S. small

businesses (para. 6). More importantly, sales totals for women-

owned and -operated firms amounted to over $1.15 trillion in

2002 (Center for Women's Business Research [CFWBR], 2002).

One area of rapid growth for women-owned businesses is

e-business. Recently the American economy has experienced a huge

shift toward e-commerce; despite significant economic downturns,

in 1999 "venture capitalists invested $1.45 billion in 107

Repeat the full title, centered, on the first page of text.

Leave a one-inch margin on all sides of the page.

There are more than six authors, so the first author's name is given followed by "et al."

The word "and" links the names of two authors in the signal phrase.

Short title and page number in upper right corner of every page

The preferred method for APA in-text citations is to include the author's name and date in the signal phrase.

For a corporate author with a long name, spell it out the first time followed by an abbreviation in brackets or parentheses.

For a direct quotation, indicate the author's name, year of publication, and the specific part of the text (separated by commas).

When paraphrase or summary is involved, you needn't indicate a page or paragraph number.

This information appeared in both sources. List them in alphabetical order separated by a semicolon.

Sheconomy.com   3

Washington area [Internet-related] companies" (Daniels, 2000,

para. 3). Of course, this occurred in the "technology capital" of

Washington state (home of Microsoft). Internet- and computer-

related business have been growing exponentially. And according

to Jones (2001), the percentage of venture capital directed toward

women-owned high-tech companies doubled in the year 2000. One

reason for this might be the 103% increase in women-owned

firms that has occurred over the past 10 years (Daniels,

2000; Haynes & Haynes, 2000). This sea change offers an

extraordinary opportunity for women to start up businesses on the

web. The ease of start-up and some of the characteristics of

e-business offer advantages for women to make their mark in

American commerce.

    First, the cost of starting a business on the web is relatively

low. This type of entrepreneur does not have to rent office space.

She just needs a computer and a phone line. E-businesses also

have lower operating costs, since e-companies can provide better

customer service at a lower cost. While a live operator costs $10

per customer contact, e-mail responses cost only $3 ("Widening,"

2000).

    Secondly, the nature of e-business makes it easier for

women, who frequently have added domestic responsibilities, to

manage. A survey conducted by the AFL-CIO indicates that many

Because this is an electronic document (no pagination), use "para." (for "paragraph").

In a parenthetical citation, an ampersand appears between the last two names of multiple authors.

When the author's name is unknown, use a shortened version of the article title and the date in the parenthetical phrase.

This electronic document doesn't have a normal paragraph structure but is divided into three clearly marked sections.

For a quote that has been quoted in another source, identify the original speaker in the signal phrase and include "as cited in" and the name of the author of the source in the parenthetical citation.

women are employed in information technology jobs. Kristina Hanna, founder of *Girl Geeks,* notes that women in Internet-related businesses are "able to work out of their homes . . . creating their own time, their own schedules, their own world" (as cited in Solomon, 2000, sec. 3). Also, unlike most traditional businesses, an e-business does not rely on a geographical location for its success. In fact, the Internet makes a business so universally accessible that customers may be from anywhere in the United States, or even from another country. This means that it is possible to run a fairly large business from a remote location, sometimes even from home. Via the Internet, Maria del Carmen Vucetich's homemade cake business receives orders from Peruvians living all over the world (San Roman, 2000). E-commerce also offers special advantages for women, since pregnancy and child rearing frequently hinders their advancement in traditional businesses. On the web, women entrepreneurs are able to work from home while they are watching their children.

For many women, the biggest drawback to starting a business is not financial or domestic, but an issue of self-esteem. Often women think they are incapable of running their own businesses. In a survey conducted at a San Diego County high school economics class, 64% of the students were either running,

Sheconomy.com 5

Use brackets to indicate words or letters that don't appear in the original wording but have been added to clarify meaning or blend the quote with your sentence.

When using a shortened title to identify a source, enclose the title in quotation marks.

or planning to run, an e-business. Among these students, only one was female ("New Netpreneures," 1999). Joanna Rees Gallanter, the founder of Venture Strategy Group, points out that "[Women] naturally put a lower value on [success in business] than men do" (as cited in Almer, 2000, para. 4). However, there is no reason for women to think they are less competent in business than men. Numerous female entrepreneurs already have proven that women can be successful in the new e-market.

For example, Olivia Ongpin, who founded Fabric8 on the web in 1996, was recognized by San Francisco Women on the Web as a female entrepreneur who has inspired people with her efforts to advance technology, contribute to the community, and set an example as a successful businesswoman on the Internet ("Top 25," n.d.). Her online shopping site contains independent designers' clothing, music, jewelry, and accessories for women.

This source, a website, didn't provide an author or date, so a shortened version of the title and the abbreviation "n.d." is used.

Another example of a woman who has been successful in ecommerce is Ann Winbland, a software industry entrepreneur and technology leader. She has been recognized by *Business Week* as a member of the "Elite 25 Power Brokers in the Silicon Valley" and by *Vanity Fair* as a member of the "Top 50 Leaders of the New Establishment" (Townsend, 2001) and is one of the most powerful women entrepreneurs in America.

Sheconomy.com   6

Women entrepreneurs like Ongpin and Winbland not only inspire other women, but also strengthen American economics. Moreover, statistics show that women-owned businesses are, on the average, more "financially sound and creditworthy" and tend to remain in business longer than the average (male-owned and -run) U.S. firm (CFWBR, 2002).

Women are the wave of the future on the Internet. As more and more computers become networked and connected to the web, more and more computer users are women. In order to meet the needs of the ever-increasing population of women on the web, there needs to be a growing cadre of e-businesswomen who create successful web businesses.

This is the second reference to the corporate name, so use the abbreviation indicated in the first citation.

Sheconomy.com   7

References

Almer, E. (2000, October 4). What women need to know about

starting up. *The New York Times.* Retrieved November 15,

2002, from ProQuest database (Article No. 03624331).

Center for Women's Business Research. (2002, November 10).

Key facts. Retrieved November 18, 2002, from

http://www.nfwbo.org/key.html

Daniels, A. (2000, November 27). The money winners: Despite

troubles, Internet companies find funding in the third quarter.

Washington Techway. Retrieved November 13, 2002, from

http://www.washingtontechway.com/news/1_22/techcap/

5292-1.html

Haynes, P. J., & Haynes, M. M. (2000, May). When bank loans

launch new ventures: A profile of the growing female

entrepreneur segment. *Bank Marketing, 32*(5), 28-35.

Retrieved November 18, 2002, from WilsonSelectPlus

database (Article No. BBPI00058667).

Jones, (2001, November 12). Silicon ceiling. *Crain's Chicago

Business,* 15-16. Retrieved November 16, 2002, from

InfoTrac College Edition database (Article

No. BBPI01089978).

Newcomb, P., Kafka, P., Egan, M. E., Murphy, V., Ridgway, N.,

Bravakis, P., et al. (2000, October 9). By the numbers.

Margin notes:

Begin your reference list on a separate page and center the title.

When a web page is part of a larger project, the organization's name appears in place of an author.

For a work by more than one author use an ampersand (&) between the last two names.

APA format requires that you list the first six authors' names, followed by "et al."

Alphabetize all entries.

This article is published only on the web.

Always double-space everything on your References page (both within each entry and between each entry).

Sheconomy.com   8

Forbes, 361-364. Retrieved April 3, 2002, from Academic

Search Premier database (Article No. 3586171).

New netpreneures will be high schoolers. (1999, December 12).

Business Wire. Retrieved April 6, 2002, from Business

Source Premier database (Article No. CX344B1219).

San Roman, (2000). Computers and cakes give confidence ◄——— This article
was previously
and cash to housewives in Peru. *International Trade Forum,*   published in
hard copy, and is
3, 30-31. Retrieved April 3, 2002, from WilsonSelectPlus   now reprinted in
a database.
database (Article No. BBPI00086539).

Solomon, (2000, March 27). The downside of 24/7 service.

Computerworld, 52. Retrieved April 5, 2002, from

WilsonSelectPlus database (Article No. BBPI00026264).

Top 25 Women on the Web. (n.d.). Retrieved April 3, 2002, from ◄——— The author and
date for this web
http://www.top25.org/winner.html   page are
unknown.

Entries that
conclude with   Townsend, (2001). *Ann Winblad, partner Hummer Winblad Venture*
a URL do not
close with   *Capital.* Retrieved April 3, 2002, from
a period.   ———► http://www.techdivas.com/annwinblad.htm

Widening the road. (2000, October 2). *Electronic Design,48*(20),

4. Retrieved April 3, 2002, from InfoTrac College Edition

database (Article No. 9711226176).

10

Documentation: CSE Format

"Art and science

have their

meeting point

in method."

EDWARD
BULWER-LYTTON

The most common forms of documentation are the MLA and APA styles. However, depending on the discipline for which you are writing, your instructor may require that you use other formats. The CSE (Council of Science Editors) style of documentation (formerly known as CBE—Council of Biology Editors—style) is used in many of the sciences (e.g., biology, geology, chemistry, mathematics, medicine, and physics). You should always check with your instructor to make sure which style he or she requires.

The CSE style of documentation is used in a wide spectrum of professional publications concerning the physical and biological sciences. As a result, the system contains a great number of variations. Some disciplines most frequently use an *author-date* format that is similar, in many ways, to the APA style of documentation.* However, the CSE format most preferred by instructors is called the *citation-sequence* system. Like other styles of documentation, it uses both an in-text citation and reference list entry to indicate a source.

---

*This format is detailed in *Scientific Style and Format: The CBE Manual for Authors, Editors, and Publishers* (6th edition, 1994), and examples of this style can be found on the web at <http://www. lib.ohio-state.edu/guides/cbegd.html> or <http://writing.colostate.edu/references/sources/cbe/index.cfm>.

CSE In-Text Citations

In the CSE citation-sequence system, all bibliographic information is given in the references list at the conclusion of the paper. Within the text, the only indication that references are being cited is numbers listed sequentially throughout the text.* These numbers correspond to the numbered entries in the references list. This method interrupts the flow of the paper the least, but it also means that readers must turn to the reference list at the end of the essay to obtain information about the sources. The reference list is organized numerically, starting with the first reference cited in the text.

Examples of CSE Citation-Sequence In-Text Citations

Some basic rules for in-text citation in the CSE citation-sequence system follow.

- Use a superscript number or a number in parentheses [e.g., (1)] following any reference to a source. (Superscript numbers are recommended because parenthetical numbers can be confused with other parenthetical statements in your essay.)

Examples:

- Reptiles captured in the wild and transported for sale as pets run a higher risk of bacterial infection.[1]

- Reptiles captured in the wild and transported for sale as pets run a higher risk of bacterial infection (1).

- Each source will have only one reference number. In other words, if your first reference is to a book by Franklin, you would indicate this with a [1] in the text of your essay, and Franklin's work would be the first entry in your references list. You would continue to use a [1] to indicate any subsequent references to Franklin's book in your paper.

Example:

- Reptiles captured in the wild and transported for sale as pets run a higher risk of bacterial infection.[1] This is because they are frequently kept in unsanitary containers or cages and fed infrequently and/or incorrectly.[2] Studies[1] show that good hygiene and a healthy diet will reduce the incidence of bacterial infections in reptiles.

The in-text reference number should immediately follow the title, word, or phrase that indicates the information or document you are citing.

*Another option is to use the name-year system, which lists the author's surname and year of publication in parentheses after the citation [e.g., (Bradley 2001)]. In this system, the references list is organized alphabetically. See *Scientific Style and Format: The CBE Manual for Authors, Editors, and Publishers* (6th edition, 1994) for guidelines.

Note that when using a superscript number, the end punctuation precedes the number. When using a number in parentheses, the end punctuation follows the parentheses. If you cite the same source later in an essay, refer to it by its original number.

e-TIPS

Typing Superscript Numbers

To create a superscript number using Microsoft Word, simply type the number into the text as you would normally do (leave **no** space between end punctuation or the end of a word and the number), then highlight the number, click on "Format" on the main menu, click on "Font" and then check the box next to the term "superscript" in the list of options and click "OK."

- If information is contained in more than one source, list the source numbers in a series.

Examples:

- As the public has become more conscious of the biological risks posed by pet reptiles, the number of salmonella infections has decreased.[1,4,7]

- Experts agree that reducing the incidence of bacterial infection in the domestic reptile population requires the cooperation of pet dealers.[2-4]

Use a comma (but no intervening spaces) to separate two numbers, or numbers that do not form a sequence. Use a hyphen to separate more than two numbers that form a sequence.

- If you are quoting from or citing a source that has been quoted in a document by a different author, record the reference number for the original document followed by the parenthetical statement "cited in" and the reference number for the secondary document.

Example:

- The first report of human salmonella infection linked to pet turtles[5(cited in 6)] occurred in Chicago.

Do not space between the first reference number and the parenthetical citation. The complete bibliographic information for BOTH sources must appear in your references list.

CSE Reference List Entries

At the conclusion of a research paper, you need to furnish a list that includes all of the references used. The heading on this list should be REFERENCES or CITED REFERENCES. Should your instructor require that you list sources you read but did not cite, include these entries (alphabetized by author's last name and unnumbered) in a separate list entitled ADDITIONAL REFERENCES.

The CSE system emphasizes brevity. Every entry on a reference list provides the same basic information—author (last name, first), year of publication, title, and publication information. However, the format differs depending on the type of source you are listing. Most instructors place a high premium on correctly formatting a reference list, so pay special attention to detail and produce a page that will boost, rather than reduce, your grade.

The following are a few *general rules* to follow in order to properly format your reference list.

- Begin a new page for your reference list after the last page of your essay.
- Center the title (REFERENCES or CITED REFERENCES) and distinguish it by using all capital letters, a bold font, or underlining.
- Double-space *everything* on the page (between the title and the first entry, within each entry, and between entries).
- Place the reference number flush with the left margin, skip two spaces, and begin the entry.
- Authors' (or editors') names should always appear last name first. Indicate first and middle initials (if given), and do not punctuate between them (i.e., there should be no comma between last name and initials, no periods after initials and no space between initials). All authors' or editors' names should appear in the entry.
- If the name of the author or editor of a work is not provided, then list the author as [Anonymous].
- The titles of books or articles should appear in sentence-style capitalization: Capitalize only the first word and all proper nouns (e.g.: Reptile care: an atlas of diseases and treatments) and do NOT underline, italicize, or enclose in quotation marks.
- The titles of journals that consist of more than one word should be abbreviated (see the Quick Check Box on page 181 for guidelines on abbreviating titles).
- Within the reference entry, skip one space after each period, comma, and colon.
- End every entry with a period.

Printed and Recorded Sources

In order to correctly format your reference list, it is important to identify the type of source that you are documenting. Standard CSE format for print sources (as opposed to electronic documents) has remained virtually unchanged for years and is readily available in numerous print and online sources. You may have a guide to basic CSE format in your textbook or access to *Scientific Style and Format: The CBE Manual for Authors, Editors, and Publishers* (6th edition, 1994) in your library.* In addition there are numerous websites to help you determine the proper format for your sources. The following are two of the best:

CSU: Council of Biology Editors (CBE) Scientific Style
<http://writing.colostate.edu/guides/sources/cbe/pop2.cfm>

The Council of Biology Editors (CBE) Style of Documentation in Science and Mathematics: Monroe Community College
<http://www.monroecc.edu/depts/library/cbe.htm>

QUICK CHECK
CSE Guidelines for Abbreviating Journal Titles
Journal titles longer than one word need to be abbreviated. Standard abbreviations used in the Index Medicus system are available online (in a PDF file) at <ftp://nlmpubs.nlm.nih.gov/online/journals/lsiweb.pdf>. Single-syllable words and words of five or fewer letters are generally not abbreviated. Retain all significant elements of the title, but remove

- Articles, conjunctions, and prepositions (unless they are part of a proper noun, a standard phrase, or a scientific or technical term—for example, the "in" from "in vitro")
- At least the final two letters, if possible. Example: Biological becomes Biol
- Internal letters. Example: Country becomes Ctry

Capitalize the initial letter of each abbreviated word and omit all punctuation (don't put periods at the ends of abbreviations).

Books:

Obtain all information from the title page (and the reverse side of the title page), not from the cover. In the CSE format, booklets, pamphlets, and brochures are all categorized as "books."

1. A Book with One Author
Basic format:

> #. Last name and initial(s) of author. Title of book. Edition. (*if given*) Place of publication: Publisher; Year of publication. Number of pages in the book.

Always list the city of publication; if the city is unfamiliar (or if it is the name of a city in more than one state), list the state as well. Use the two-letter ZIP code abbreviation in parentheses, but do not use a comma to separate the city from the state abbreviation.

---

*CBE Manuals for Authors, Editors, and Publishers 7th edition is scheduled to release in the summer of 2006.

Example:

> 1. Cloudsley-Thompson, JL. The diversity of amphibians and reptiles: an introduction. New York: Springer; 1999. 254 p.

2. A Book with One Editor

Basic format:

> #. Last name and initial(s) of editor, editor. Title. Edition. (*if given*) Place of publication: Publisher; Year of publication. Number of pages in the book.

Example:

> 2. Fudge AM, editor. Laboratory medicine: avian and exotic pets. Philadelphia: Saunders; 2000. 486 p.

3. A Book with Two or More Authors or Editors

Basic format:

> #. Last name and initial(s) of authors or editors (*separated by commas*), editors. (*if editors, not authors*) Title. Edition. (*if given*) Place of publication: Publisher; Year of publication. Number of pages in the book.

Examples:

> 3. Zug GR, Vitt LJ, Caldwell JP. Herpetology: an introductory biology of amphibians and reptiles. 2nd ed. San Diego: Academic Press; 2001. 630 p.
>
> 4. Wright KM, Whitaker BR, editors. Amphibian medicine and captive husbandry. Malabar (FL): Krieger; 2001. 499 p.

4. A Book with a Translator

Basic format:

> #. Last name and initial(s) of author(s) (*separated by commas*). Title. Edition *(if given)*, Last name and initial(s) of translator, translator; Last name and initial(s) of editor, editor (*if given*), Place of publication: Publisher; Year of publication. Number of pages in the book. Translation of Original title.

Example:

> 5. Piaget J. Biology and knowledge, an essay on the relations between organic regulations and cognitive processes. Walsh B, translator. Chicago: University of Chicago Press; 1971. 384 p. Translation of Biologie et connaissance: essai sur les relations entre les régulations organiques et les processus cognitifs.

5. A Volume in a Multivolume Work (Separate Title)

Notice that this format is used if you intend to cite the entire volume—not an article in a multivolume work.

Basic format:

> #. Last name and initial(s) of author(s) or editors(s) of volume (*separated by commas*), editor(s). (*if editors, not authors*) Title of volume. Volume number, Title of multivolume work. Edition. (*if given*) Place of publication: Publisher; Year of publication.

Example:

> 8. Schlager N, editor. Reptiles. Volume 7, Grzimek's animal life encyclopedia. 2nd ed. Detroit: Gale; 2003.

6. A Chapter or Article in a Larger Work (with different authors or editors)

Basic format:

> #. Last name and initial(s) of author(s) of chapter or article (*separated by commas*). Title of chapter or article. In: Last name and initial(s) of authors or editor(s) of book (*separated by commas*), editors. Title of book. Edition. (*if given*) Place of publication: Publisher; Year of publication. p (*pages on which the chapter or article appears*).

Example:

> 6. Auffenburg W, Iverson JB. Demography of terrestrial turtles. In: Harless M, Morlock H, editors. Turtles: perspectives and research. New York: John Wiley and Sons; 1979. p 541-96.

7. A Chapter or Article in a Larger Work (with same author)

Basic format:

> #. Last name and initial(s) of author(s) of chapter or article (*separated by commas*). Title of book. Volume, (*if given*) Edition. (*if given*) Place of publication: Publisher; Year of publication. Part or chapter title; p (*pages on which the chapter or article appears*).

Example:

> 7. Davidson OG. Fire in the turtle house: the green sea turtle and the fate of the ocean. Cambridge, MA: Perseus Books; 2001. An elusive virus; p 137-46.

Periodicals:

For journal titles longer than one word, abbreviate the title according to CSE guidelines (see the Quick Check Box on page 181).

8. A Journal Article (with continuous pagination)

Basic format:

> #. Last name and initial(s) of author(s) (*separated by commas*). Title of article. Title of Journal Year of publication; volume #: Page numbers.

Example:

> 9. Bradley T, Angulo F, Mitchell M. Public health education on salmonella and reptiles. J Am Vet Med Assoc 2001; 219: 754-5.

Abbreviate page ranges (e.g., 233-45; 76-9); if an article appears on non-contiguous pages, list all pages or page ranges (e.g., 23-7, 44, 46-9).

9. A Journal Article (each issue begins with page 1)

Basic format:

> #. Last name and initial(s) of author(s) (*separated by commas*). Title of article. Title of Journal Year and month of publication; volume # (issue #): Page numbers.

Example:

> 10. Herbst LH, Klein PA. Green turtle fibropapillomatosis: challenges to assessing the role of environmental cofactors. Envir Health Persp Sup 1995 Dec; 103 (4): 27-30.

10. A Magazine Article

Basic format:

> #. Last name and initial(s) of author(s) (*separated by commas*). Title of article. Title of Magazine Year and Month of publication: Page numbers.

If the author's name is not given, substitute "[Anonymous]."

Examples:

> 11. Williams T. The terrible turtle trade. Audubon 1999 Mar-Apr: 44, 59.
>
> 12. [Anonymous]. Salmonella in pet reptiles—still a problem. Child Health Alert 2000 Jan: 4-5.

For a magazine published monthly or every two months, indicate the year and month. Use a three-letter abbreviation for each month, but do not conclude with a period. For a magazine published weekly, indicate the year, month, and day. If a magazine lists volume and issue numbers, these may be used in lieu of the month and day, following, the same format as journal articles in example 9.

13. Padgett T, Liston B. Tickled about turtles. Time 2000 Feb 28: 76.

OR

14. Padgett T, Liston B. Tickled about turtles. Time 2000 Feb; 155 (8): 76.

11. A Newspaper Article

Basic format:

\#. Last name and initial(s) of author(s) (*separated by commas*). Title of article. Newspaper Title Year Month Day of publication; Section information: Page number (column number).

If the author's name is not given, substitute "[Anonymous]."

Examples:

15. Aeppel T. Seeking ways to rid turtles of salmonella. Wall Street Journal 1996 May 30; Sect B: 3 (col 1).

16. Tunstall J. Saving turtles is slow work. Tampa Tribune 2002 Oct 7; Metro: 2 (col 4).

17. [Anonymous]. U.S. to appeal trade ruling on turtles. New York Times 1998 Jul 14; Sect A: 4 (col 2).

Other Types of Sources:

12. A Conference Presentation

Basic format:

\#. Last name and initial(s) of author(s) (*separated by commas*). Title of paper. In: Last name and initial(s) of editor(s) (*separated by commas*), editor(s). Title of proceedings. Title of Conference; Year Month and Days of conference; Conference location. Place of publication: Publisher; Year of publication. p (*pages on which the chapter or article appears*).

Examples:

18. Buech RR, Hanson LG, Nelson MD. Identification of wood turtle nesting areas for protection and management. In: Van Abbema J, editor. Conservation, restoration, and management of tortoises and turtles. Proceedings of the 1993 International Conference on the Conservation, Restoration, and Management of Tortoises and Turtles; 1993 July 11-16; State University of New York at Purchase, NY. Hauppauge (NY): New York Turtle and Tortoise Society, 1997. p 383-91.

13. A Government Report

Basic format:

> #. Name of government organization (country of origin abbreviated) [Abbreviation of name of government organization]. Title and description of report. Place of publication: Publisher; Year and month of publication. Number of pages of report.

Example:

> 19. Food and Drug Administration (US) [FDA]. Code of federal regulations-21-1240.62: Turtles intrastate and interstate requirements. Washington, DC: GPO, 2001 Apr. 2 p.

14. A Corporate (non-government) Report

Basic format:

> #. Name of corporation or organization [abbreviation of corporation organization]. Title and description of report. Place of publication: Publisher; year and month of publication. Report number. (*if given*) Number of pages.

Example:

> 20. Sea Turtle Survival League [STSL]. Florida sea turtle & coastal habitation program: an educator's guide. Gainesville (FL): Caribbean Conservation Corporation. 1999 Jul. 48 p.

15. A Dissertation

Basic format:

> #. Last name and initial(s) of author. Title of dissertation or thesis [dissertation/thesis]. Place of degree-granting institution: Degree-granting institution; Year of degree. Number of pages.

For dissertations published on microfilm by University Microfilms International (UMI), or Dissertations Abstract International (DAI), include that information as well as the microfilm number.

Example:

> 21. Conway KM. Human use of two species of river turtles (Podocnemis spp.) in lowland eastern Bolivia [dissertation]. Gainesville (FL): University of Florida; 2004. 176 p. Available from: University Microfilms, Ann Arbor. AAT 3145384.

16. A DVD or Videotape

Basic format:

> #. Title of DVD or videocassette [DVD or videotape]. Last name and initial(s) of editor(s) (*separated by commas*), editor(s). Name of producer (*if corporate and different from publisher*), producer. Place of publication: Publisher; Year of publication.

Example:

> 22. Sea turtles: ancient nomads [videotape] Palmer CN, De Nixon R, Kelly K, editors. National Audubon Society, producer. Stamford (CT): Vestron Video; 1989.

17. A CD or Audiocassette

Basic format:

> #. Title of CD or audiocassette [CD or audiocassette]. Last name and initial(s) of editor(s) (*separated by commas*), editor(s). Name of producer (*if corporate and different from publisher*), producer. Place of publication: Publisher; Year.

Example:

> 23. Hamburg concert: Turtle Island string quartet. [CD]. Herzog M, producer. Eslohe (Germany): CCn'C Records; 1998.

Electronic Sources

One challenge confronting the research paper writer in the age of the Internet is that the essential components of a reference list entry (author's name, title, date of publication) may be missing from electronic documents or may be present in a form that must be converted into something that makes sense in the CSE formatting system (e.g., a URL and the date when a site was last updated might have to replace more standard publication information). Last, but not least, information that has been "reprinted" on the web might lack complete documentation about the original source.

e-TIPS

Tricks for Finding Citation Information

If some information (the creator of the website, when a site was last updated, a sponsoring organization or institution) isn't immediately available on a web page, you can sometimes locate these facts by clicking on a hyperlink that takes you to a home page (sometimes labeled "About Us"). Also, you can often discover a home page (and more information about the source) by "backtracking." Try deleting the last portions of a URL to get to previous pages. Remember that a reference is only as good as its source. If you cannot locate a credible author or organization, you may not want to include the reference at issue in your research project.

Yet another obstacle to correctly formatting a reference list is identifying the type of source being used. Remember that the dual purpose of documentation is to give credit to the author *and* to enable a reader to find the material cited. Therefore, you need to determine first whether the source is available via the web (so it has a URL that can be accessed by anyone with a browser), or if it is delivered via a computer but available only through a licensing agreement or password (such as a subscription database, subscription service like AOL, or a CD-ROM). Reference list entries in the former category will include a URL, whereas those in the latter group will not.

e-TIPS

Accurate URLs

It is extremely important that the URL is accurate (otherwise the reader cannot access the page). Because URLs are often confusing and difficult to reproduce, it is always a smart idea to copy and paste (rather than try to type them) into your reference list entry.

However, the greatest obstacle to correctly formatting electronic documents in the CSE style is that little guidance has been provided. Because the CSE style manual hasn't been updated since 1994, many of the types of documents now available via the Internet are not included.* The manual covers electronic sources such as electronic journals and books (delivered either via the Internet or CD-ROM), but it does not include examples of web pages or databases. The examples that follow are based on the citation formats outlined by the *National Library of Medicine Recommended Formats for Bibliographic Citation [NLM]* for Internet sources—a format to which the updated CSE manual should closely adhere.** In addition to distinguishing how a text is delivered via a computer, there are some general rules to follow when using CSE format to document electronic sources on a references list.

- Because there are no regulations concerning publication on the web, many sites do not clearly state the author's name. Do not assume that the webmaster or contact person is the author (or even the editor). Many sites are maintained by organizations that should be considered the publishers, not the authors, of the sites. The NLM does not recommend the use of [Anonymous] in citations when you cannot locate the author of a web page.

- If the information has appeared previously in print form, include print information with the other (electronic) information necessary to locate a source.

- If a URL is long and must "wrap" onto the next line, DO NOT insert any punctuation (such as a hyphen). Instead, divide the electronic address in a logical place, such as at a slash ("/"), period, or hyphen.

---

*A seventh edition of Scientific Style and Format is due out soon; information and updates are available at the official CSE website, <http://www.councilscienceeditors.org/publications/style.cfm>.

**A complete guide to documentation of Internet sources according to NLM format is available at <http://www.nlm.nih.gov/pubs/formats/internet.pdf>.

- URL and e-mail addresses should not appear as hyperlinks. (Often, word processing programs will automatically transform a web address into a hyperlink. A quick way to change it back to normal type is to click on "Edit" and "Undo.")

- Occasionally, the last update is not provided on the home page. To determine the last update, enter <javascript:alert(document.lastModified)> (without the angle brackets) in the address field and then press "Enter." The last update information will appear in a window.

- If a URL is the final element, the entry does not conclude with a period unless the URL ends with a slash.

Electronic Documents Available on the Web. The following examples are for documents that are available to anyone with a browser. Complete information is not always available on web pages, but you should cite as much of the required information as you can reasonably obtain (**see Figure 10.1**).

FIGURE 10.1 Here is an excellent example of how difficult it is to correctly classify web documents to cite them correctly. This page is part of a larger collection entitled *Melissa Kaplan's Herp Care Collection*. However, the information on Kaplan's home page reveals that she is a layperson and that the page is not part of any professional project. That means that this page should be documented as a single, website, authored by Melissa Kaplan.

e-TIPS

Determine Last Updates

Frequently web editors will not include the last update on a web page. To determine this, type <javascript:alert(document.lastModified)> in the address field of the web page and press "Enter." The last update information should appear in a window.

18. A Single Web Page

A single web page is complete in itself and is not connected to a larger, professional web project.

Basic format:

> #. Last name and initial(s) of author(s). Title of site (*Use a descriptor such as* Home page—*neither underlined nor in quotation marks—if there is no title*) [Internet]. [updated year month day; cited year month day]. Available from: URL

Examples:

> 24. Kaplan M. Cryptosporidium: health threat to humans and reptiles [Internet]. [updated 2002 Aug 17; cited 2002 Oct 24]. Available from: http://www.anapsid.org/cryptosporidium.html

> 25. Fife R. Salmonella and your privilege to keep reptiles to be reviewed by the FDA [Internet]. [updated 2003 Mar 3; cited 2003 Jul 7]. Available from: http://personal.riverusers.com/~richardfife/page20.html

> 26. Power T. Salmonella in reptiles and amphibians [Internet]. [updated 2001 Feb 19; cited 2001 Dec 12]. Available from: http://www.icomm.ca/dragon/salmonella.htm

19. A Secondary Web Page

A secondary web page is part of a larger, professional web project. The page has a title but features the name of the project as well (**see Figure 10.2**).

Basic format:

> #. Last name and initial(s) of author(s). Title of page. Title of Web Project. [Internet]. Name of any organization or institution associated with the site; [updated year month day; cited year month day]. Available from: URL

Examples:

> 27. Kuhrt T. Trachemys scripta. Animal Diversity Web. [Internet]. University of Michigan Museum of Zoology; [updated 2001 May 2; cited 2001 Dec 2]. Available from: http://animaldiversity.ummz.umich.edu/accounts/trachemys/t._scripta$narrative.html

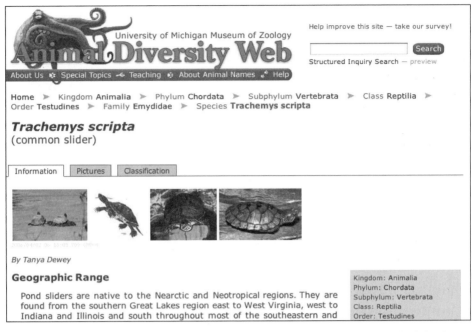

FIGURE 10.2 This website page is one page in a larger project (Animal Diversity Web) that is sponsored by the University of Michigan (the electronic "publisher") of the site.

28. Salmonella infection (salmonellosis) and animals. National Center for Infectious Diseases. [Internet]. Centers for Disease Control and Prevention; [updated 2002 Oct 7; cited 2002 Oct 24]. Available from: http://www.cdc.gov/healthypets/diseases/salmonellosis.htm

20. An Online Journal Article

An online journal article is the electronic text of a previously printed article (now available on the web) or a document available only on the Internet.

Basic format:

#. Last name and initial(s) of author(s). Title of article. Title of journal [Internet]. Year of publication [cited year month day]; vol. # (issue #): (*if each issue begins at page 1*) page numbers. Available from: URL

Examples:

29. Levy C, Finnerty M, Hansen G, Cory J, McGuill M, Matyas B, DeMaria A, Schmunk G, Grantham J, Archer J, Kazmierczak J, Davis J. Reptile-associated salmonellosis—selected states, 1996-1998. Morb and Mort Wkly Rpt [Internet]. 1999 [cited 2001 Dec 12]; 48: 1009-13. Available from: http://www.cdc.gov/epo/mmwrpreview/mmwrhtml/mm4844a1.htm

30. Rosner E. Salmonellosis from a trip to the zoo. Phys Wkly [Internet]. 1996 [cited 2001 Dec 13]; 13 (39). Available from: http://www.physweekly.com/archive/96/10_21_96/cu4.html

For articles that have been previously published, include page numbers. Because electronic documents do not have pagination, you will not indicate page numbers.

21. An Online Magazine Article

An online magazine article is the electronic text of a previously printed article (now available on the web) or a document available only on the Internet.

Basic format:

#.   Last name and initial(s) of author(s). Title of article. Title of Magazine [Internet]. Year of publication [cited year month day]: Page numbers. Available from: URL

Examples:

31. Turk MP. New food rules for pregnancy. Parents [Internet]. 2001 [cited 2001 Dec 13]: 32-3. Available from: http://www.parents.com/articles/pregnancy/1186.jsp

32. Williams W. Turtle tragedy: demand in Asia may be wiping out turtle populations worldwide. ScientificAmerican.com [Internet]. 1999 [cited 2002 Oct 21]; Available from: http://www.sciam.com/article.cfm?articleID=00043E38-66A6-1C72-9EB7809EC588F2D7& pageNumber=2&catID=2

22. An Online Newspaper Article

An online newspaper article is the electronic text of a previously printed article (now available on the web) or a document available only on the Internet.

Basic format:

#.   Last name and initial(s) of author(s). Title of article. Newspaper Title [Internet]. Year month day of publication [cited year month day]: section information page number (*if available*) [Number of paragraphs]. Available from: URL

Examples:

33. Hoy C. Sea turtles use a natural compass to find their way. USA Today [Internet]. 2001 Oct 12 [cited 2002 Dec 18]: [8 paragraphs]. Available from: http://www.usatoday.com/news/science/aaas/2001-10-11-turtles.htm

34. Lelis L. Turtles arrive in state—with help. Sun Sentinel [Internet]. 2002 Dec 20 [cited 2002 Dec 22]: [10 paragraphs]. Available from: http://www.sunsentinel.com/news/local/florida/ orlloccoldturtle20122002dec20.story

23. An Online Encyclopedia Entry

Basic format:

#. Last name and initial(s) of author(s). (*if given*) Title of entry. Title of Online Reference [Internet]. City of publication: Publisher; Year of publication. [cited year month day]. Available from: URL

Example:

35. Salmonellosis. Encyclopedia Britannica [Internet]. Chicago: Encyclopedia Britannica Premium Service; 2006. [cited 2006 Jul 10]. Available from: http://www.britannica.com/eb/article?eu=66794

24. An Online Government Publication

An online government publication is the electronic text of a previously printed article (now available on the web) or a document available only on the Internet.

Basic format:

#. Name of the government. Name of the government agency. [Internet]. City of publication: Publisher; Date of publication. [cited year month day]. Title of publication. Available from: URL

Example:

36. Utah. Department of Health. [Internet]. Salt Lake City: Bureau of Epidemiology; 2001. [cited 2001 Dec 8]. Reptile-associated salmonellosis. Available from: http://hlunix.hl.state.ut.us/els/epidemiology/epifacts/reptile.html

25. An Online Corporate (non-government) Report

An online (non-government) corporate publication is the electronic text of a previously printed article (now available on the web) or a document available only on the Internet.

Basic format:

#. Name of Corporation or organization [abbreviation of corporation or organization]. Title and description of report. [Internet] Place of publication: Publisher; Date of publication. [cited year month day]. Available from: URL

Example:

> 37. National Environmental Trust [NET]. Destined for extinction: the fate of Chilean sea bass. [Internet]. Washington, DC: Mount Vernon Printing; 2001. [cited 2005 Sep 1]. Available from: http://www.net.org/marine/csb/grassroots/materials/whitepaper.pdf

26. An Online Book

An online book may be the electronic text of part or all of a printed book (now available on the web) or a book-length document available only on the Internet.

Basic format:

> #. Last name and initial(s) of author(s) or editor(s). (*if editor, not author*) Chapter title (*if given*). In: Title of book [Internet]. Edition. (*if given*) Place of publication: Publisher; Year of publication [updated year month day; cited year month day]. Page numbers. Available from: URL

Examples:

> 38. Ernst CH, Zug GR. Should I keep a snake (or any other reptile) as a pet? In: Snakes in question: the Smithsonian answer book [Internet]. Washington, DC: Smithsonian Institute Press; 1996 [updated 2001 Dec 22; cited 2002 Oct 13]. p. 149-51. Available from: http://www.emblheidelberg.de/~uetz/db-info/snakes_as_pets.html

> 39. Drugge R. The electronic textbook of dermatology [Internet]. New York: Internet Dermatological Society; 2000 [updated 2002 Jul 6; cited 2002 Oct 24]. Available from: http://www.telemedicine.org/stamford.htm

27. An Online Forum Posting

Basic format:

> #. Last name and initial(s) of author. Title of posting. In: Name of Forum [Internet]; Year month day, time of posting [cited year month day]. Available from: URL

Example:

> 40. Peteralbrian. Treating parasites without fecals. In: Herpetological Health Forum [Internet]; 2003 Apr 23, 16:49:31[cited 2003 Jul 7]. Available from: http://forum.kingsnake.com/health/messages/5960.html

Electronic Documents with Restricted Access. These entries usually do not include a URL because they require a subscription, password, or CD-ROM to access them. Cite as much of the required information as you can reasonably obtain.

28. A Journal Article from a Database

Basic format:

> #. Last name and initial(s) of author(s). Title of article. Title of Journal Year and month of publication; vol. # (issue #): (*if each issue begins at page 1*) page numbers. In: Name of Database [database]. [cited year month day]. Available from: Name of Service. Name of library or URL of provider

Example:

> 41. Herbst LH, Klein PA. Green turtle fibropapillomatosis: challenges to assessing the role of environmental cofactors. Envir Health Prsp Sup 1995 Dec; 103 (4): 27-30. In: Academic Search Premier [database] [cited 2002 Oct 27]. Available from: EBSCOhost. Seminole Community College Library.

29. A Magazine Article from a Database

Basic format:

> #. Last name and initial(s) of author(s). Title of article. Title of Magazine Year month day (*if weekly*) of publication: Page numbers. In: Name of Database [database]. [cited year month day]. Available from: Name of Service. Name of library or URL of provider

Example:

> 42. Williams W. The deadly shell game. Animals 1999 May: 16. In: InfoTrac College Edition [database]. [cited 2002 Nov 15]. Available from Gale Group. http://www.infotrac-college.com

30. A Newspaper Article from a Database

Basic format:

> #. Last name and initial(s) of author(s). Title of article. Newspaper Title Year month day of publication; Section information: Page numbers. In: Name of Database [database]. [cited year month day]. Available from: Name of Service. Name of library or URL of provider

Example:

43. Webb T. New weapon against salmonella. Philadelphia Inquirer 1998 Mar
    20:n.p. In: SIRSResearcher [database]. [cited 2001 Dec 13]. Available from:
    FirstSearch. Seminole Community College Library.

If page numbers aren't provided, use "n.p." to indicate the information is
unavailable.

31. An E-Book from a Database

Basic format:

#. Last name and initial(s) of author. Title of Book. Edition. (*if given*) Place of
    publication: Publisher; Year of publication. Number of pages in the book. In:
    Name of database [database]. [cited year month day]. Available from: Name of
    service. Name of library or URL of provider.

Example:

44. Torrey, E F, & Yolken, RH. Beasts of the earth: animals, humans, and disease.
    New Brunswick, N.J: Rutgers UP; (2005). 191 p. In: NetLibrary [database].
    [cited 2005 Mar 22]. Available from: OCLC. Seminole Community College
    Library.

32. A Magazine Article from an Online Subscription Service (such as AOL)

Basic format:

#. Last name and initial(s) of author(s). Title of article. Title of Magazine Year
    month day (*if weekly*) of publication: Page numbers. In: Name of Subscription
    Service [online service]. [cited year month day]. Keyword: search phrase.

Example:

45. Hogan D. Rage for reptiles. Current Science 1997 Nov 14:8. In: AOL [online
    service]. [cited 2001 Dec 15]. Keyword: reptiles AND salmonella.

33. An Encyclopedia Article from a CD-ROM

Basic format:

#. Last name and initial(s) of author(s) of article. (*if given*) Title of entry. Title of
    Encyclopedia. Edition or version. [CD-ROM]. Name of Vendor; Year of elec-
    tronic publication. [cited year month day].

Example:

46. Salmonella. Compton's Interactive Encyclopedia. Ver 2000Dlx. [CD ROM].
    Compton's NewMedia; 2000. [cited 2001 Dec 12].

34. An E-Mail Message

Basic format:

> #. Last name and initial(s) of sender. Subject of message [electronic mail on the Internet]. Message to: Name of recipient. Year month day, time of transmission [cited year month day].

Example:

> 47. Peppers J. Salmonellosis in turtles [electronic mail on the Internet]. Message to: Frank Bonner. 2000 May 10, 11:30 am [cited 2002 Jun 30].

Sample Research Paper Using CSE Style

The following paper uses CSE documentation style and provides an example of how to correctly incorporate both print and electronic documents into the text and the Cited References page of a research paper. Annotations are provided to comment on some of the more complicated aspects of documentation.

A research paper should *look* like an academic work. Resist the urge to become creative with "desktop publishing." Don't include colored type, "fancy" fonts, graphics, or pictures (unless they are tables, graphs, or illustrations related to your project). You may think they add interest to your project, but most professors will consider this type of augmentation distracting and unscholarly.

The Plight of the Patagonian Toothfish

Christian Rogman

Your title page should include the title of your paper, your name, the title of the course, your professor's name, and the date the assignment is due—all centered and in a normal (12-point/Times New Roman) font.

Biology and Environment

Professor Kellen

November 20, 2005

Toothfish   2

Headings
announce the
organization of
the essay.

Abstract

This paper contends that growing market demand for the

Patagonian toothfish has threatened this species with extinction

and disrupted oceanic ecosystems. Despite international efforts to

regulate catches and prevent overfishing, poaching is widespread.

Studies indicate that overfishing may have irreparably unbalanced

the lifecycle of the toothfish and disturbed the delicate balance of

the ocean's food web. Legal intervention has thus far proven

ineffective. The solution lies in improved international enforcement,

increased consumer awareness, and better cooperation from

fisheries.

The abstract
introduces the
purpose and
scope of the
essay.

Each page (other
than the title
page) should
include an
abbreviated form
of the paper title
and the page
number in the
upper right
corner.

Introduction

Fine dining is a pleasure enjoyed around the world. Yet few

think carefully about what is on their plate. Take, for example, the

Patagonian toothfish, a delectably moist, white-fleshed fish served

in many fine restaurants. Toothfish is not found by name on any

menu: it is listed instead as Chilean sea bass, a marketing ploy to

make the dish sound more appealing. This gambit has been

effective: Increased popularity of Chilean sea bass has increased

the market price to nearly fifteen dollars a pound.[1] The high price

means big profits and has sparked a frenzy among fisheries, even

at the expense of the species. The National Environmental Trust

(NET) estimates that overfishing of the Patagonian toothfish may

Leave a one-inch
margin on all
sides of the
page.

An introduction
should
command your
readers'
attention *and*
plainly introduce
the topic of the
paper.

Superscript numbers (listed sequentially) correspond to numbered entries on the reference list.

Toothfish 3

ultimately lead to its extinction.[2] Profit, it seems, is more important than sustaining the species or maintaining the ecosystem. But for seafood lovers, fishermen, scientists, and environmentalists alike, the exploitation of this species could leave a very bad taste if action to prevent overfishing is not taken soon.

The thesis succinctly summarizes the goals and organization of the essay.

The Effects of Overfishing

Subheadings differentiate between sections of the essay. Use italics to distinguish these from the formal headings.

The toothfish (Latin name *Dissostichus eleginoides*) lives in the southern hemisphere, where the oceans converge in arctic waters.[3-6] It grows slowly and takes a decade to reach maturity. Undisturbed, it can grow to nearly two meters and live for fifty years.[4] Commercial fishing of the toothfish began in the late 1980s. Prior to that time, the species was considered "bycatch"[2]—undesired fish captured in trawl nets seeking more valuable catch, such as squid. However, once the commercial value of toothfish became known, fisheries began to harvest them using longlines, systems of up to ten thousand baited hooks sunk to depths where toothfish is abundant, 700-1,500 meters below the surface.[5]

If information is found in more than one reference, cite all entries. Use a hyphen to indicate continuous numbers.

The in-text reference number should immediately follow the information you are citing.

According to the Food and Agricultural Organization (FAO), the number of harvested toothfish increased eightfold between 1984 and 1992.[5] As more boats attempt to catch what has become known as "white gold"[2,6] the toothfish remaining in the ocean have decreased at an alarming rate. Yet available numbers do not accurately represent the actual quantities of toothfish harvested, for

When citing more than one entry (and the numbers are nonsequential), separate them with a comma

Names of organizations should be spelled out the first time (followed by the abbreviation in parentheses). Use the abbreviation for any subsequent mention.

Toothfish 4

they account only for legal catches reported. A study conducted by the NET concluded that, in 2002, the legal catch (30,000 metric tons) was exceeded by the unreported catch (33,000 metric tons). This was a conservative estimate.[2] Such illegal and unregulated activity undermines the efforts of those working to curb overfishing.

Poaching Is Big Business

As the demand for toothfish has grown, poachers have become more cunning. One common strategy involves transferring illegal catches to properly licensed ships at sea.[7] Some poachers camouflage their boats by changing the name or color to elude suspicion; most often, they simply fly "flags of convenience"—flags of countries not bound to international fishing laws and quotas.[6] Others hide behind governments and large corporations willing to pay penalties if they are caught. One frustrated Australian official says, "To put it plainly, we are up against organized crime, bureaucrats versus big business."[8] Although many countries are working together toward the conservation of the Patagonian toothfish, the lucrative financial rewards make it difficult to regulate effectively and eliminate overfishing.

Disrupting the Food Web

Overfishing does not affect the targeted species alone. Food webs begin with the largest predators at the top and the smallest prey at the bottom, with numerous levels between. The

When the superscript reference number occurs at the end of a sentence, the end punctuation *precedes* the number.

Introduce direct quotation with a signal phrase that indicates the speaker of the words. Don't just "plop" the quotation into your essay.

predator/prey relationships between species are delicate. When larger predator fish are removed, less food remains for those higher up in the food web. Additionally, the species normally consumed by these predators no longer get eaten. This changes the entire ecosystem. Lower-level organisms thrive and even take over, while the largest predators leave to find food elsewhere.[9] One report notes that seabirds and marine mammals have faced increased competition with commercial fisheries and that overfishing has a direct relationship to decreases in their populations.[10(cited in 11)] Animals that feed on toothfish include penguins, sea lions, sperm whales, and elephant seals: Fewer toothfish result in less food for these animals. Additionally, there could be an escalation in populations of organisms the toothfish would normally maintain—crustaceans, squid, and small fishes.[3] Overfishing removes the organisms that have the important function of both eating and being eaten; these species are what keep the ecosystem in harmony.

The fishery and numerous pirate vessels that scour the ocean for toothfish may inflict so much damage that this species will never recover.[2,5-7] To avoid extinction, toothfish populations must be allowed to replenish. When fishermen have depleted a species to such an extent that they are harvesting only immature fish, the result is a phenomenon known as "fishing down."[10,12] As

If you are referencing a work that has been cited in a work by a different author, assign a reference number to the original source followed by "cited in" and the secondary source reference number in parentheses. [*Both* sources must appear in your reference list.]

No matter where you cite a source in the essay, refer to it by its original number.

Reference numbers *not* in sequence are separated by commas. Numbers *in* sequence are separated by a hyphen.

the numbers of adult toothfish diminish, fishermen settle for smaller juveniles to meet the demand and more of the smaller fish are needed to meet expected weights. Because the toothfish grows at such a slow rate, catches increasingly contain fish that have not yet reached sexual maturity and spawned.[2,7,8,13] This means that fewer and fewer toothfish reproduce, a process fundamental to the survival of every species.

Conclusions

Intervention is crucial. The Commission for the Conservation of Antarctic Marine Living Resources (CCAMLR) is leading the effort by setting limits on annual catches. It dictates how much toothfish vessels can procure; it requires that they prove it was done legally.[14] Other nations have deployed patrols in the Southern Ocean to monitor fishing and intercept pirate vessels. To combat poaching, a global group of toothfishermen is offering a $100,000 reward for the capture of illegal fishermen.[14] Consumers, chefs, and seafood dealers can participate in the campaign to "Take a Pass on Chilean Sea Bass," a boycott coordinated by the NET to reduce demand; environmentalists feel that educating consumers about overfishing may be essential to alleviate the overfishing problem.[7]

While many chefs have stopped serving Chilean sea bass, others continue to offer it. Some remain unconvinced there's a problem; others are unwilling to lose their business to others. "It's our second-biggest seller after salmon filets, and at retail you have to have it," claims one owner of a New York seafood market.[7]

It is the fishermen, in the end, who control the fate of the Patagonian toothfish and other species affected by overfishing. Their cooperation could lead to solutions and restoration of a sustainable fishery. Toothfish populations must be replenished before they are wiped out completely. If generations of toothfish are allowed to mature, fishermen may once again see a 200 pound toothfish on the end of a fishing line.

The conclusion presents a summary of analysis and research and frequently offers a call for future action.

Toothfish   8

CITED REFERENCES

1. Longmore M. Australian officials board ship suspected of poaching rare fish. Assoc Press Wrldstrm 2003 Aug;59: 1370-84. In: LexisNexis Academic [database]. [cited 2005 Sep 1]. Available from: Elsevier. University of Central Florida Library.

2. National Environmental Trust. [NET]. Black market for white gold: the illegal trade in Chilean sea bass. [Internet]. Washington, DC: Mount Vernon Printing; 2004 Sep. [cited 2005 Sep 1]. Available from: http://www.net.org/reports/csb_report.pdf

3. Pilling GM, Purves MG, Daw TM, Agnew DA, Xavier JC. The stomach contents of patagonian toothfish around South Georgia (South Atlantic). J Fish Biol 2001 Nov; 59 (5): 1370-84. In: ScienceDirect [database]. [cited 2005 Sep 1]. Available from: Elsevier. University of Central Florida Library.

4. Yau C, Collins MA, Bagley PM, Everson I, Nolan CP, Priede IG. Estimating the abundance of patagonian toothfish dissostichus eleginoides using baited cameras: a preliminary study. Fshrs Res 2001 May; 51 (2-3): 403-12. In: ScienceDirect. [database]. [cited 2005 Sep 1]. Available from: Elsevier. University of Central Florida Library.

5. Collins MA, Belchier M, Everson I. Why the fuss about toothfish? Biologist 2003; 50 (3): 116-19. In: Academic

References should be numbered and appear in the same order as in the paper.

This is the electronic text of a previously printed pamphlet (now available on the web) from a nonprofit organization.

Double-space everything—within entries and between entries.

Begin a new page and center the title (References or Cited References) and distinguish it by using all capital letters, a bold font, or underlining.

When a URL appears at the end of a citation, it is NOT followed by a period.

Journal titles should be abbreviated according to the standard method used in the Index Medicus system.

Articles from a database accessed from a school library should conclude with the name of the library rather than the URL of the library site.

Toothfish   9

Search Premier [database]. [cited 2005 Sep 1]. Available

from: EBSCOHost. University of Central Florida Library.

6.   Daley B. With fish piracy on rise, agents cast worldwide net.

B Globe 2003 May 18:A1. In: LexisNexis Academic

[database]. [cited 2005 Sep 1]. Available from: Elsevier.

University of Central Florida Library.

7.   Fabricant F. Chilean sea bass: more than an identity problem.

NY Times 2002 May 29:F4. In: InfoTrac College Edition

[database]. [cited 2005 Sept 1]. Available from: Gale Group.

http://www.infotrac-college.com

Articles from a database accessed via a personal subscription on the WWW should conclude with the URL of the database.

8.   Shaw J. Australia casts net for fish poachers. NY Times 2002

Sep 8:14. In: LexisNexis Academic. Available from: Elsevier.

University of Central Florida Library.

9.   [Anonymous]. Year of the ocean. Discov 2002 Jan; 23 (1):

35-8. In: Academic Search Premier [database]. [cited 2005

Sep 1]. Available from: EBSCOHost. University of Central Florida

Library.

If the author of a source is unnamed, then list the author as "[Anonymous]."

For an indirect source, indicate the original publication as well as the publication in which you accessed the information.

10.   Anderson DW, Gress F. Brown pelicans and the anchovy

fishery off southern California. In: Nettleship DN, Sanger A,

Springer PF, editors. Marine birds: their feeding ecology and

commercial fisheries relationships. Ottawa: Canadian Wildlife

Service; 1984. p 128-35.

11.   Goldsworthy SD, He X, Tuck GN, Lewis M, Williams R. Trophic

interactions between the patagonian toothfish, its fishery,

Toothfish   10

and seals and seabirds around Macquarie Island. Mar Ecol

Prog Ser 2001 Aug; 218: 283-302. In: EBSCOHost Electronic

Journals [database]. [cited 2005 Sep 1]. Available from: Gale

Group. University of Central Florida Library.

12.   Pauly D, Watson R. Counting the last fish. Sci Am 2003

Jul; 289 (1): 42-7. In: Academic Search Premier [database].

[cited 2005 Sep 1]. Available from: EBSCOHost. University of

Central Florida Library.

13.   Handwerk B. U.S. chefs join campaign to save Chilean sea

bass. Natl Geogr News [Internet]. 2002 May 22 [cited 2005

Sep 1]. Available from: http://news.nationalgeographic.com/

news/2002/05/0522_020522_seabass.html

14.   Gable E. Fisheries: NMFS announces new rules to monitor

Chilean sea bass imports. Greenwire 2003 May 2. In:

LexisNexis Academic [database]. [cited 2005 Sep 1]

Available from: Elsevier. University of Central Florida Library.

This is an article from a credible online magazine with a listed author.

For articles from a database, indicate the name of the database as well as the publisher.

Documentation: CMS Format

The most common forms of documentation are the MLA and APA styles. However, depending on the discipline for which you are writing, your instructor may require that you use other formats. *The Chicago Manual of Style* (CMS) is used in history and some social science and humanities disciplines. You should always check with your instructor to make sure which style he or she requires.

The CMS form of documentation was once widely used in many social science and humanities disciplines. Today it is employed to a much more limited extent. However, some professors continue to require that you document according to this system. The CMS format uses a combination of footnotes or endnotes and a bibliography that appears at the end of the essay.

CMS Footnotes, Endnotes, and Bibliographies

In CMS format, complete bibliographic information is given in the text of the paper (either at the bottom of the page on which the reference appears—in a footnote—or at the end of the essay—in the endnotes) as well as on the bibliography page at the conclusion of the essay. Within the text, a superscript numeral is used to indicate that a quotation, paraphrase, or summary is being employed. That numeral corresponds to a footnote or endnote (you must choose one method and use it consistently throughout the essay) that provides complete publication information. The first note (footnote or endnote) includes all essential information for the work cited. Subsequent notes about the same work are brief, including only the author's last name, a brief version of the title, and the page number on which the information or quotation appears. In CMS format, footnotes or endnotes may also contain commentary (further observations, explanations, or clarifications) in addition to the bibliographic information. In some cases, a footnote or endnote may be composed entirely of commentary.

- Footnotes should be provided at the bottom of the page on which the citation appears.

- Endnotes should be provided on their own page, immediately following the last page of the essay.

NOTE: Many professors prefer endnotes pages rather than footnotes, and despite the vast improvements made in word processing programs for footnoting, footnoting remains a bit tricky. Therefore, unless your professor specifies that you *must* use footnotes, I recommend that you choose the endnote format.

Some Basic Rules for Footnotes and Endnotes in the CMS

- Begin a new page for your endnotes after the essay
- Center your title (Notes) one inch from the top of the page.
  - Number this page consecutively with the rest of your paper.
- Use a superscript number following any reference to a source.
  - Notes are numbered consecutively as they appear in the text.
  - End punctuation precedes the note number within the text.

Example:

Reptiles captured in the wild and transported for sale as pets run a higher risk of bacterial infection.[1] This is because they are frequently kept in unsanitary containers or cages and fed infrequently and/or incorrectly.[2]

e-TIPS

Footnotes and Endnotes and Word Processing

If you have a recent version of Microsoft Word, it is simple to create footnotes or endnotes using the automatic formatting system. (If you don't have Word or you have an outdated version of Word, spend a few minutes in the "Help" section of your word processing program and learn how your program works.) For most versions, click on "Insert" on the main menu, then on "reference," and then on "footnote." (Once this window opens, you can choose endnotes instead of footnotes.) Using this system will make it easy to "keep track" of your notes. If you delete a note or add one later, the program will automatically adjust the numbering and positioning of the notes on the pages. Make sure that you choose settings that agree with the CMS formatting requirements. A few minutes acquainting yourself with your program's system is time well spent; it could save you a lot of headaches later.

■ The number in the text corresponds to a footnote or endnote.
   □ Indent the first line of each note five spaces. Then place the number that corresponds to the reference in the text (normally-sized, *not* superscript) followed by a period and one space.
   □ Single-space within notes and double-space between them.

Basic format:

   1. Author, (*first name, first*) ed., (*if there is an editor instead of an author*) *Title*, volume and/or edition number, (*if there is one*) (Place of publication: Publisher, date of publication), page #.

Examples:

   1. Harmut Wilket, *Turtles: Everything about Purchase, Care, Nutrition, and Diseases* (Woodbury, NY: Barron's, 1983), 83.

   2. Douglas R. Mader, ed., *Reptile Medicine and Surgery* (Philadelphia: W. B. Saunders, 1996), 36.

■ CMS style discourages using more than one note at a single text location (i.e., "These risks can be reduced.[3,4]"). Instead, combine the material to create one single note. If the subject matter changes within the new note, indicate this by starting a new paragraph at the change.

Example:

   As the public has become more conscious of the biological risks posed by pet reptiles, the number of salmonella infections has decreased.[3]

   3. Birgitta De Jong, Yvonne Andersson, and Karl Ekdahl, "Effect of Regulation and Education on Reptile-associated Salmonellosis," *Emerging Infectious Diseases* 11, no. 3 (2005): 398-403, and Jonathan Mermin et al., "Reptiles, Amphibians, and Human Salmonella Infection: A Population-Based, Case-Control Study," *Clinical Infectious Diseases* 38 (2004): 253-61, indicate that recent efforts at education have resulted in significant reductions in infection rates.

- If you are citing from a source that has been quoted in a subsequent document, record one reference number. In your note, include both works, using "quoted in."

Example:

The first report of human salmonella infection linked to pet turtles[4] occurred in Chicago.

    4. Tad Hardy, "The Tortoise and the Scare," *Bio Science* 38, no. 2 (1988): 76-9, quoted in Ted Williams, "The Terrible Turtle Trade," *Audubon,* March/April (1999): 44.

The complete bibliographic information for BOTH sources must appear in your bibliography.

- For subsequent references to a source you have already cited, give only the author's name, a shortened version of the title (shorten titles more than four words long—italicize if it is a book title or use quotation marks if it is the title of an article), and the pages cited. When you cite the same source in *consecutive* notes, use the term "Ibid." (meaning "the same place") for the subsequent notes and the page number (for the same page number, use "Ibid.," alone).

Examples:

    5. Mader, *Reptile Medicine and Surgery*, 32.

    6. De Jong, Andersson and Ekdahl, "Effect of Regulation," 399.

    7. Ibid., 401.

Bibliography Pages in the CMS Style

- Begin a new page for your bibliography (after the essay if using footnotes or after the endnotes page(s) if using endnotes). Center your title (Bibliography) one inch from the top of the page.
- Single-space each entry and double-space between entries.
- Alphabetize the entries according to authors' last names.
- If no author's name is given, alphabetize according to the first significant word in the title (ignore *A, An,* and *The*).
- Should you reference more than one work by the same author, arrange the works alphabetically. The first entry should follow the prescribed format, but in subsequent works, use three dashes followed by a period instead of the author's name.
- Note that CMS prefers to italicize rather than underline.
- Begin each entry at the left margin. Subsequent lines in that entry should be indented five spaces.

CMS Footnote/Endnote and Bibliography Format

The format for footnote/endnote entries and bibliography entries is very similar. In fact, at first glance they seem almost identical (*take special note of the differences in indentation, order of author's or editor's first and last names, and punctuation*). Because they are so alike, the two formats (note entry and bibliography entry) are best understood when seen together. Therefore, in the following examples of CMS formatting, the model note entry appears first, followed by the model bibliography entry.

Printed and Recorded Sources

As with every other form of documentation, it is important to identify the type of source that you are documenting. Standard CMS format for print and audiovisual sources (as opposed to electronic documents) has remained virtually unchanged for years and is readily available in numerous print and online sources. There are numerous websites to help you determine the proper format for your sources. The following are two of the best.

The Chicago Manual of Style Website
<http://www.chicagomanualofstyle.org/tools.html>

Michael Harvey's *The Nuts and Bolts of College Writing*: Chicago Document Formats
<http://nutsandbolts.washcoll.edu/chicago.html>

Books:

Obtain all information from the title page (and the reverse side of the title page), not from the cover.

Basic format for footnote/endnote of a book:

1. Author (*first name first*), ed., (*if there is an editor instead of an author*) *Title*, edition and/or volume number, (*if there is one*) ed. or trans. (*editor's or translator's name, first name first, if there is one*) (Place of publication: Publisher, year of publication), page.

Basic format for bibliography entry of a book:

Author (*last name, first*), ed. (*if there is an editor instead of an author*) *Title*. Edition and/or volume number. (*if there is one*) Edited by or Translated by (*editor's or translator's name, first name first, if there is one*). Place of publication: Publisher, year of publication.

1. A Book with One Author or Editor

Endnote/Footnote:

>   1. Frederic L. Frye, *Biomedical and Surgical Aspects of Captive Reptile Husbandry,* 2nd ed. (Malabar, FL: Krieger, 1991), 26.

>   2. Alan F. Fudge, ed., *Laboratory Medicine: Avian and Exotic Pets* (Philadelphia: Saunders, 2000), 143.

Bibliography:

> Frye, Frederic L. *Biomedical and Surgical Aspects of Captive Reptile Husbandry.* 2nd ed. Malabar, FL: Krieger, 1991.
> Fudge, Alan F., ed. *Laboratory Medicine: Avian and Exotic Pets.* Philadelphia: Saunders, 2000.

If no author's or editor's name is given for a work, begin both the note and the bibliography entry with the title of the book (italicized). When alphabetizing the work in the bibliography, ignore beginning words like "A," "An," and "The."

2. A Book with Two or Three Authors or Editors

Endnote/Footnote:

>   3. C. Wray and A. Wray, *Salmonella in Domestic Animals* (New York: CABI Publications, 2000), 52.

>   4. Clifford Warwick, Fredric L. Frye, and James B. Murphy, eds., *Health and Welfare of Captive Reptiles* (New York: Chapman and Hall, 1995), 137.

Bibliography:

> Warwick, Clifford, Fredric L. Frye, and James B. Murphy, eds. *Health and Welfare of Captive Reptiles.* New York: Chapman and Hall, 1995.

> Wray, C., and A. Wray. *Salmonella in Domestic Animals.* New York: CABI Publications, 2000.

3. A Book with Four or More Authors or Editors

Endnote/Footnote:

>   5. Karl Garbrisch et al., eds., *Atlas of Diagnostic Radiology of Exotic Pets: Small Mammals, Birds, Reptiles and Amphibians* (London: Wolfe Pub., 1991), 39.

Bibliography:

> Garbrisch, Karl, G., Alexander Rübel, Ewald Isenbügel and Pim Wolvekamp, eds. *Atlas of Diagnostic Radiology of Exotic Pets: Small Mammals, Birds, Reptiles and Amphibians.* London: Wolfe, 1991.

When there are four or more authors or editors, only indicate the first named author or editor in the footnote or endnote (followed by "et al."— the Latin abbreviation for "and others"); however, in the bibliography entry, list all of the authors or editors.

4. A Book with an Author and an Editor

Endnote/Footnote:

> 6. Geoffrey Chaucer, *The Canterbury Tales,* ed. Paul G. Ruggiers (Norman: University of Oklahoma Press, 1987), 103.

Bibliography:

> Chaucer, Geoffrey. *The Canterbury Tales.* Edited by Paul G. Ruggiers. Norman: University of Oklahoma Press, 1987.

5. A Book with an Author and a Translator

Endnote/Footnote:

> 7. Massimo Capula, *Simon and Schuster's Guide to Reptiles and Amphibians of the World,* trans. John Gilbert (New York: Simon and Schuster, 1989), 128.

Bibliography:

> Capula, Massimo, *Simon and Schuster's Guide to Reptiles and Amphibians of the World.* Translated by John Gilbert. New York: Simon and Schuster, 1989.

6. A Selection from a Collection or an Anthology

Endnote/Footnote:

> 8. Kay Ryan, "Turtle," in *Literature: An Introduction to Fiction, Poetry, and Drama,* 8th ed., ed. X. J. Kennedy and Dana Gioia (New York: Longman, 2002), 874.

Bibliography:

> Ryan, Kay. "Turtle." In *Literature: An Introduction to Fiction, Poetry, and Drama,* 8th ed., Edited by X. J. Kennedy and Dana Gioia, 874. New York: Longman, 2002.

If you are citing more than one selection from the same collection or anthology, create a separate bibliographic entry for each one. Do not cross-reference them (as you would in MLA format).

7. The Introduction, Foreword, Preface, or Afterword of a Book

Endnote/Footnote:

> 9. Nat B. Frazer, foreword to *Turtle Conservation*, by Michael W. Klemens (Washington, DC: Smithsonian Institution Press, 2000).

Bibliography:

> Frazer, Nat B. "Foreword" in *Turtle Conservation*, by Michael W. Klemens. Washington, DC: Smithsonian Institution Press, 2000.

Notice that the footnote/endnote format does not include a page number for the quotation or information cited. The designation (i.e., "Introduction," "Foreword," "Preface," or "Afterword") stands in for the page number(s).

8. A Volume in a Multivolume Work

Endnote/Footnote:

> 10. Peter L. Lutz, John A. Musick, and Jeanette Wyneken, eds., *The Biology of Sea Turtles*, vol. 2 (Boca Raton, FL: CRC Press, 1995), 11.

Bibliography:

> Lutz, Peter L, John A. Musick, and Jeanette Wyneken, eds. *The Biology of Sea Turtles.*
>   Vol. 2. Boca Raton, FL: CRC Press, 1995.

9. An Entry in a Dictionary or Encyclopedia

Endnote/Footnote:

> 11. *New Encyclopedia Britannica*, 15th ed., s.v. "Turtle."

The abbreviation "s.v." is for the Latin *sub verbo* (under the word).

Bibliography:

According to CMS format, reference works (like encyclopedias and dictionaries) are not included in bibliographies.

10. A Work with a Corporate Author

Endnote/Footnote:

> 12. Sea Turtle Survival League, *Florida Sea Turtle and Coastal Habitation Program: An Educator's Guide* (Gainesville, FL: Sea Turtle Survival League, 2003), 5.

Bibliography:

> Sea Turtle Survival League, *Florida Sea Turtle and Coastal Habitation Program: An Educator's Guide.* Gainesville, FL: Sea Turtle Survival League, 2003.

11. A Letter in a Published Collection

Endnote/Footnote:

> 13. Gilbert White to Thomas Pennant, 4 May 1767, in *The Portrait of a Tortoise*, ed. Sylvia Townsend (London: Chatto and Windus, 1946), 14.

Bibliography:

> White, Gilbert. Gilbert White to Thomas Pennant, 4 May 1767. In *The Portrait of a Tortoise*, Edited by Sylvia Townsend. London: Chatto and Windus, 1946.

12. A Sacred Text

Endnote/Footnote:

> 14. Song of Sol. 2:12 (King James Version).

Sacred book titles are not italicized. Subsequent notes would abbreviate the version (e.g., KJV).

Bibliography:

    According to CMS format, sacred texts (like the Bible, the Koran, the Talmud, etc.) are not included in bibliographies.

Periodicals:

13. A Journal Article

Endnote/Footnote:

    15. Tad Hardy, "The Tortoise and the Scare," *BioScience* 38, no. 2 (1988): 78.

Bibliography:

    Hardy, Tad. "The Tortoise and the Scare." *BioScience* 38, no. 2 (1988): 76-9.

14. A Magazine Article

Endnote/Footnote:

    16. Peter Pritchard, "Tickled about Turtles," *Time,* February 28, 2000, 77.

    17. Ted Williams, "The Terrible Turtle Trade," *Audubon,* March/April 1999, 44.

Bibliography:

    Pritchard, Peter. "Tickled about Turtles." *Time,* February 28, 2000.

    Williams, Ted. "The Terrible Turtle Trade." *Audubon,* March/April 1999.

If the page numbers of an article are not sequential, do not indicate page numbers.

15. A Newspaper Article

Endnote/Footnote:

    18. Timothy Aeppel, "Seeking Ways to Rid Turtles of Salmonella," *Wall Street Journal,* May 30, 1996.

Page numbers are usually omitted from notes related to newspaper articles.

Bibliography:

    Aeppel, Timothy. "Seeking Ways to Rid Turtles of Salmonella." *Wall Street Journal,* May 30, 1996, sec. B.

16. A Book Review

Endnote/Footnote:

    19. Romain Pizzi, "Chelonian Medicine and Surgery," review of *Medicine and Surgery of Tortoises and Turtles,* by Stuart McArthur, Roger Wilkinson, and Jean Meyer, *Veterinary Record: Journal of the British Veterinary Association* 155 (2004): 30.

Bibliography:

> Pizzi, Romain. "Chelonian Medicine and Surgery." Review of *Medicine and Surgery of Tortoises and Turtles*, by Stuart McArthur, Roger Wilkinson, and Jean Meyer. *Veterinary Record: Journal of the British Veterinary Association* 155 (2004): 30-31.

Other Types of Sources:

17. A Government Document

Endnote/Footnote:

> 20. U.S. Food and Drug Administration, *Code of Federal Regulations—Title 21, 2001* (Washington, DC: GPO, 2005), 254.

Bibliography:

> U.S. Food and Drug Administration. *Code of Federal Regulations—Title 21, 2001.* Washington, DC: GPO, 2005.

18. A Pamphlet

Endnote/Footnote:

> 21. Blair Witherington, *Sea Turtles and Lights* (Tallahassee, FL: Florida Power and Light, 2005) 2.

Bibliography:

> Witherington, Blair. *Sea Turtles and Lights.* Tallahassee, FL: Florida Power and Light, 2005.

19. A Dissertation

Endnote/Footnote:

> 22. Manjula Tiwari, "Density-Dependent Effects on Hatchling Production in the Green Turtle Nesting Population in Tortuguero, Costa Rica" (Ph.D. diss., University of Florida, 2004), 31.

Bibliography:

> Tiwari, Manjula. "Density-Dependent Effects on Hatchling Production in the Green Turtle Nesting Population in Tortuguero, Costa Rica." Ph.D. diss., University of Florida, 2004.

20. A Lecture or Conference Paper

Endnote/Footnote:

> 23. Padmini Srikantiah, "An Outbreak of Salmonella Javiana Associated with Amphibian Contact" (paper presented at the International Conference on Emerging Infectious Diseases, Atlanta, GA, March 25, 2002), 11.

Bibliography:

> Srikantiah, Padmini. "An Outbreak of Salmonella Javiana Associated with the Amphibian Contact." Paper presented at the International Conference on Emerging Infectious Diseases, Atlanta, GA, March 25, 2002.

21. A Personal Interview or Communication

Endnote/Footnote:

Include brief identifying information when appropriate.

> 24. James Spotila, letter to author, September 15, 2005.

> 25. E. Anne McGee (president, Seminole Community College), interview with the author, April 7, 2004.

Bibliography:

According to CMS format, personal communications are not included in bibliographies.

22. A Radio or Television Program

Endnote/Footnote:

> 26. *Sleeper Cell*, episode no. 1 (first broadcast December 4, 2005, by Showtime), directed by Clark Johnson and written by Cyrus Voris and Ethan Reiff.

Bibliography:

> *Sleeper Cell.* Episode no. 1, first broadcast December 4, 2005, by Showtime. Directed by Clark Johnson and written by Cyrus Voris and Ethan Reiff.

Consult <http://epguides.com/> for information on episode numbers and broadcast dates.

23. A Movie

Endnote/Footnote:

> 27. *The Turtle Diary*, directed by John Irvin (Los Angeles: Samuel Goldwyn, 1985).

Bibliography:

> *The Turtle Diary*. Directed by John Irvin. Los Angeles: Samuel Goldwyn, 1985.

24. A DVD or Videotape

Endnote/Footnote:

> 28. *Sea Turtles: Ancient Nomads*, videotape, directed by Christopher N. Palmer (Stamford, CT: Vestron Video, 1989).

Bibliography:

> *Sea Turtles: Ancient Nomads*. Videotape. Directed by Christopher N. Palmer. Stamford, CT: Vestron Video, 1989.

25. A CD or Audiocassette

Endnote/Footnote:

> 29. Sting, *Dream of the Blue Turtles,* compact disc, produced by Sting and Pete Smith (A&M Records).

Bibliography:

> Sting. *Dream of the Blue Turtles.* A&M Records, 1985. Compact disc.

26. An Advertisement

Endnote/Footnote:

> 30. Turtle Wax, "Clean Cars Run Better," magazine advertisement. *Car and Driver*, November 2005, 113-14.

Bibliography:

> Turtle Wax. "Clean Cars Run Better." Magazine advertisement. *Car and Driver*, November 2005, 113-14.

Electronic Sources

The Internet has made it possible to transmit information in new ways, and these methods and modes are in a constant state of flux. The challenge confronting the research paper writer in the age of the World Wide Web is that the essential components of documentation entries (author's name, title, publication information) may be missing from electronic documents, or they might be present in a form that must be converted into something that makes sense in the CMS formatting system. For example, a website may not indicate an author (or the author might use an alias). The layout of an online document might make it difficult to distinguish between two or three possible titles, or there might be no title. A URL and the date when a site was last updated might have to replace more standard publication information. Last, but not least, information that has been "reprinted" on the web might lack complete documentation about the original source.

e-TIPS

Tricks for Finding Citation Information

If some information (the creator of the website, when a site was last updated, a sponsoring organization or institution) isn't immediately available on a web page, you can sometimes locate these facts by clicking on a hyperlink that takes you to a home page (sometimes labeled "About Us"). Also, you can often discover a home page (and more information about the source) by "backtracking." Try deleting the last portions of a URL to get to previous pages. Remember that a reference is only as good as its source. If you cannot locate a credible author or organization, you may not want to include this reference in your research project.

Yet another obstacle to correctly formatting a references list is identifying the type of source being used. Remember that the dual purpose of documentation is to give credit to the author *and* to enable a reader to find the material cited. Therefore, you need to determine first whether the source is available via the web (so it has a URL that can be accessed by anyone with a browser), or if it is delivered via a computer but available only through a licensing agreement or password (such as a subscription database, subscription service like AOL, or a CD-ROM). References list entries in the former category will include a URL, whereas those in the latter group will not.

In addition to distinguishing how a text is delivered via a computer, there are some general rules to follow when using CMS format to document electronic sources.

- If the information has appeared previously in print form, include print information with the other (electronic) information necessary to locate a source.

- For a website, include the name of the author, title of the site, any institution or corporation associated with the site, and the site's URL. When no author is named, treat the institution or corporation as the author.

- If a URL is long and must "wrap" onto the next line, DO NOT insert any punctuation (such as a hyphen). Instead, divide the electronic address after a slash ("/"), or before a period or hyphen.

- URLs and e-mail addresses should not appear as hyperlinks. (Often word processing programs will automatically transform a web address into a hyperlink. A quick way to change it back to normal type is to click on "Edit" and "Undo.")

- Because URLs are often confusing and difficult to reproduce (but *must* be accurate), copy and paste them into your notes and bibliographic entries.

- CMS format doesn't *require* the date of access, but it does permit it. Including this (enclosed in parentheses) is a good idea, as web pages are "time sensitive" (meaning they are often edited and availability and content can change).

Electronic Documents Available on the Web. The following examples are for documents that are available to anyone with a browser. Complete information is not always available on web pages, but you should cite as much of the required information as you can reasonably obtain.

QUICK CHECK
CMS Web Page Basic Format
Web page entries should include the following information:
- Author's or editor's name
- Title of document, in quotation marks
- Title of larger web project (if relevant), in italics
- Institution or corporation that is associated with the site
- URL (in plain type, *not* as a hyperlink)
- Date of access (in parentheses) may be included (but is not required)

27. A Single Web Page

A single web page is complete in itself and is not connected to a larger, professional web project.

Endnote/Footnote:

> 31. Tricia Power, "Salmonella in Reptiles and Amphibians," http://www.icomm.ca/dragon/salmonella.htm (accessed November 14, 2002).

Bibliography:

> Power, Tricia. "Salmonella in Reptiles and Amphibians." http://www.icomm.ca/dragon/salmonella.htm (accessed November 14, 2002).

28. A Secondary Web Page

A secondary web page is part of a larger web project. The page has a title but also features the name of the project as well.

Endnote/Footnote:

> 32. Trudy Kuhrt, "Trachemys Scripta," *Animal Diversity Web*, University of Michigan Museum of Zoology. http://animaldiversity.ummz.umich.edu/accounts/trachemys/t._scripta$narrative.html (accessed November 14, 2005).

Bibliography:

> Kuhrt, Trudy. "Trachemys Scripta." *Animal Diversity Web*. University of Michigan Museum of Zoology. http://animaldiversity.ummz.umich.edu/accounts/trachemys/t._scripta$narrative.html (accessed November 14, 2005).

29. An Online Journal Article

An online journal article is the electronic text of a previously printed article (now available on the web) or a document available only on the Internet.

When an article has appeared previously in print:

Endnote/Footnote:

> 33. C. Levy et al., "Reptile-Associated Salmonellosis—Selected States, 1996-1998," *Morbidity and Mortality Weekly Report* 48 (1999), http://www.cdc.gov/mmwr/PDF/wk/mm4844.pdf (accessed November 14, 2005).

Bibliography:

> Levy, C. J. Sakala, L. Heatong, and L. I. Lee. "Reptile-Associated Salmonellosis—Selected States, 1996-1998." *Morbidity and Mortality Weekly Report* 48 (1999): 1009-13, http://www.cdc.gov/mmwr/PDFwk/mm4844.pdf (accessed November 14, 2005).

Since electronic documents don't have page numbers, it makes pinpointing where a quotation or information is located tricky. When an article has appeared in print previously, you should include page range information in your bibliography entry. CMS recommends that you use a "locator" (such as a paragraph number or a subheading) in your footnote or endnote to indicate where in the article the information appears. (See Endnote/Foot-note #34 and Endnote/Footnote #42 for examples of this.) The document in the example above (note #33) is a PDF file, so page numbers can be listed—both for the location of the specific information or quotation in the footnote or endnote and in the bibliographic entry for the range of the entire article.

When an article has never been published in print, but appears only in an online publication:

Endnote/Footnote:

> 34. Elsie Rosner, "Salmonellosis from a Trip to the Zoo," *Physician's Weekly* 13, no. 39 (1996): par. 4, http://www.physweekly.com/archive/96/10_21_96/ cu4.html (accessed November 14, 2005).

Bibliography:

> Rosner, Elsie. "Salmonellosis from a Trip to the Zoo." *Physician's Weekly* 13, no. 39 (1996). http://www.physweekly.com/archive/96/10_21_96/cu4.html (accessed November 14, 2005).

30. An Online Magazine Article
An online magazine article is the electronic text of a previously printed article (now available on the web) or a document available only on the Internet.

When an article has appeared previously in print:

Endnote/Footnote:

> 35. Michelle Pullia Turk, "New Food Rules for Pregnancy." *Parents*, July 2001. http://www.parents.com/parents/story.jhtml?storyid=/templatedata/parents/story/data/ 1186.xml (accessed November 14, 2005).

Bibliography:

> Turk, Michelle Pullia. "New Food Rules for Pregnancy." *Parents*, July 2001. http://www.parents.com/parents/story.jhtml?storyid=/templatedata/parents/ story/data/1186.xml (accessed November 14, 2005).

When an article has never been published in print, but appears only in an online publication:

Endnote/Footnote:

> 36. "Is Your Child Safe from Salmonella?" *Medscape Health for Consumers*, February 2000, http://cbshealthwatch.aol.com/cx/viewarticle/210245 (accessed November 14, 2005).

Bibliography:

> "Is Your Child Safe from Salmonella?" *Medscape Health for Consumers*, February 2000. http://cbshealthwatch.aol.com/cx/viewarticle/210245 (accessed November 14, 2005).

31. An Online Newspaper Article

An online newspaper article is the electronic text of a previously printed article (now available on the web) or a document available only on the Internet.

When an article has appeared previously in print:

Endnote/Footnote:

> 37. Rick Hampson, "Tiny Turtle Has Friends and Foes," *USA Today*, April 30, 1999, http://pqasb.pqarchiver.com/USAToday/tinyturtle.htm (accessed December 14, 2005).

Bibliography:

> Hampson, Rick. "Tiny Turtle Has Friends and Foes." *USA Today*, April 30, 1999. http://pqasb.pqarchiver.com/USAToday/tinyturtle.htm (accessed December 14, 2005).

When an article has never been published in print, but appears only in an online publication:

Endnote/Footnote:

> 38. Austin Ripley, "Salmonella and Reptile Pets," *Earth Times News Service*, September 26, 2002, http://earthtimes.org/sep/healthsalmonellafromsep17_01.htm (accessed December 16, 2005).

Bibliography:

> Ripley, Austin. "Salmonella and Reptile Pets." *Earth Times News Service*, September 26, 2002.http://earthtimes.org/sep/healthsalmonellafromsep17_01.htm (accessed December 16, 2005).

32. An Online Encyclopedia Article

Endnote/Footnote:

> 39. *Encyclopedia Britannica*, s.v. "salmonellosis," http://www.britannica.com/eb/article?eu=66794 (accessed November 14, 2005).

The abbreviation "s.v." is for the Latin *sub verbo* (under the word).

Bibliography:

According to CMS format, reference works (like encyclopedias and dictionaries) are not included in bibliographies.

33. An Online Government Publication

Endnote/Footnote:

> 40. Utah Department of Health, *Reptile-Associated Salmonellosis* (Salt Lake City: Bureau of Epidemiology, 2001), par. 2, http://hlunix.hl.state.ut.us/els/epidemiology/epifacts/reptile.html (accessed November 14, 2005).

Bibliography:

> Utah Department of Health. *Reptile-Associated Salmonellosis* (Salt Lake City: Bureau of Epidemiology, 2001). http://hlunix.hl.state.ut.us/els/epidemiology/epifacts/reptile.html (accessed November 14, 2005).

34. An Online Book

Like online journal, magazine, or newspaper articles, online books may be "reprints" of hardcover publications (see Endnote/Footnote #41) or documents appearing only on the Internet (see Endnote/Footnote #42). If a book has been previously published, supply the original publication information as well as the URL of the Internet version you accessed.

Endnote/Footnote:

> 41.   John Milton, *Paradise Lost*, ed. Roy Flanagan (New York: Macmillan, 1992), bk. 3 ln. 650-653, http://darkwing.uoregon.edu/~rbear/lost/pl3.html (accessed December 16, 2005).

For poems and plays, indicate the location of a quotation by the divisions used in these works (e.g., book, canto, verse, stanza, act, scene, line, etc., separated by periods) rather than by page numbers. In the preceding example, the quotation appears in Book 3, lines 650–653.

Bibliography:

> Milton, John. *Paradise Lost.* Edited by Roy Flanagan. New York: Macmillan, 1992. http://darkwing.uoregon.edu/~rbear/lost/pl3.html (accessed December 16, 2005).

35. A Portion of an Online Book

Endnote/Footnote:

> 42.   F. Wayne King and Russell L. Burke, eds., "Checklist of Crocodilians, Tuatara, and Turtles of the World," in *Crocodilian, Tuatara, and Turtle: An Online Taxonomic and Geographic Reference*, under "Pseudemys floridana," http://www.flmnh.ufl.edu/natsci/herpetology/turtcroclist/chklst7.htm (accessed December 16, 2005).

If paragraph divisions are not clear, you can indicate the location of a quotation by a subtitle or a heading (e.g., under "Pseudemys floridana" in the previous note). This information is *not* included in the bibliography entry.

Bibliography:

> King, F. Wayne and Russell L. Burke, eds. "Checklist of Crocodilians, Tuatara, and Turtles of the World." In *Crocodilian, Tuatara, and Turtle: An Online Taxonomic and Geographic Reference*. http://www.flmnh.ufl.edu/natsci/herpetology/turtcroclist/chklst7.htm (accessed December 16, 2005).

36. An Online Forum Posting

Endnote/Footnote:

> 43.   David Starkey, "North American Herp Tissues Needed," July 18, 2003, http://www.cnah.org/forum/display_message.asp?mid=229 (December 20, 2005).

Bibliography:

According to CMS format, online postings are not included in bibliographies.

Electronic Documents with Restricted Access. These documents require a subscription or password to access them (and are not freely available on the WWW). Often these documents have been made available in print previously and have been "reprinted" electronically (in either html or PDF format). For this reason, the formats for these sources are a "hybrid" of the print-version information and the digital source information. (If you are confused about formatting, check the CMS format for the type of "hard copy" document it was prior to being transformed into its "digital" form.) As always, cite as much of the required information as you can reasonably obtain.

CMS format for database articles requires the URL of the homepage of the service. This is easy if you are using a database to which you have personally subscribed (like the subscription to InfoTrac College Edition that may come with this text). For this database you must point your browser to a specific web address (i.e., http://www.infotrac-college.com). However, many of the databases you will use in your research are services to which your school or public library subscribe. In these cases, you access the database via the library's site and the web address of the database service will never appear in your browser's window. See the "e-tip" on "Identifying Database URLs" (page 227) for help with this.

37. A Journal Article from a Database

Endnote/Footnote:

> 44. Carol Lewis, "The Fright of the Iguana," *FDA Consumer* 31, no. 7 (1997): par. 10, http://search.epnet.com (accessed November 21, 2005).

Bibliography:

> Lewis, Carol. "The Fright of the Iguana." *FDA Consumer* 31, no. 7 (1997): 33-36. http://search.epnet.com (accessed November 21, 2005).

38. A Magazine Article from a Database

Endnote/Footnote:

> 45. Peter Pritchard, "Tickled About Turtles," *Time,* February 28, 2000: par. 3, www.infotrac-college.com (accessed November 24, 2005).

> 46. Ted Williams, "The Terrible Turtle Trade," *Audubon*, March 1999: par. 1, http://firstsearch.oclc.org/ (accessed December 8, 2005).

Bibliography:

> Pritchard, Peter. "Tickled About Turtles." *Time,* February 28, 2000. www.infotrac-college.com (accessed November 24, 2005).

> Williams, Ted. "The Terrible Turtle Trade." *Audubon*, March/April 1999. http://firstsearch.oclc.org/ (accessed December 8, 2005).

e-TIPS

Identifying Database URLs

If you are accessing a database via your school or public library (rather than through a personal subscription like the InfoTrac College Edition subscription you may have received with the purchase of this text), the URL that appears in your browser window will **NOT** be the home page of the database service. It requires that you do a little "detective work" to discover what service supplies the database you are using. Usually the name of the service appears on the hyperlink directory to databases supplied by your library and/or as part of the title information once you access the database. The four major suppliers of databases to libraries are EBSCO, OCLC, Gale, and Wilson (and there are a few smaller services like CQpress <http://library.cqpress.com/>, LexisNexis <http://web.lexis-nexis.com/>, and ProQuest <http://www.proquest.com/>). The following are the home page URLs of these services and a partial list of some of the databases they supply. Consult a reference librarian if you are unsure of the service that supplies the database you are using.

EBSCO <http://search.epnet.com>

Academic Search (Elite or Premier); Business Source (Complete, Corporate, Elite, or Premier); Humanities International Index; Library, Information Science and Technology Abstracts; Military and Government Collection; Nursing and Allied Health Collection (Basic, Comprehensive, or Expanded); Psychology and Behavioral Sciences Collection; SocINDEX.
[For a complete listing of EBSCO service databases, go to <http://www.epnet.com/titleLists.php?topicID=380&tabForward=titleLists&marketID=>.]

OCLC <http://firstsearch.oclc.org/>

ABI/INFORM; AGRICOLA; Applied Science and Technology Index; ArticleFirst; Arts and Humanities Search; BioDigest; BusDateline; BusManagement; EconLit; GEOBASE; MLA International Bibliography; SIRSResearcher.
[For a complete listing of OCLC service databases, go to <http://www.oclc.org/firstsearch/content/databases/databaselist.htm>.]

Gale <http://galenet.galegroup.com/>

Biography Resource Center; Computer Database; CWI; Custom Newspapers InfoTrac College Edition; Expanded Academic; General Business File; General Reference Center; InfoTrac College Edition OneFile; Literature Resource Center; MLA International Bibliography; Science Resource Center; Twayne's Authors Online.
[For a complete listing of Gale service databases, go to <http://www.gale.com/title_lists/index.htm>.]

Wilson <http://vnweb.hwwilsonweb.com/>

Applied Science and Technology; Art; Biological and Agricultural Index; Book Review Digest Plus; Business; Education; Essay and General Literature Index; General Science; Humanities; Legal Periodicals and Books; Library Literature and Information Science; Reader's Guide; Science Full Text Select; Social Sciences; Wilson Omni-File.
[For a complete listing of Wilson service databases, go to <http://www.hwwilson.com/ftabsind_alpha.htm>.]

39. A Newspaper Article from a Database

Endnote/Footnote:

47.   Peter Genovese, "'Sinatra of Salmonella' Sings of Food Safety," *The Star Ledger*, September 30, 2005, http://galenet.galegroup.com/ (accessed December 5, 2005).

Bibliography:

> Genovese, Peter. " 'Sinatra of Salmonella' Sings of Food Safety." *The Star Ledger*, September 30, 2005. http://galenet.galegroup.com/ (accessed December 5, 2005).

40. An E-Book from a Database

Endnote/Footnote:

> 48. E. Fuller Torrey and Robert H. Yolken. *Beasts of the Earth: Animals, Humans, and Disease*. (New Brunswick, N.J: Rutgers UP, 2005), 82. http://www.oclc.org (accessed March 22, 2007).

Bibliography:

> Torrey, E. Fuller and Robert H. Yolken. *Beasts of the Earth: Animals, Humans, and Disease*. (New Brunswick, N.J: Rutgers UP, 2005). http://www.oclc.org (accessed March 22, 2007).

41. An E-Mail Message

Endnote/Footnote:

> 49. Laura Ross, e-mail message to author, June 30, 2005.

Bibliography:

According to CMS format, e-mail messages are not included in bibliographies.

Sample Research Paper Using CMS Style

The following paper uses CMS documentation style and provides an example of how to correctly incorporate both print and electronic documents into the text, endnotes page, and bibliography page of a research paper. Annotations are provided to comment on some of the more complicated aspects of documentation.

A research paper should *look* like an academic work. Resist the urge to become creative with "desktop publishing." Don't include colored type, "fancy" fonts, graphics, or pictures (unless they are tables, graphs, or illustrations related to your project). You may think they add interest to your project, but most professors consider this type of augmentation distracting and unscholarly.

CMS style dicates a one-inch margin on all sides of the paper.

A Critical Analysis of Athenian Democracy

During the Golden Age, 480 BC to 431 BC

Michael McConville

IDH 1613

Dr. C. Robbins

April 20, 2004

Your title page should include the title of your paper, your name, the title of the course, your professor's name, and the date the assignment is due—all centered and in a normal (12-point/Times New Roman) font.

The writer of this paper has chosen to include an epigraph (italicized) to set if off from the main body of the paper.

An introduction should command your readers' attention *and* plainly introduce the topic of the paper. This introduction is two paragraphs long and concludes with the thesis sentence of the essay.

The thesis succinctly summarizes the goals and organization of the essay.

Each page (other than the title page) should include the paper writer's last name and the page number in the upper right corner.

Superscript numbers (listed sequentially) correspond to numbered entries on the endnotes page(s).

McConville   2

It has been said that democracy is the worst form of government except all the others that have been tried.

—Sir Winston Churchill

The origins of democracy can be found in its etymology. The Greek word *dêmokratia* is a compound of two Grecian concepts. The first is *demos*, or "the people"; the second is *kratos*, or "power." Democracy is literally "the people's power," and its influence is seen in many modern-day political systems. In one form, it has become the representative democracy (republican) government of the United States, where, theoretically, the needs of the people are met by elected officials who act as a voting proxy for their constituents. In its purest form, a democracy is a system of government in which the members of a city, county, province, parish, state, territory, or country vote directly on laws and referenda. According to Fred Edwards, in Athens, "democracy wasn't merely a practical procedure for passing laws and placing government officials in office" but the "empowerment of the governed by the governed."[1]

The Athenians of ancient Greece first implemented democracy into government. From its beginnings with Solon and Cleisthenes to its heyday with Pericles in the mid-fifth century BC, democracy grew as an important means of governing the people. However, while democracy provided Athens with a relatively stable

McConville 3

government, it is a system prone to many problems that even today have not been solved.government, it is a system prone to many problems that even today have not been solved.

The roots of the Athenian democratic system are found in the reforms instituted by the leader Solon after his election to the executive position of *archon* in 594 BC. According to R. K. Sinclair, Solon's main mission as leader was to "restore stability to his native city when it was threatened by bitter civil strife."[2] To achieve this goal, asserts David Stockton, Solon established "objective property qualifications for the different classes of Athens' citizens."[3] And in *Politics*, Aristotle sums up Solon most succinctly: "[Solon] put an end to the exclusiveness of the oligarchy, emancipated the people, established the ancient Athenian democracy, and harmonized the different elements of the state."[4] This was accomplished, in large part, by Solon's establishment of the Council of Four Hundred, for it provided a way for the Athenian people to put forth proposals to be heard in the general assembly.[5] Three decades after Solon left office, the Greek tyrant Pisistratus rose to power with the backing of the Athenian oligarchy. As a testament to the efficacy of Solon's reforms, Pisistratus left them largely intact.[6]

Use brackets to indicate words or letters that don't appear in the original wording but have been added to clarify meaning or blend the quote (grammatically) with your sentence.

Introduce direct quotation with a signal phrase that indicates the speaker of the words. Don't just "plop" the quotation into your essay.

Endnotes may include commentary as well as bibliographic information. This endnote expands on the claim made in the text of the essay.

Limit the amount of direct quotation by smoothly incorporating remarkable or striking phrases into your own sentences.

When a quote is long (more than four typed lines), set it off from the text by indenting it. In this case, omit quotation marks (the indentation indicates direct quotation).

McConville   4

However, the main catalyst for the introduction of democracy into Athenian politics was Cleisthenes, who came to power in 510 BC. Known as the "Father of Democracy," Cleisthenes abolished the old system of tribes and redistricted Athens into ten sections, known as *demes*. J. M. Moore notes that this redistricting allowed "those whose citizenship was questioned by the narrow oligarchs [aristocrats]" to back Cleisthenes.[7] Thus empowered, Cleisthenes transformed the *boule*, the advisory councils of ancient Athens, into the Council of Five Hundred, which included 50 legislators from each *deme*. Thus the government was altered from an aristocratic institution into a "random and representative cross-section"[8] of the populace so that the laws passed would suit more than the nobles. Barry Strauss notes that the strength of Athenian democracy

> was embodied in . . . a legislative and deliberative body open to all adult male citizens, as well as in jury courts, magistracies, and a Council that served as a sort of executive committee. Each of these institutions was large, thereby offering every one of Athens' adult male citizens (a number that fluctuated between c. 25,000 and 50,000 in the two centuries of Athens' democratic regime) a chance to play at least a small part in self-government.[9]

Use present tense verbs in signal phrases.

When you omit words from a quotation, indicate this with ellipsis points (three dots separated by spaces).

McConville   5

By no means was the democratic system of Cleisthenes a flawless one, however. Some of the *demes* were in poorer and more distant areas of Athens, and since involvement in the *boule* required vast amounts of free time, A. H. M. Jones argues that, in reality, the Council never represented the general populace.[10] The resulting government was comprised of a vocal minority (the nobles and aristocracy) who fully participated in proceedings— giving policy speeches and proposing (and passing) new laws— and a mostly silent majority of "ordinary" members who—because of distance or work responsibilities—were unable to attend sessions and/or wholly engage in the legislative process.[11]

Mid-fifth century BC marked the "Golden Age" of Athens and heralded changes that significantly impacted the evolving democratic system. Under Pericles, Athens prospered and extended its influence. The Delian League, once meant to serve as a military "cooperative" of 200 city-states in case of invasion by an outside force, was subjugated under the growing power of the Athenian polis. These allies were now required to pay "tribute" to the Athenians.[12] But as Pericles used Athenian military might to intimidate and overpower his allies, he simultaneously empowered the ordinary citizenship of Athens. Most importantly, he instituted payment to citizens for work done for the government.[13] This increased the active involvement of the "ordinary" members of the Council who pushed through legislation (like the use of Delian

Paraphrase (as well as direct quotation) must be acknowledged in an endnote.

When the superscript reference number occurs at the end of a sentence, the end punctuation *precedes* the number.

McConville   6

resource to build the Parthenon) that was unpopular with the aristocrats of Athens. Plutarch states that Pericles "was never seen to walk in any street but that which led to the market-place and council-hall," two places where he could associate with the common Athenian.[14]

Despite these democratizing modifications and a leadership bent on increasing its sphere of influence, Athenian democracy had pitfalls. Most damning was the exclusion of vast numbers of the Athenian population from voting privileges. Of the 400,000 or so people living in Athens during the fifth century, only one-tenth of the population had voting rights.[15] Since an even smaller number of eligible citizens actually participated, elections were determined by a small percentage of the Athenian population.

For this reason, there were numerous critics of democracy both during and after the Golden Age. Thucydides sounded his concern that dissolute men could manipulate the system in order to assume leadership. His tirade against the populist Cleon in *The History of the Peloponnesian War* demonstrates his contempt for a system that had supported "Cleon . . . the most violent man at Athens."[16] However, Thucydides was not totally hostile to democracy. Stockton notes that Thucydides was an "admirer of Pericles, even perhaps in some respects an insufficiently critical admirer" of the politician.[17]

"Sandwich" direct quotation or paraphrase between your claim (that it is supporting) and follow-up clarification of significance

The first mention of an author should include his/her *full* name. Subsequent mention should be by *last* name only.

McConville   7

It is ironic that Athenian democracy helped to produce one of its most ardent opponents, Plato. Born into an aristocratic and politically active family, Plato aspired to political office, but he grew jaded with the political atmosphere of Athens in the early fourth century BC. "For Plato," M. I. Finley states, "the condemnation of Socrates symbolized the evil of any open or free society, not just a democratic one."[18] There are three main criticisms of democracy discussed by Plato in *The Republic*. The first claims it is foolish to believe that a common man has the ability to rule effectively, for "the desires of the less reputable majority are controlled by the desires and wisdom of the superior minority."[19] The second criticism concerns the complete absence of women in the public sector. He insists that woman can do as much as most men, for "there is no special faculty of administration in a state which a woman has because she is a woman, or which a man has by virtue of his sex, but the gifts of nature are alike diffused in both."[20] The third criticism is the possible devolution of democracy into anarchy. Plato states that "tyranny naturally arises out of democracy, and the most aggravated form of tyranny and slavery out of the most extreme form of liberty."[21]

It has been over 2,400 years since the Golden Age of Athens ended, but the innovations that arose during that time still affect the lives of people today. The Greeks of antiquity gave the world

Vary the signal phrase by placing it in the middle of a quotation.

McConville   8

much, and history shows that democracy has adapted well to modernity. Democracy serves as the basis for many governments around the world, including that of the United States. To many, it is the strongest form of government now existing. But as has been shown, democracy does have problems that are inherent in its design and implementation. In the end, it is up to the leaders of democracy (and the voters who elect them) to make the most prudent decisions concerning its use. After all, it is "the people's power."

The conclusion presents a summary of analysis and research and frequently offers a call for future action.

McConville   9

Endnotes

1. Fred Edwards, "The Democratic Ideal Versus the State of the Union," The Humanist 64, no. 2 (2004): par. 2, http://vnweb.hwwilsonweb.com/ (accessed April 3, 2004).

2. R. K. Sinclair, *Democracy and Participation in Athens* (Cambridge: Cambridge University Press, 1988), 1.

3. David Stockton, *Classical Athenian Democracy* (Oxford: Oxford University Press, 1990), 6.

4. Aristotle, *Politics,* trans. Benjamin Jowett (New York: Colonial Press, 1900), bk. 2. ln. 12, http://classics.mit.edu/ Aristotle/politics.2.two.html (accessed March 9, 2004).

5. This innovation in political participation is attested to by Plutarch in his *Lives*, but no mention of the Council is found in Aristotle's *Politics*. See Stockton, *Classical Athenian Democracy,* 28.

6. See Herodotus, *The History of Herodotus*, trans. George Rawlinson (New York: Tudor Publishing, 1956), bk. 1. ln. 432-450, http://classics.mit.edu/Herodotus/history.html (accessed March 9, 2004).

7. J. M. Moore, *Aristotle and Xenophon on Democracy and Oligarchy* (Berkeley: University of California Press, 1975), 237.

8. Stockton, *Classical Athenian Democracy*, 29.

9. Barry Strauss, "American Democracy Through Ancient Greek Eyes," *History Today* 44, no. 4 (1994): par. 4, http://search.epnet.com (accessed April 3, 2004).

10. A. H. M. Jones, *Athenian Democracy* (Baltimore, MD: Johns Hopkins University Press, 1957), 106.

McConville   10

11. Ibid., 108.

12. In fact, in 454 BC the League's treasury was relocated from the temple of Apollo on Delos to the temple of Athena in Athens. See Sinclair, *Democracy and Participation,* 7.

13. Ibid., 37.

14. Plutarch, *The Lives of the Noble Grecians and Romans*, vol. 1, trans. John Dryden (New York: Modern Library, 1992), 187.

15. The remaining 360,000 residents were women, underage males, slaves, and freemen of foreign birth. See Joe Allman and Walt Anderson, *Evaluating Democracy: An Introduction to Political Science* (Pacific Palisades: Goodyear Publishing, 1974), 7.

16. Thucydides, *The History of the Peloponnesian War*, trans. Richard Crawley (New York: E. P. Dutton, 1950), bk. 3. chap. 9, http://classics.mit.edu/Thucydides/pelopwar.3.third.html (accessed March 9, 2004).

17. Stockton, *Classical Athenian Democracy*, 167.

18. M. I. Finley, *Democracy: Ancient and Modern* (New Brunswick, NJ: Rutgers University Press, 1973), 96.

19. Sean Sayers, *Plato's Republic: An Introduction* (Edinburgh: Edinburgh University Press, 1999), 27.

20. Plato, *The Republic*, trans. Benjamin Jowett (New York: P. F. Collier and Son, 1901), bk. 2, http://etext.library.adelaide.edu.au/p/plato/p71r/ (accessed March 16, 2004).

21. Ibid., bk. 5.

When citing the same source in *consecutive* notes, use the term "Ibid." and the page number.

In CMS endnote format, the author's name is *not* inverted.

Single-space entries and double-space between them.

McConville   11

Bibliography

Allman, Joe, and Walt Anderson. *Evaluating Democracy: An Introduction to Political Science.* Pacific Palisades, CA: Goodyear Publishing, 1974.

Aristotle. *Politics.* Translated by Benjamin Jowett. New York: Colonial Press, 1900. http://classics.mit.edu/Aristotle/politics.2.two.html (accessed March 9, 2004).

Edwards, Fred. "The Democratic Ideal Versus the State of the Union." *The Humanist* 64, no. 2 (2004): 10-15, http://vnweb.hwwilsonweb.com/ (accessed April 3, 2004).

Finley, M. I. *Democracy: Ancient and Modern.* New Brunswick, NJ: Rutgers University Press, 1973.

Herodotus. *The History of Herodotus.* Translated by George Rawlinson. New York: Tudor Publishing, 1956. http://classics.mit.edu/Herodotus/history.html (accessed March 9, 2004).

Jones, A. H. M. *Athenian Democracy.* Baltimore, MD: Johns Hopkins University Press, 1957.

Moore, J. M. *Aristotle and Xenophon on Democracy and Oligarchy.* Berkeley: University of California Press, 1975.

Plato. *The Republic.* Translated by Benjamin Jowett. New York: P. F. Collier and Son, 1901. http://etext.library.adelaide.edu.au/p/plato/p71r/ (accessed March 16, 2004).

Plutarch. *The Lives of the Noble Grecians and Romans.* Vol. 1. Translated by John Dryden. New York: Modern Library, 1992.

Sayers, Sean. *Plato's Republic: An Introduction.* Edinburgh: Edinburgh University Press, 1999.

Center heading at the top of page

Alphabetize entries by author's last name.

Database articles should include the URL of the home page of the database.

Begin bibliography on a separate page, numbered like the others.

CMS doesn't require access dates for electronic documents, but is does allow their inclusion at the end of the entry.

Single-space entries and double-space between them.

For documents located on the Internet, include original publication information as well as the URL of the website.

McConville   12

Sinclair, R. K. *Democracy and Participation in Athens.* Cambridge:
    Cambridge University Press, 1988.

Stockton, David. *Classical Athenian Democracy.* Oxford: Oxford
    University Press, 1990.

Strauss, Barry. "American Democracy Through Ancient Greek
    Eyes." *History Today* 44, no. 4 (1994): 32-37.
    http://search.epnet.com (accessed April 3, 2004).

Thucydides. *The History of the Peloponnesian War.* Translated
    by Richard Crawley. New York: E. P. Dutton, 1950.
    http://classics.mit.edu/Thucydides/pelopwar.3.third.html
    (accessed March 9, 2004).

Entries of
articles accessed
via a database
must include all
of the original
publication
information.

Index

Credits